GENDER REPLAY

MW01485614

CRITICAL PERSPECTIVES ON YOUTH SERIES
General Editors: Amy L. Best, Lorena Garcia, and Jessica K. Taft

Fast-Food Kids: French Fries, Lunch Lines, and Social Ties
Amy L. Best

White Kids: Growing Up with Privilege in a Racially Divided America
Margaret A. Hagerman

Growing Up Queer: Kids and the Remaking of LGBTQ Identity
Mary Robertson

The Kids Are in Charge: Activism and Power in Peru's Movement of Working Children
Jessica K. Taft

Coming of Age in Iran: Poverty and the Struggle for Dignity
Manata Hashemi

The World Is Our Classroom: Extreme Parenting and the Rise of Worldschooling
Jennie Germann Molz

The Homeschool Choice: Parents and the Privatization of Education
Kate Henley Averett

Growing Up Latinx: Coming of Age in a Time of Contested Citizenship
Jesica Siham Fernández

Unaccompanied: The Plight of Immigrant Youth at the Border
Emily Ruehs-Navarro

The Sociology of Bullying: Power, Status, and Aggression Among Adolescents
Edited by Christopher Donoghue

Gender Replay: On Kids, Schools, and Feminism
Edited by Freeden Blume Oeur and C. J. Pascoe

Gender Replay

On Kids, Schools, and Feminism

Edited by

Freeden Blume Oeur *and* C. J. Pascoe

NEW YORK UNIVERSITY PRESS

New York

NEW YORK UNIVERSITY PRESS
New York
www.nyupress.org

Library of Congress Cataloging-in-Publication Data
Names: Blume Oeur, Freeden, 1981– editor. | Pascoe, C. J., 1974– editor.
Title: Gender replay : on kids, schools, and feminism / edited by Freeden Blume Oeur and
C.J. Pascoe.
Description: New York : New York University Press, [2023] | Series: Critical perspectives on
youth series | Includes bibliographical references and index.
Identifiers: LCCN 2022041772 | ISBN 9781479813360 (hardback) | ISBN 9781479813377
(paperback) | ISBN 9781479813384 (ebook) | ISBN 9781479813391 (ebook other)
Subjects: LCSH: Thorne, Barrie. Gender play. | Sex differences in education—United States. |
Youth—United States. | Feminism—United States.
Classification: LCC LC212.92.T46 G46 2023 | DDC 370.15/1—dc23/eng/20221011
LC record available at https://lccn.loc.gov/2022041772

New York University Press books are printed on acid-free paper, and their binding materials
are chosen for strength and durability. We strive to use environmentally responsible suppli-
ers and materials to the greatest extent possible in publishing our books.

Manufactured in the United States of America

10 9 8 7 6 5 4 3 2 1

Also available as an ebook

To Barrie: for always encouraging us to sing our song.

Children's interactions are not preparation for life; they are life itself.

As adults, we can help kids, as well as ourselves, imagine and realize different futures, alter institutions, craft new life histories. A more complex understanding of the dynamics of gender, of tensions and contradictions, and of the hopeful moments that lie within present arrangements, can help broaden our sense of the possible.

—Barrie Thorne, *Gender Play: Girls and Boys in School* (1993)

To use a metaphor I have long used and enjoyed . . . feminist academic spaces are oases from which we water surrounding deserts, create tools for survival, and nurture a next generation of scholars and teachers.

—Barrie Thorne, Interview with Laurence Bachmann (2013)

CONTENTS

Introduction

Playing with Gender

FREEDEN BLUME OEUR AND C. J. PASCOE

During research at a school for her groundbreaking book, *Gender Play: Girls and Boys in School* (1993), the sociologist Barrie Thorne had quite an unexpected moment. She listened one day as the school loudspeaker blared, *"Barrie Thorne, the Principal would like to speak with you."* That commanding request, familiar to many of us from childhood, transported Thorne back to her own elementary school days. She would later recall her "middling status" as a kid (Smith and Greene 2014). The announcement likely provoked feelings of embarrassment and worry, perhaps even shame as "tugs of memory" (Thorne 1993:24) brought back impressions of Thorne's child self. This poignant moment of self-reflection is a reminder that adults who study youth have one important thing in common: they were once children themselves. These childhood memories are both resources for and challenges to studying kids. Young people were the central actors of Thorne's book—how they together create and experience gender, within school settings that constrain and enable gendered possibilities—but adults who study them become a part of their social worlds. Kids throughout the school likely giggled at the thought of Thorne being called to the principal's office. She may have even wondered if the gatekeepers at the school were intending to scold her for some research violation! Thorne's reflections in *Gender Play* are honest and personal, and they urge the same transparency of other youth researchers.

Our volume offers critical reflections on and celebrates *Gender Play*— its many lessons for feminism, childhood studies, the study of schools, and thinking on gender—as well as the larger research, teaching, and mentoring legacy of *Barrie*, its author.[1] By providing an intimate view of the worlds of kids, in the thirty years since its publication *Gender Play* has

1

had a lasting impact on how we understand the socialization of gendered lives, the place of children in feminist thought, and how schools often, in Barrie's memorable words, "divide in a familiar geography of gender" (Thorne 1993:1). We are joined in this volume by a feminist community of authors—representing a wide range of interests, career stages, and professional and personal connections to Barrie—that will revisit and critically assess the insights from the book and help gift it to new audiences.

The Play of Gender

The images on the front cover of *Gender Play* convey much more than the title alone. Across the top and bottom of the cover are photographs of a schoolyard, spliced together like a photo reel. In the bottom at the center stands Barrie: leaning against a basketball hoop, staring at the camera, and flashing a wide grin. The movement of children surrounds her, a scene "thick with moving bodies," as she wrote (Thorne 1993:14). You can hear the children laughing and shrieking, the pitter patter of feet, rubber balls bouncing on asphalt. You might be carried back to the playgrounds and schoolyards in your own past and feel those memories of play. And play is not the superfluous stuff of childhood. It is, rather, as Barrie explains, how kids make sense of, re-create, and resist the adult worlds they move in and out of.

Gender Play was the result of two periods of fieldwork in two different public elementary schools: at a school Barrie calls Oceanside in California during the 1976–77 school year; and at another she calls the Ashton school in Michigan in 1980. Barrie embarked on her research concerned with making sense of "group life," or how young people "actively come together to help create, and sometimes challenge, gender structures and meanings" (Thorne 1993:4). Barrie was dissatisfied with models of socialization that viewed children as incomplete adults or as individuals who were passively undergoing the process of becoming adults. In this deterministic view, children are "appropriated" by society and placed on future, linear paths (Corsaro 2018).[2] Instead of seeing kids as people in the process of becoming, Barrie took them seriously as social actors. The book traces the implications of kids' play and introduces the generative concept of borderwork to understand how kids negotiate gender and their often-unequal relations.

Play and Borderwork

Barrie's book offers four clusters of meanings for the word "play." Resonating with the idea that gender is "done" in the tradition of symbolic interactionism (West and Zimmerman 1987), the first meaning of play concerns action and engagement. This understanding of play "provides an antidote to the view of children as passively socialized" and embraces the view of children as actors in their own right (Thorne 1993:5). A second cluster of meanings underscores the notion of play as a kind of performance. A third meaning captures the sheer complexity of play, imbued with contradictory meanings as play refracts "crosscutting lines of difference and inequality" (Thorne 1993:5). Out of this prism emerge rays of possibility, including opportunities for social change. The final cluster of meanings suggests that play is also a grave matter. Young people laugh, act, speak, and move in ways that carry risks and consequences. An emphasis on play as trivial may therefore hide "serious and fateful encounters" (Thorne 1993:5). "Play" in this instance resonates with other well-known uses of the metaphor in a "deep" sense, where the stakes of collective action are high (Geertz 1972).

A central insight of *Gender Play* is how actors, including kids, take part in activities that reinforce and sometimes dissolve boundaries between the genders. Barrie identified three different forms of "borderwork," a term inspired by the Norwegian social anthropologist Fredrik Barth's research on ethnic classification.[3] The first involves contests, in which boys and girls are separated into opposing teams for games and competitions. These more official games are supplemented by other games that are no less serious and become commonplace and help organize the everyday of school life. In these situations, for example, boundaries are reinforced through chasing and pollution rituals.[4] A third form of boundary work is invasions, where boys disrupt girls' activities, often with impunity. Boys learn of the male privilege of property ownership through these incursions into girls' spaces.

Gender Play's reputation as advancing an "interactionist" view of gender—a careful view of the small and repetitive moments that make gender meanings, or the "micropolitics" that make up the social world (Henley 1977)—risks shortchanging Barrie's robust view of gender as both an essential part of people's lives and an analytic category. As Barrie

(2002) observed, an interactionist approach to gender brings together several related sociological traditions, including ethnomethodology, symbolic interactionism, and sociolinguistics. An interactionist view carries many advantages, including showing how gender is a constituent part of everyday life and not a function of biology. Similarly, theories of gender performativity, in the hands of leading scholars such as Judith Butler (1990), would echo the insights of dramaturgical approaches to interaction (Goffman 1959) and attract a wide audience within sociology and across the social sciences and humanities. However, Barrie has cautioned against the "one-sidedness" of approaches that focus on face-to-face interaction at the expense of the "crossroads" (Thorne 2002:8) between interactionism and other levels of analysis, including the psyche, social structure, and history. These various crossroads at once penetrate even more deeply into the self (revealing, for example, gender's affective dimensions, not easily accessed through macro-level analyses) while encouraging a more expansive and dynamic view of gender that is attentive to multiple levels of analysis and their respective advantages and limitations. To put it differently, Barrie's "interactionist" approach is not merely concerned with the face-to-face interactions between people but also with the interaction between this level of analysis and those attuned to social structures. This "fuller" account of gender, as Barrie has described it, acknowledges a "loose coupling" between interaction and structures, an anticategorical approach that does not necessarily assume that people's positions in larger structures (along lines of race, gender, social class, sexuality, and so on) determine in any rigid way how people will necessarily behave and act as they go about their daily lives. In a word, people play with gender in a manner that conforms to and resists larger social patterns and histories. The challenge for ethnographers is to be sensitive to when, how, and why gendered meanings and their implications change across situations (Thorne 2013).

Feminist Childhood Studies

In the thirty years since it was published, *Gender Play* has become an essential text in the growing and dynamic field of childhood studies. One of *Gender Play*'s major contributions has been to help tear down the unnecessary walls between feminist thought and childhood studies.

The book was the culmination of Barrie's decades-long work to situate youth—their concerns and playfulness, their standpoints, their agency and subordination—squarely in feminist concerns. While the study of childhood and children held a marginal location in mainstream sociology during the period when Barrie collected data for her book, feminism provided a language for Barrie to draw out issues of power, marginalization, and dependency (see also Best 2007). Like the ways in which feminist theory called into question a variety of dualisms (Ortner 1974), a feminist childhood studies approach troubled the dualisms of adult and child, independence and dependence, agency and passivity, and the public and the private. In Barrie's work this unsettling appears when young people are treated as experts on their own lives and as having experiences from which adults could learn. Viewing young people as legitimate social actors in these ways has ramifications for the ethics of research on youth. For example, in her 1980 essay "'You Still Takin' Notes?'" Barrie reflected on how the notion of "informed consent" fails to capture the complexities of ethical judgments that researchers are forced to make when studying young people. While it is true that hearing from kids is important so that the adults in their lives are not always speaking on their behalf, the process of making proper accommodations for young people remains laden with power dynamics. For example, childhood scholars have found that the impulse to share what consent means to young people is sometimes motivated more by a desire to protect the interests of adult researchers. And in the process of sharing this information—replete with the technical language of "rights" and "dangers" typical of Institutional Review Board materials—researchers may find themselves talking down to young people and inducing conformity in them (David, Edwards, and Alldred 2001).

Why "Gender Replay"?

The chosen name for our book, *Gender Replay*, has several meanings that capture the aims for the edited volume. It is, first, a "replay" in the sense that it reflects on the legacy of Barrie's 1993 book. This retrospective situates *Gender Play* in Barrie's own larger strands of research: on feminism and families, feminism and children, schools, and childhoods in the United States and abroad. We view our volume as a reflection on *Gender Play* as a "feminist life history," to borrow from the focus of another influential 1997 volume Barrie coedited with Barbara Laslett, titled *Feminist Sociology: Life Histories of a Movement*.[5] This approach encourages immersion in the "blurred genre" of sociological writing where "personal narratives and social theory come together" (Laslett and Thorne 1997:4). In fact, for several of the contributors, *Gender Play* was among the first influential books they read as undergraduate students, and one that helped motivate them to pursue a career studying and working with children.

Second, our volume reflects on the development of "play" in theorizing on gender, feminism, sexuality, and youth. Serious play—the kind that often parodies gender but sometimes challenges traditional gender categories and categories of difference—remains a vital metaphor in influential research (e.g., Ito et al. 2010; Pascoe 2007). Children, as Barrie wrote, engage in borderwork that marks and reinforces boundaries (e.g., through "contamination rituals" such as labeling others for having cooties). Yet young people also transgress boundaries, most powerfully illustrated by Jessie, the tomboy who played sports with the boys in *Gender Play*.[6] In fact, scholars are increasingly documenting the way in which trans, queer, and gender-fluid young people are reconfiguring gendered boundaries many adults have long seen as fixed and timeless.[7]

Third, our volume reconsiders an important cluster of meanings of play from the original text: that which acknowledges the "sheer complexity of gender relations" and, within those relations, "possibilities for social change" (Thorne 1993:5). There have been exciting developments in topics related to the book (e.g., on men and masculinities, and the privatization of public schooling), as well as heightened visibility of nonnormative gender identities (e.g., trans youth) since the publication of *Gender Play*. In a section titled "Looking Ahead," our volume will consider how the text continues to have an impact in newer areas of research. Another section is dedicated to examining the relevance of "play" in scholarship on race and ethnicity both within and outside of the United States.

The Making of *Gender Play*

Understanding what inspired us to create *Gender Replay* requires a better sense of how *Gender Play* came to exist in the first place. From her early undergraduate training as an anthropologist, Barrie developed a penchant for storytelling, a deep concern for the human condition, and a commitment to respecting the dignity of research participants. Even as Barrie changed disciplines, anthropology would remain close to her heart. Later, Barrie and her collaborator, Judith Stacey, in their 1985 call for a feminist revolution in sociology, would draw on the lessons of anthropology, which had earlier embraced the paradigm-shifting insights of feminism (Stacey and Thorne 1985).[8] The "play" of biography and feminism is crucial here, and so it helps here to situate *Gender Play* in Thorne's own *feminist life history*. As Barrie and her coauthor Barbara Laslett wrote, feminist life histories weave biographies and personal narratives with established knowledge and social theory. They are deeply human and emphasize vulnerability, revealing how emotions animate intellectual projects. And they are sensitive to historical context and change, and the "contingency, contradiction, and ambivalences" of life events (Laslett and Thorne 1992:3). In her own chapter in the *Feminist Sociology* volume, Barrie describes growing up in northern Utah, the second-oldest of five children and the daughter of parents who both held PhDs and who had met each other at Mormon Sunday School. As an undergraduate at Stanford University, Barrie grew distant from the LDS Church and was later sought out for excommunication (a story she shared often with delight and pride). Barrie's new convictions were ideas and theory. She later enrolled in 1965 at Brandeis University for her PhD in sociology. The program was relatively new, and she found in Everett Hughes a supportive advisor. Barrie describes Brandeis during that time as a "generative institution" with a spectacular menagerie of characteristics: the program was deeply indebted to both European social thought and American phenomenology and pragmatism, invested in the teaching of qualitative field methods, and committed to nurturing a critical and political consciousness in its department members.

Against the backdrop of the Vietnam War and the professional field of sociology that at the time was resolutely conservative (Burawoy 2005), Barrie and several friends became involved in a women's caucus and local women's collectives, which eventually led them to found Bread and Roses, one of the first women's liberation organizations in New England (see figure 1.1). The name for the organization drew inspiration from the famous poem by the suffragist Helen Todd. At the Women's March in Boston in 2017, long after the organization had folded, those marching would continue to call for bread and roses.[9] Barrie and her colleagues used their new feminist community to organize what they called "zap actions"—protests and other open acts of defiance against authority and patriarchal traditions—which Barrie would continue to embrace as a faculty member.[10] Barrie's deep involvement in feminist and antiwar activism led her to write a dissertation on the draft-resistance movement. It was not until Barrie had children herself that she began looking at children with "an ethnographic eye" (Smith and Greene 2014:219). She was at that time surprised and disappointed to find that the feminist literature on children was so limited.

After Barrie had completed her fieldwork for *Gender Play*, she continued to build a feminist agenda for studying young people, which resulted in what she called her "manifesto," the essay "Re-Visioning Women and Social Change: Where Are the Children?," published in *Gender and Society* as an update to the 1986 Cheryl Allen Miller Lecture she had earlier given at Loyola University in Chicago. As Barrie argued, taking children seriously was principally a feminist concern because "the fates and definitions of children have been closely tied with those of women" (1987:86). For example, in much the same way that patriarchal customs characterize women as dependent and subordinate, an adult ideological viewpoint views children as helpless and *in terms of* adults (i.e., as "adults in the making"). The study of children, Barrie argued, shares with feminism a concern with how marginalized persons construct knowledge that is often dismissed or overlooked. And like feminism, the critical study of childhood seeks to problematize taken-for-granted dualisms that reinforce systems of power and deny agency to historically marginalized groups (Thorne 2009; see also Pugh 2014 for a review).

Barrie's scholarship was inspired by a social-constructivist branch of childhood studies that emerged from Europe (in places like the United Kingdom and Scandinavia) in the 1980s. At the invitation of sociologist and fellow scholar of childhood William Corsaro, Barrie traveled to Trondheim, Norway, in 1987 for a conference on children and ethnog-

Figure I.1. Women's Bread and Roses March in Boston, Massachusetts, 1970. Courtesy of the *Boston Globe* and the Northeastern University Archives and Special Collections Department.

raphy, the first of many trips to Norway for her. From there Barrie met Hanne Haavind, a psychologist at the University of Oslo, who became a friend and collaborator and who helped introduce Barrie to a wider community of childhood and gender scholars in the region. Shortly after the publication of *Gender Play* in 1993, Barrie befriended Harriet Bjerrum Nielsen, a contributor to this volume; through this relationship, Barrie met other researchers and new collaborators at the Centre for Gender Research at the University of Oslo, where she was later an adjunct professor (Nielsen, this volume). As editor of the journal *Childhood*, housed at the Norwegian Centre for Childhood Research, Barrie would work closely with scholars across Scandinavia and Europe. These relationships led to Barrie's involvement with helping found research sections for the study of children and childhood for both the American Sociological Association and the International Sociological Association. While Barrie's primary research was conducted in the United States, she was committed to cross-national research in collaborations with scholars from different countries; see, for example, a 2015 study of Chinese American girls that Barrie wrote with researchers from Norway, Sweden, and the United Kingdom (Haavind, Thorne, Hollway, and Magnusson 2015). Barrie was also committed to destabilizing Western and Eurocentric views of childhood in her own classes and to highlighting writings on the Global South.[11]

A Legacy of Mentorship

Gender Replay will also reflect on Barrie's legacy of feminist mentoring. When research productivity and individual achievement in the academy are valorized above all else, it is easy to overlook the labor, time, and care that go into supporting the lives and careers of others. Mentoring is especially important for students from historically marginalized groups, who may have been denied access to cultural capital and models of professional success in the academy. While the third section of the book, "Feminist Praxis," is dedicated to these topics, mentorship is a thread that runs throughout the book. With Barrie's own life and work as models, we describe below our own feminist life histories and how our lives have intersected with Barrie's.

Freeden's Story

I arrived at the University of California–Berkeley in 2005 as an excited and nervous twenty-four-year-old. I had just completed two years as a sixth-grade teacher in Philadelphia, a member of the city's inaugural cohort of Teach For America (TFA) instructors. At the time, I was aware of the strong criticisms of TFA but was not totally prepared for the level of scrutiny the organization would face in the coming years. My coursework in sociology and education (and particularly courses and topics on antiracism and feminism) urged me to think more critically about my own positionality: the politics and ethics surrounding what it meant that I was an outsider who had taught in West Philly and had intentions of studying the historical dynamics of racially segregated public schooling.

The impostor syndrome that first year of graduate school was debilitating. I gave serious thought to leaving graduate school. I spent my first two years of graduate school spending a lot of time away from campus, at a record store in Oakland. I was curious about how the store brought together people from within and beyond the community, just as the Bay Area was gaining national recognition for its distinctive brand of hip-hop, called "hyphy." A lucky thing happened: I took a course on participant observation with the wonderful Dawne Moon, who helped me to sharpen my ethnographic sensibilities. My original research question (How does a record store create a sense of community for men who pass through its doors?) evolved, with Moon's encouragement, into, How are women artists positioned in the Bay Area music scene?

My growing interest in the study of gender led me to Raka Ray, who assured me I had a home in the Sociology Department. I soon found myself in Barrie's seminar on feminist theory, an experience like none other for me in graduate school. Intense and rollicking discussions were punctuated often by laughter. We viewed authors as full people with noble ambitions but with their own biases and flaws, and class participants were challenged to build and reimagine the serious work of theory. I took the questions raised in Moon's seminar and (without yet having the language of feminist life histories to guide me) asked them of myself and my own work. How had misogyny and gendered power structured my own upbringing in a Cambodian American family? What were the relations between gender, on the one hand, and race and class, on the other, the latter being more familiar coordinates in discussions of inequality in public schooling?

These new ways of considering the "twists of gender" (to borrow a favorite phrase of Barrie's)—and how gender boundaries are maintained and sometimes challenged—in a history of racially segregated schools motivated me to study single-sex public education targeted to Black children. It became the topic of my final paper in Barrie's seminar and later the subject of my dissertation. After I shared my new interest with Barrie that semester, she arrived to class one day with a large bag overflowing with materials that were relevant to the topic: articles, unpublished manuscripts, reports, grant proposals, policy briefs, clippings of newspaper articles . . . even copies of email correspondences with other scholars! The margins of these materials were full of her scribbled comments, and there were pages of handwritten notes torn out of notebooks. More than an archive of knowledge that helped launch my dissertation, those materials became for me a model for how to approach research.

The pages were full of passion, attention to detail, an eagerness to listen and learn, and humor.[12] And I came to understand from the documents that Barrie had played a major part in early debates on public single-sex education. While she was intimately familiar with the topic, she never imposed her point of view on me. She instead encouraged me to read widely and carefully and to be attentive to history and to the demands of the current political moment. Barrie encouraged me to fight for the story I believed in telling. One of the highest compliments I can offer Barrie is that, though I was her advisee, she urged me to write a book that is likely very different from one she would have written on the same topic.[13]

Like Barrie, I had been an anthropology major in college and had come to graduate school wanting to study the human condition with great care. In *Gender Play* I found an exemplar in how to think about the ways people in the rituals and daily pacing of life spin "webs of significance," and how ethnographers can use metaphors (including that of "play") to give meaning to those moments (Geertz 1973).[14] Barrie taught me that theory need not be some abstraction divorced from the details of everyday life but can be a way of organizing those many details and helping craft a story out of life's moments. She encouraged me to think imaginatively about my work and to stay clear of borderwork between sociology and other fields. And she taught me to think boldly and creatively and to think "out of the box," actually; to mention one of my favorite Barrie sayings, she encouraged her students to avoid doing their work as if it were a crossword puzzle, merely switching letters to fit boxes that others had created.

Barrie's mentoring has also shaped how I relate to my own students. While it took some time for me to develop this language, I came to understand that feminist notions of care shaped Barrie's teaching and mentoring. The same spirit animates the teaching and mentoring I now aspire to, but with my own "twists." These forms of care require transparency concerning hierarchies and power relations between faculty and students. They urge paying careful attention to student work, and the wisdom to know when a critical approach or a gentler touch is needed in working with students and advisees (see Pugh's chapter in this volume). I find myself helping students learn not just to speak up with confidence in intellectual conversations but to listen well to others: a skill rarely taught and valued in the academy. And Barrie taught me that good teaching and mentoring require a dedication to self-care: to attend to our own needs and personal well-being so that we can create healthy relationships with others.

CJ's Story

Of the many types of discussions I had with Barrie over the years, one genre in particular stands out: discussions reflecting on our own versions of "gender play" over warm bowls of soup in a café next to our department at UC–Berkeley. Barrie would marvel at my shifts in gendered styles, from a period of wearing fitted black shirts and baggy cargo pants with combat boots to one sporting long, highlighted hair and the occasional dress. For my part, I expressed wonder at her dedication to gender-neutral clothing and short, nondescript haircuts. These discussions circled around our shared identity as feminist scholars and activists, while simultaneously revealing our different, often generational, engagements with what it meant to be feminist. Our feminism, our sociological imaginations, and perhaps our forms of gender play were forged in similar intellectual and activist traditions and reflected generational engagements with those traditions. Both of us were Brandeis University graduates (her graduate training, my undergraduate), and, as such, we had been steeped in a tradition that placed liberationist approaches like feminist theory at the center of the intellectual project. While this training launched me as a naïve twenty-two-year-old into one of the most prestigious universities in the country, it led me there with very little understanding of sociology as a discipline. I had been taught Marx, sure, but only, as per the Frankfurt tradition that characterized Brandeis Sociology at that time, along with Freud. I had only a passing acquaintance with Durkheim and had never heard of Weber. In my first year of graduate study, I could still talk to you in great depth about repressive desublimation but had little understanding of organizations or collective action.

Thankfully I found Barrie, whose Brandeisian subjectivity shone through her pedagogy and mentorship. Take, for example the story she often told about the response she would have liked to have given when a colleague told her, "You're not a scientist." In retrospect, she wished she had said, "Okay, you can have science; I approach sociology like an art-ist" (Laslett and Thorne 1997:119). This creative, playful, and flexible ap-proach characterized not only her research but her mentorship as well. Rather than impart some sort of methodological dogma or strict bound-aries around what counted as sociology, Barrie instead encouraged me and her other advisees to "sing your song." Rather than setting her graduate students up to write about her own data or enforcing particu-lar visions on her graduate students' projects, Barrie, even if unfamiliar with or even skeptical of my theoretical approach, always provided me with an array of intellectual possibilities, processed them with me, and allowed me to chart my own path. Nowhere was this approach more evident than in the manuscripts I had received from Barrie, covered in all manner of comments, musings, linkages, suggestions, and the oc-casional drop of sweat due to Barrie's proclivity for reading while on the Stairmaster. These little drops always reminded me of her dedication to her graduate students, letting us and our sometimes brilliant and some-times inane ideas intrude on her solo time. The meetings that accompa-nied these responses were free-flowing brainstorms and sometimes rant sessions, occasionally punctured by a moment in which Barrie would underscore a comment that was important and should be heeded. Never directing my research, even if she was not particularly sure of my desire to bring together symbolic-interactionist approaches with queer-theory ones, she continually encouraged me to sing my own song.

Of course, singing my own song as a graduate student was not an entirely rosy experience. It meant that Barrie allowed me to make my own mistakes and was ready with words of support and wisdom when I did so. I wince when I think about some early missteps on my part. I, as my publication record suggests, have a penchant for provocative titles, a penchant that Barrie generously let me develop. An important part of becoming an academic is figuring out what concepts are boundary pushing, which are derivative, and which are just stupid, and thank-fully Barrie allowed us to figure out how to discern the difference. Most importantly, Barrie empowered me and her other advisees to succeed. She continually passed on opportunities for research, funding, academic talks, publications, and media appearances without once needing ac-claim, instead beaming in support as she watched her students go out into the world to carry on the intellectual traditions she has passed to us.

Just looking at the varied work Barrie's students have produced speaks to what she has bequeathed to us intellectually. Her focus on the embodied and lived experiences of gender, sexuality, race, nation, class, and *age*, as well as her encouragement to attend to the complexity, conflict, and emotion in these experiences appears in all of our work. Whether our work is about young people's romantic relationships, the experiences of immigrant kids in schools, or young people's use of technology, we all learned from Barrie the ethnographic skill of taking kids seriously as social actors and as social analysts.

Whether celebrating my successes or picking me up from, yet another, failure, Barrie always offered a soft place to land. I may have been over the moon with excitement about a new publication, job offer, or book contract, or crying about the job market, a particular tough review, or just graduate school in general. Regardless, Barrie was ready with tea, chocolate, and an appropriate dose of feminist fury. In fact, one of my favorite memories was visiting her office, teary and rageful about a particularly sexist insult levied by a man in the department. Fuming, I interrupted Barrie and Arlene Kaplan Daniels midconversation. Both of them responded with hugs, sage advice about the "old girls' network," and stories of how they too had encountered these sorts of things and worse. I carry with me this wonderful moment of three generations of feminists, Arlene with her "just one of the boys" attitude and flair; Barrie with her gentle, righteous anger; and me, as usual, in tears. Indeed, the bonds joining these feminist generations across shared experiences, from encountering sexually exploitative male professors at our shared alma mater to grappling with sexism at UC–Berkeley to insisting that children's concerns should be central to feminist concerns in activism and scholarship, all shape the legacy of Barrie's intellectual work, activism, and mentorship. It is a legacy that I hope to pass on to my own students.

A Feminist Community of Authors

To help explain the enduring influence of *Gender Play* and Barrie's overall body of scholarship in the "abundant present" (to borrow Barrie's words) of childhood studies, *Gender Replay* has assembled a talented group of contributors, working inside and outside the United States. The authors come from a range of institutions, from research universities to liberal arts colleges to organizations outside the academy, and an array of disciplinary backgrounds. Barrie herself, while trained as a sociologist and so eager to help cultivate a sociological imagination in others, expressed ambivalence towards the increasing disciplinarity of sociology and its tendency to impose constraints (and therefore constrain creativity) in seeking legitimacy (see Thorne 1997). We have envisioned the process of curating a list of contributors as an act of feminist community building, which was at the heart of Thorne's work, teaching, and mentoring.

The fourteen essays in our volume are organized into four sections. The first section, "Kids as Actors, Studying Kids," highlights how adult researchers can approach young people as meaning-making agents in their own worlds, and the possibilities and challenges of doing research with and on children. The leading gender theorist Raewyn Connell opens this volume with an overview and introduction to *Gender Play* in her essay, "The Play of Gender in School Life." Connell places *Gender Play* in the context of its time, describing how it was part of a larger and ongoing intellectual transformation in gender studies. In "With Love and Respect for Young People," Marjorie Elaine Faulstich Orellana addresses the analytic power of Barrie's discussion of the "adult ideological viewpoint" (Speier 1976) as the one that shapes research and what we think we know about young people. This essay makes clear how Barrie's work helps us to center, honor, and value the perspectives of those who have fewer years on the planet and how this helps reframe our own perspectives, encouraging us to imagine new possibilities. Eréndira Rueda, in her essay, "From Classrooms to Bathrooms," documents how the approaches in *Gender Play* helped her to find a way out of the "resistance" narratives that for so long dominated research on youth and education. Under Barrie's mentorship, Rueda learned to study from and with kids, and to use asset-based frames that view children as seeking a sense of belonging in their schools.

Barrie (1993:9) confesses that she was "less sensitive to [the] interconnections" among race, ethnicity, and gender than she should have been while doing fieldwork for the book. Her school sites were predominantly (about three-quarters) white and working-class.[15] In the second section of our volume, "Racial and Ethnic Borderwork and Play," the authors consider the relevance of *Gender Play* for issues of race and ethnicity in schools. Jessica S. Cobb's essay, "Playing to Resist," explains how patterns of criminalization in the United States have denied Black and Brown youth the privileges of childhood, including the freedom to make mistakes and to play. Cobb describes how movements led by marginalized youth fought back against surveillance tactics in the Los Angeles Unified School District, "subverting authority, crossing into forbidden spaces, and upholding their right to exuberant joy." In "Learning from Kids," Margaret A. Hagerman and Amanda E. Lewis draw on their respective and influential ethnographic studies—Hagerman's study of how affluent white children learn about race in their everyday lives, and Lewis's study of schools as race-making institutions—to challenge the long-held assumption that young people are passively socialized into accepting messages about race. Instead, Hagerman and Lewis find that young people's views of race and racism are sometimes at odds with those of the adults in their lives. The next chapter, "From Gendered Borderwork to Ethnic Boundaries," is also a collaborative effort featuring two different research studies. After completing their independent research in schools in Oslo, Norway, Ingrid Smette (who studied a junior high school) and Ingunn Marie Eriksen (who observed a high school) came together and discovered important differences. Smette and Eriksen update the concept of "borderwork" to explain how distinctions between who counts as "Norwegian" and who counts as a "foreigner" harden as young people move into their high school years.

The third section, "Feminist Praxis," reflects on Thorne's legacy of mentoring and advising.[16] As Barrie shared in an interview with Laurence Bachmann, "Feminist academic spaces are oases from which we water surrounding deserts, create tools for survival, and nurture a next generation of scholars and teachers" (Bachmann 2013:9). The essays in this section show how Barrie carried out this work. Michael A. Messner, in his essay "Breaking Up the Pavement," expands on this verdant growth metaphor in his description of "feminist sproutings." He links Barrie's mentorship practices with a feminist approach to theorizing in which a commitment to a collective democratic future and feminist love opens up space for creative and progressive intellectual work. Allison J. Pugh's reflections exemplify a rich ethnographic tradition in her essay "The Legacy of Relationship." She explores the question of what constitutes feminist mentoring by returning to her past communications with Barrie. In doing so she demonstrates that cultivating interpretive sensitivity through feedback, conflict, and disappointment is central to feminist mentorship. Next, Christo Sims reflects on his experience of joining Barrie at a protest in New York City and how that illustrated the ethic of care that is central to *Gender Play*. In "Living Theory" he proposes that *Gender Play* productively troubles boundaries between work and life. The following chapter, "Teaching Education, Talking Childhood, Troubling Gender," by Ingrid E. Castro and her students at Massachusetts College of Liberal Arts, is a unique example of feminist praxis in action. Castro documents a conversation about *Gender Play* with her students and their reflections about the gendered generational forces that shape children's lives—and, indeed, how those forces have shaped their own lives.

Barrie could not have anticipated the ways in which our understanding of gender has changed for children since the publication of her book. "Looking Ahead," the final section of our volume, shines a light on *Gender Play* in our contemporary moment, showing the book's enduring influence while opening new lines of inquiry and reflection. To revise Barrie's own language in *Gender Play*, all research projects have their own borders: outer limits that may preclude alternative viewpoints or confront unforeseen issues, or walls in need of building on (or dismantling) to meet the needs of today. At the close of *Gender Play*, Barrie charged adults with helping young people to disinvest from arrangements of oppositional gender and to seek out "sources of resistance, of opposition, of alternative arrangements based on equality and mutuality" (Thorne 1993:172). That spirit animates these final essays.

In the first chapter in this section, "Making Space," Cassidy Puckett and Brian E. Gravel take us inside a high school's makerspace, a creative and collaborative workspace designed for young people to explore forms of technology and engineering. The experiences of a group of Haitian girls revealed how the ambiguous categorization and valuation of certain activities inside makerspaces promoted more equitable schooling and challenged historically male-dominated STEM spaces. The next chapter, "Nordic Gender Play?" by Harriet Bjerrum Nielsen, explains how progressive changes in gender relations in Norway beginning in the 1980s likely resulted in the construction of gender categories in schools that do not necessarily square with Barrie's own observations. Through dialogue and later collaboration, Nielsen and Barrie merged situational views of play and borderwork with understandings of socialization found outside of a US context. In "Changing Youth Worlds," Amy L. Best draws on several of her own ethnographic studies to reveal the "new co-ordinates shaping youth worlds" since the publication of *Gender Play*. In the face of growing challenges—a dwindling sphere of youth autonomy, increased surveillance, and intensive parenting—young people struggle to fashion and refashion their identities, and to lead lives of dignity on their own terms. Near the end of *Gender Play*, Barrie urges a "fluid and contextual approach" to understanding gender and power, one that embraces "play as possibilities" (Thorne 1993:159). Hava Rachel Gordon's "When Kids 'Play' Politics," the volume's final essay, takes up this very call in its reflections on youth activism. By encouraging intersectional and age-diverse coalitions, young people's political engagements, Gordon demonstrates, represent the "serious stuff" of play.

The Continuing Play of Gender

Our book, *Gender Replay*, is a retrospective on Barrie's classic text and how the book has continued to shape how we think about kids, feminism, and schools. We—Freeden and CJ—have been blessed with Barrie and *Gender Play*. Our volume is our own small contribution to the feminist gift economy—to use one of Barrie's favorite sayings—which helps sustain a feminist community of researchers. As we put the finishing touches on *Gender Replay*, we at last had an opportunity to talk about our book with Barrie and to present it as a gift to her. This book is *very Barrie* in the sense that it is guided by generosity and great care, resolutely committed to feminist principles, dedicated to craft, and welcoming to all. Our work and all it entails—our scholarship, our teaching, our mentoring, the support and encouragement we offer—are gifts we give one another, with the hope that our mutual relations will spur social change and build feminist futures. To return to and revise (with love) Barrie's own language one final time, as we traverse the concrete of academic theorizing, we hope our volume encourages creative sproutings, lining new paths to change amid the continuing and evolving play of gender, in ways that will help students, researchers, activists, and classroom instructors—young and old.

NOTES

1   We have chosen to refer to Barrie by her first name in this introduction. Partly this is to convey a sense of intimacy, as we and many of our contributors have been close to Barrie (and so using her last name, particularly later in the introduction, when we share our own personal stories and how we met her, would be awkward). We also imagine that she would want to be referred to in that way. At the same time, we acknowledge that this practice risks undermining Barrie's earned authority as a scholar and professional. We have left it to the discretion of each of the authors in their own chapters to choose how they wish to refer to her.

2   Barrie's work can be situated here in a new sociology of childhood that is critical of traditional views of socialization and more open to the view of childhood as "interpretive reproduction," or how young people are creative actors who participate actively in cultural production (Corsaro 2018; see also James, Jenks, and Prout 2005).

3   In the United States, Barth's research has been foundational in comparative theories of ethnicity (e.g., Wimmer 2013). Barrie drew on Barth's writings with the encouragement of the anthropologist of education Frederick Erickson.

4   While same-gender chasing is unremarkable (and reveals gendered patterns themselves, e.g., boys are more physically aggressive), cross-gender chasing made for lively discussion. In pollution rituals, girls as a group are viewed as more contaminating than boys (e.g., as having "cooties"). Barrie has joked that she is the world's leading expert on cooties.

5   While doing preliminary research for this volume, Freeden found that he had misplaced his copy of *Feminist Sociology*. He purchased a used copy online and was stunned to find that it had once been owned by Dorothy E. Smith, who had written an inscription—"The fault line bifurcated at last!"—inside the front cover. (The comment is a play on Smith's notion of a "bifurcated consciousness," referring to the tension women academics feel between their own life experiences and the scientific vocabularies that have historically failed to account for those experiences, a rupture Smith [1987] has called a "line of fault.") Laslett and Thorne had hoped that Smith, a leading feminist theorist, could contribute a chapter to their volume. Smith was unable to but her influence can be felt throughout the pages of *Feminist Sociology*. In 1992, Laslett and Thorne had organized a symposium aimed at showing how Smith's writings could help tear down the "wall of science between . . . sociological theory and feminist theory" (1992:60). In 2021, Freeden was able to connect with Smith (on Twitter!) and to chat about how much she influenced Barrie's own work, and to let her know about the present volume. We had hoped to give Smith a copy of *Gender Replay* once it was published. Smith passed away on June 3, 2022, shortly before we submitted the final manuscript to our publisher.

6   In her book *Dude, You're a Fag* (2007), CJ named one of her respondents—an athletic, lesbian homecoming queen—Jessie in homage to the girl of the same name in *Gender Play*.

7 See, for example, Tey Meadow's book *Trans Kids: Being Gendered in the 21ˢᵗ Century* (2018) and Ann Travers's book *Trans Generation: How Trans Kids (and Their Parents) Are Creating a Gender Revolution* (2018).

8 As Judith Stacey and Barrie observed, anthropology's abiding concern with kinship is one reason why issues of sex and gender have long been more central concerns for this field than for the other social sciences. The family would remain a scholarly interest for Barrie. With Marilyn Yalom, Barrie gathered anthropologists and sociologists together to assess the family through a feminist prism in the volume *Rethinking the Family: Some Feminist Questions* (1982).

9 Posters at the march read, "We Still Want Bread and Roses." See the Digital Repository Service of the Northeastern University Library. Available at https:// repository.library.northeastern.edu.

10 For example, in 2011 Barrie was involved in the Occupy Wall Street Movement and related efforts, including the fight against tuition hikes at UC–Berkeley. These efforts serve as the backdrop to Christo Sims's chapter in this volume.

11 A favorite book of Barrie's to teach was Tobias Hecht's *At Home in the Street: Street Children in Northern Brazil* (Thorne 2013). *Gender Play* has been influential outside of Europe as well. A Korean translation of the book appeared in 2014.

12 In one exchange Barrie had with several women colleagues about a scheduled panel on single-sex education, they joked that their participation in the "semin-ar" (highlighting the popular media narratives at the time about a boys' crisis in schools and a men's crisis more generally) was more accurately a "semin(ovul)ar."

13 Barrie had been a consultant for the National Organization for Women, which had in the early 1990s challenged efforts by the city of Detroit to open all-male academies targeted to Black boys. Freeden's own book, *Black Boys Apart* (2018), opens with a discussion of NOW's legal challenges. The title of the book nods to Barrie's favored language of "with and apart" to describe gender integration and separation (Bachmann 2013).

14 I (Freeden) am not at all trying to reduce Barrie's own interpretivist approach to that of the well-known anthropologist Clifford Geertz. The writings of the latter, in fact, emerged and became influential contemporaneously with Barrie's time in graduate school and in her early years as a junior faculty member at Michigan State University. Reading Geertz—including "Deep Play" (1972)—in college, however, sensitized me to microscopic approaches to the social world, and later, with Barrie's guiding hand, how a feminist perspective deepens understanding of how emotions saturate the "webs of significance" (in Geertz's words) that people spin. And as my own scholarship has evolved to consider feminist questions for African American history and politics, I remain interested in how writers can use metaphors to explain the social world like a text. (Several authors in this volume reflect on Barrie's special gift for using metaphors.) However, I have learned that this work should be done with great care since metaphors can hide as much as they reveal (e.g., Blume Oeur 2021).

15 Barrie expressed regret for not spending more time with and listening to the Spanish-speaking children at these schools.

16 In 2011, Barrie was recognized with the Distinguished Faculty Mentor Award from UC–Berkeley. She retired the following year.

REFERENCES

Bachmann, Laurence. 2013. "Watering Surrounding Deserts: A Lifetime of Spreading Feminist Insights; An Interview with Barrie Thorne, UC Berkeley." Sociograph Working Paper. Université de Gèneva.

Barth, Fredrik. 1998. *Ethnic Groups and Boundaries: The Social Organization of Culture Difference*. Long Grove, IL: Waveland Press.

Best, Amy L., ed. 2007. *Representing Youth: Methodological Issues in Critical Youth Studies*. New York: NYU Press.

Blume Oeur, Freeden. 2018. *Black Boys Apart: Racial Uplift and Respectability in All-Male Public Schools*. Minneapolis: University of Minnesota Press.

———. 2021. "Fever Dreams: W. E. B. Du Bois and the Racial Trauma of COVID-19 and Lynching." *Ethnic and Racial Studies* 44(5):735–45.

Burawoy, Michael. 2005. "For Public Sociology." *American Sociological Review* 70(1):4–28.

Butler, Judith. 1990. *Gender Trouble: Feminism and the Subversion of Identity*. New York: Routledge.

Corsaro, William A. 2018. *The Sociology of Childhood*, 5th ed. Thousand Oaks, CA: Sage.

David, Miriam, Rosalind Edwards, and Pam Alldred. 2001. "Children and School-Based Research: 'Informed Consent' or 'Educated Consent.'" *British Educational Research Journal* 27(3):347–65.

Ferguson, Ann Arnett. 2000. *Bad Boys: Public Schools in the Making of Black Masculinity*. Ann Arbor: University of Michigan Press.

Geertz, Clifford. 1972. "Deep Play: Notes on the Balinese Cockfight." *Daedelus* 101(1):1–37.

———. 1973. *The Interpretation of Cultures*. New York: Basic Books.

Goffman, Erving. 1959. *The Presentation of Self in Everyday Life*. New York: Anchor Books.

Haavind, Hanne, Barrie Thorne, Wendy Hollway, and Eva Magnusson. 2015. "'Because Nobody Likes Chinese Girls': Intersectional Identities and Emotional Experiences of Subordination and Resistance in School Life." *Childhood* 22(3):300–315.

Hecht, Tobias. 1998. *At Home in the Street: Street Children of Northeast Brazil*. Cambridge: Cambridge University Press.

Henley, Nancy. 1977. *Body Politics: Power, Sex, and Nonverbal Communication*. New York: Prentice Hall.

Ito, Mizuko, Sonja Baumer, Matteo Bittanti, danah boyd, Rachel Cody, Becky Herr-Stephenson, Heather A. Horst, Patricia G. Lange, Dilan Mahendran, Katynka Martinez, C. J. Pascoe, Dan Perkel, Laura Robinson, and Lisa Tripp. 2010. *Hanging*

Out, Messing Around, and Geeking Out: Kids Living and Learning with New Media. Cambridge, MA: MIT Press.

James, Allison, Chris Jenks, and Alan Prout. 2005. "Theorizing Childhood." Pp. 138–60 in *Childhood: Critical Concepts in Sociology,* edited by C. Jenks. New York: Taylor & Francis.

Laslett, Barbara, and Barrie Thorne, eds. 1992. "Considering Dorothy Smith's Social Theory: A Symposium" (essays by Charles Lemert, Patricia Hill Collins, R. W. Connell, and Dorothy E. Smith). *Sociological Theory* 10(1):60–98.

———. 1997. *Feminist Sociology: Life Histories of a Movement.* New Brunswick, NJ: Rutgers University Press.

Meadow, Tey. 2018. *Trans Kids: Being Gendered in the 21st Century.* Oakland: University of California Press.

Ortner, Sherry B. 1974. "Is Female to Male as Nature Is to Culture?" Pp. 68–87 in *Woman, Culture, and Society,* edited by M. Rosaldo and L. Lamphere. Stanford, CA: Stanford University Press.

Pascoe, C. J. 2007. *Dude, You're a Fag: Masculinity and Sexuality in High School.* Berkeley: University of California Press.

Pugh, Allison. 2014. "The Theoretical Costs of Ignoring Childhood: Rethinking Independence, Insecurity, and Inequality." *Theory and Society* 43:71–89.

Smith, Carmel, and Sheila Greene. 2014. "Barrie Thorne." Pp. 219–27 in *Key Thinkers in Childhood Studies,* edited by C. Smith and S. Greene. Bristol, UK: Policy Press.

Smith, Dorothy E. 1987. *The Everyday World as Problematic: A Feminist Sociology.* Toronto: University of Toronto Press.

Speier, Matthew. 1976. "The Adult Ideological Viewpoint in Studies of Childhood." Pp. 168–86 in *Rethinking Childhood: Perspectives on Development and Society,* edited by A. Skolnick. New York: Little, Brown.

Stacey, Judith, and Barrie Thorne. 1985. "The Missing Feminist Revolution in Sociology." *Social Problems* 32(4):301–16.

Thorne, Barrie. 1975. "Women in the Draft Resistance Movement." *Sex Roles* 1(2):179–95.

———. 1980. "'You Still Takin' Notes?': Fieldwork and Problems of Informed Consent." *Social Problems* 27(3):284–97.

———. 1987. "Re-Visioning Women and Social Change: Where Are the Children?" *Gender and Society* 1(1):85–109.

———. 1993. *Gender Play: Girls and Boys in School.* New Brunswick, NJ: Rutgers University Press.

———. 1997. "Brandeis as a Generative Institution: Critical Perspectives, Marginality, and Feminism." Pp. 103–25 in *Feminist Sociology: Life Histories of a Movement,* edited by B. Laslett and B. Thorne. New Brunswick, NJ: Rutgers University Press.

———. 2002. "Gender and Interaction: Widening the Scope." Pp. 3–18 in *Gender in Interaction: Perspectives on Femininity and Masculinity in Ethnography and Discourse,* edited by B. Baron and H. Kotthoff. Amsterdam: John Benjamins.

———. 2009. "Childhood: Changing and Dissonant Meanings." *International Journal of Learning and Media* 1(1):19–27.

———. 2012. "*Pricing the Priceless Child* as a Teaching Treasure." *Journal of the History of Childhood and Youth* 5(3):474–80.

———. 2013. "Children and Gender." Pp. 185–201 in *The New Psychology of Gender*, edited by M. Gergen and S. Davis. New York: Routledge.

Thorne, Barrie, and Marilyn Yalom. 1982. *Rethinking the Family: Some Feminist Questions*. New York: Longman.

Travers, Ann. 2018. *Trans Generation: How Trans Kids (and Their Parents) Are Creating a Gender Revolution*. New York: NYU Press.

West, Candance, and Don H. Zimmerman. 1987. "Doing Gender." *Gender & Society* 1(2):125–51.

Wimmer, Andreas. 2013. *Ethnic Boundary Making: Institutions, Power, Networks*. New York: Oxford University Press.

PART I

Kids as Actors, Studying Kids

1

The Play of Gender in School Life

Reflections on Barrie Thorne's Classic Book

RAEWYN CONNELL

I came to know Barrie Thorne by teaching with her. In spring semester 1989 I was visiting the United States as a very temporary professor in gender studies, in the Program for the Study of Women and Men in Society (referred to as "swims") at the University of Southern California. This was an implausible place to find either of us, a wealthy private college swimming in oil and Hollywood money. But feminist women at USC had managed to establish and fund one of the most flourishing gender studies centers in the country, perhaps the only one at the time that mentioned men in its name. I had recently published some sociological work about masculinities, and about class and gender in schools, that connected with Barrie's work. I was also interested in a promising young scholar by the name of Michael Messner, another contributor to this volume, who was teaching in the same program and writing unusual papers about masculinities in sport.

Barrie made our family warmly welcome, offering a kindness to wandering foreigners who needed to find a place in North American culture. She suggested combining the introduction-to-gender-studies units she and I were both scheduled to teach. I was very glad to do this, as I had no experience with teaching American undergraduates, let alone an introductory class. Teaching together was a pleasure and a revelation. Barrie is one of the best and most interactive teachers I have ever seen in action. She has an extraordinary capacity for keeping the wandering attention of a bunch of students focused; for getting the discussion to move ahead, and transform from a random expression of opinions into a collective process of exploration; and for making all the participants, whatever their background or level of sophistication, feel they have something of value to add.

These talents as a teacher, combining quick empathy with sharp intelligence, overlap with the capacities needed for good ethnography. When *Gender Play* appeared a few years later, Barrie's talent as a field researcher was fully revealed.

Some years after that, I was invited by my UK publishers to prepare a second edition of my book, *Gender and Power*. I tried to do this, spending many months planning and drafting new chapters, but the project would not come together. I became very frustrated, not understanding why. Myra Marx Ferree (2018) has given a good explanation—the problems themselves were shifting historically, so patching up the original framework was not really possible. But I did not want to waste all that work! When the publishers launched a series of "short introductions" to different fields, and asked me to write for it, I agreed. I imagined that an introductory text should do some introducing. I have always tried to get beginning students to meet some examples of first-class research very early. It has to be chosen carefully, as cutting-edge stuff is often difficult for beginners to understand. No problem here. In the new book, the first example of gender research that I presented was Barrie Thorne's *Gender Play*.

What follows in this chapter are my reflections on *Gender Play* that I wrote for my book *Gender* (2002), now out of print.[1] At the end, I have added some thoughts on the significance of Barrie's book in the history of gender research.

The Play of Gender in School Life

One of the most difficult tasks in social research is to take a situation that everyone thinks they understand and illuminate it in new ways. This is what the US ethnographer Barrie Thorne achieves in her subtly observed and highly readable book about school life, *Gender Play* (1993).

At the time Thorne started her work, children were not much discussed in gender research. When they were mentioned, it was usually assumed that they were being "socialized" into gender roles, in a top-down transmission from the adult world. It was assumed that there are two sex roles, a male one and a female one, with boys and girls getting separately inducted into the norms and expectations of the appropriate one. This idea was based on a certain amount of research using paper-

and-pencil questionnaires, but not on much actual observation of gender in children's lives.

Thorne did that observation. Her book is based on fieldwork in two elementary (primary) schools in different parts of the United States. She spent eight months in one, three months in another, hanging about in classrooms, hallways, and playgrounds, talking to everyone and watching the way the children interacted with each other and with their teachers in work and play.

Ethnography as a method sounds easy, but in practice is hard to do well. Part of the problem is the mass of information an observer can get from just a single day "in the field." You need to know what you are looking for. But you also need to be open to new experiences and new information, able to see things that you did not expect to see.

As an observer Thorne was certainly interested in transmission from older people, in the ways children pick up the details of how to do gender. Her funniest (and perhaps also saddest) chapter is called "Lip Gloss and 'Goin' With,'" about how preadolescent children learn the techniques of teenage flirting and dating. She was also interested in the differences between the girls' and the boys' informal interactions—the games they played, spaces they used, words they spoke, and so on.

But Thorne was able to see beyond the patterns described in conventional gender models. She became aware how much these models predisposed an observer to look for difference. She began to pay attention, not only to the moments in school life when the boys and girls separated but also to the moments when they came together. She began to think of gender difference as *situational,* as created in some situations and ignored or overridden in others. Even in recess-time games, where the girls and boys were usually clustered in separate parts of the playground, they sometimes moved into mixed activities without any emphasis on difference. There were many "relaxed cross-sex interactions" in the school's daily routine. Clearly, the boys and girls were not permanently in separate spheres, nor permanently enacting opposite "sex roles."

Recognizing this fact opened up a number of other issues. What were the situations where gender was emphasized or deemphasized? Thorne noticed that, though teachers sometimes emphasized gender—for instance, arranging a classroom learning game with the girls competing against the boys—most teacher-controlled activities deemphasized gender. This is true, for instance, of the commonest teaching technique in schools, the "talk-and-chalk" method where the teacher at the front of the room demands the attention of all the pupils to an exposition of some lesson that they all have to learn. In this situation the basic division is between teacher and taught, not between groups of pupils; so girls and boys are in the same boat.

Next, how did the children establish gender difference when they did emphasize it? Thorne began to identify a kind of activity she called "borderwork": "When gender boundaries are activated, the loose aggregation 'boys and girls' consolidates into 'the boys' and 'the girls' as separate and reified groups. In the process, categories of identity that on other occasions have minimal relevance for interaction become the basis of separate collectivities" (1993:65).

There are different kinds of borderwork in a primary school. One of the most interesting is chasing, a kind of game that is sometimes very fluid and sometimes not. I remember a chasing game at my primary school, a rather intimidating game called "cocky-laura," which was extremely rule bound. One of the implicit rules was that only boys could play, because the girls were forbidden by the school to be in the part of the playground where a big eucalyptus tree stood that was one of the bases for the game. In the schools Thorne studied, boys and girls could play together, and often chased each other, playing "girls-chase-the-boys" and "boys-chase-the-girls." Indeed, the one game would often merge into the other, as the chased turned around and became the chasers. Thorne notes that often boys chased boys, or girls chased girls, but these patterns attracted little attention or discussion. However, girls-chasing-boys/boys-chasing-girls often resulted in lively discussion and excitement. It was a situation in which "gender terms blatantly override individual identities, especially in references to the other team ('Help, a girl's chasin' me'; 'C'mon Sarah, let's get that boy'; 'Tony, help save me from the girls'). Individuals may call for help from, or offer help to, others of their gender. And in acts of treason, they may grab someone from their team and turn them over to the other side. For example, in an elaborate chasing scene among a group of Ashton third graders, Ryan grabbed Billy from behind, wrestling him to the ground. "Hey girls, get 'im,' Ryan called" (1993:69). Thorne's observation of children might alert us to parallel processes among adults. Borderwork is constantly being done to mark gender boundaries, if not by chasing then by jokes, dress, forms of speech, etc. Gender difference is not something that simply exists. It is something that happens, and must be made to happen—something, also, that can be unmade, altered, made less important.

The games in which the children make gender happen do something more. When the girls chase the boys and the boys chase the girls, they seem to be acting equally, and in some respects they are—but not in all respects. For a rough-and-tumble version of the chasing game is more common among the boys. Boys normally control more of the playground space than the girls do, more often invade girls' groups and disrupt the girls' activities than the girls disrupt theirs. That is to say, the boys more often make an aggressive move and a claim to power, in the limited sense that children can do this.

In the symbolic realm, too, the boys claim power. They treat girls as a source of contamination or pollution, for instance, calling low-status boys "girls" or pushing them next to the space occupied by girls. The girls do not treat the boys that way. Girls are more often defined as giving the imaginary disease called "cooties," and low-status girls may get called "cootie queens." A version of cooties played in one of the schools is called "girl stain." All these may seem small matters. But as Thorne remarks, "Recoiling from physical proximity with another person and their belongings because they are perceived as contaminating is a powerful statement of social distance and claimed superiority" (1993:75).

So there is an asymmetry in the situations of boys and girls, which is reflected in differences among the boys and among the girls. Some boys often interrupt the girls' games, other boys do not. Some boys have higher status, others have lower. Some of the girls move earlier than others into "romance." By fourth grade, homophobic insults—such as calling another boy a "fag"—are becoming common among the boys, most of whom learn that this word is a way of expressing hostility before they know what its sexual meaning is. At the same time, however, physical contact among the boys is becoming less common—they are learning to fear, or be suspicious of, displays of affection. In short, the children are beginning to show something of the differentiation of gender patterns, and the gender and sexual hierarchies, that are familiar among adults.

There is much more in Thorne's fascinating book, including a humorous and insightful discussion of what it is like for an adult to do research among children. For me, the most important lesson her book teaches is about these American children's *agency* in learning gender. They are not passively "socialized" into a sex role. They are, of course, learning things from the adult world around them: lessons about available identities, lessons about performance, and—regrettably—lessons about hatred. But they do this actively, and on their own terms. They find gender interesting and sometimes exciting. They move into and out of gender-based groupings. They sometimes shore up, and sometimes move across, gender boundaries. They even play with and against the gender dichotomy itself. Gender is important in their world, but it is important as a human issue that they deal with, not as a fixed framework that reduces them to puppets.

Reflections

Well before publishing *Gender Play*, Barrie Thorne had been a critic of the "sex role" model for understanding gender (Lopata and Thorne 1978). The sex-role model was important because it provided a serious alternative to the biological-determinist doctrine that women's and men's reproductive difference accounted for their different social positions, attitudes, psychological characteristics, and more. Commonsense biological determinism conveyed the powerful political message that women should accept what they had because their situation was fixed by nature. In that ideological atmosphere, the sex-role concept was a breath of fresh air. If gendered situations were determined by social norms, then they were not fixed forever in the same pattern. They could be changed by shifting the norms.

That was a very important message, from the 1950s to the 1970s, and it is not surprising that many feminists picked it up with enthusiasm (see the literature in the massive compendium by Maccoby and Jacklin 1975). Reform agendas to change sexist norms, stereotypes, and cultural assumptions about gender were worked out for schools, academia, journalism, advertising, children's books, employment practices, promotions, and so on. Indeed, this work is still going on. The current campaign to get more girls and women into STEM courses and jobs still works largely on the let's-change-the-norms model.

But the sex-role model had troubling limitations. Most formulations assumed there was just one female role and one male role, so the model did not encourage concern with race or class situations, or with diversity in gender itself. To US women who had grown up in the era of civil rights struggle, had campaigned against the ghastly American war in Vietnam, and then had become activists in the women's liberation movement, the most striking problem with the sex-role model was that it had almost nothing to say about power. It presumed a more or less benign reciprocity between the male role and the female role—"instrumental" v. "expressive" in Talcott Parsons's famous version—which made little sense of women's experiences of economic inequality, cultural denigration, institutional exclusion, domestic violence, and other forms of abuse.

So critiques of the sex-role model multiplied. But as we know from other cases, showing the flaws in an interpretive model is not enough. We have to offer credible alternatives to it. And that is what Barrie Thorne did in *Gender Play*, on the sex-role model's home ground: the learning of gender. None of the radical theories of gender produced in the women's liberation decades—models of patriarchal domination, ideological reproduction of capitalism, psychoanalytic accounts of language and culture, gender as discourse—gave a convincing account of how women and men arrived in adulthood ready to dominate or be dominated, reproduce or labor, speak or be spoken of. Childhood, conceptually speaking, went missing. So the socialization model remained as the only effective alternative to biological determinism.

Gender Play reads like an affectionate memoir, even a novel: it has a cast list, it tells a story, it has incident and humor. But underneath it is a steely agenda. Barrie is stripping away the myth-making about gender formation and making us look at the young people involved not as bearers of genetic messages, not as victims of social pressure, but as *people*. Like any other people, they are faced with a situation and respond to it as best they can. They are busy steering through pain and pleasure, constructing a life that is socially recognizable because they live in a social world, but is not quite what anybody else constructs because they are their own people. There is more than a touch of existentialism in Barrie's ethnography, I think, and it is all the better for it.

In my 2002 account of *Gender Play* I used a bit of sociological jargon to catch what was distinctive in Barrie's work, saying that she emphasized the children's *agency* in the learning of gender. I now think that underestimates what she was doing. The children's agency needs to be understood in connection with Barrie's documentation of the changing situational emphasis on gender, and the situations where gender division is muted or effectively overridden and others where it is very salient. She is not saying that gender is simply "performative," a term that was rapidly coming into favor in gender studies at the time through many readings and misreadings of Judith Butler's work. Barrie never forgets the social-structural dimension of gender. The schools she is describing are gendered institutions, the children are learning the language of vicious prejudice, the boys are learning about power, the girls are learning about heterosexual desirability even before they reach puberty.

Gender-as-structure in *Gender Play* is not one of the neat geometrical models offered by the structuralist theorists of Barrie's youth (and mine)—Piaget, Lévi-Strauss, Lacan, Althusser—taken up by women's liberation theorists such as Juliet Mitchell (1974) and Gayle Rubin (1975). Barrie's version is more turbulent, more effortful; sometimes salient, sometimes not; sometimes accepted, sometimes contested, even both at once. Gender in this vision is *historical*, to use a language I am more inclined towards now. It is a structure that comes into existence through time, and will transform in time, just as sex-role theorists believed—though with more blood, sweat, and tears than campaigns around role norms usually recognize. It is also an *embodied* structure, and the physicality of gender is brilliantly conveyed in *Gender Play*'s narratives of chasing games, the contrast of playground and classroom, the girls' experiments with cosmetics, and more.

If I am correct in these readings, then we can see *Gender Play* as part of an intellectual transformation in gender studies that is still working its way through. Barrie does not talk about hybridity, but she shows it as a feature of practices, not just identities. Her treatment of everyday gender boundary crossing and boundary defense, the kind of action she calls "borderwork," has never been bettered. Her approach is, I think, entirely consistent with the idea of intersectionality, and in her later work on California childhoods, she developed this dimension vigorously. *Gender Play* is a conceptual resource as well as a beautifully crafted ethnography. I hope new generations of scholarship will learn from it as much as our generation has.

NOTE

1 Text reproduced by kind permission of Polity Books.

REFERENCES

Connell, Raewyn. 2002. *Gender*. Cambridge, UK: Polity Press.

Ferree, Myra Marx. 2018. "'Theories Don't Grow on Trees': Contextualizing Gender Knowledge." Pp. 13–34 in *Gender Reckonings: New Social Theory and Research*, edited by J. M. Messerschmidt, P. Y. Martin, M. A. Messner, and R. Connell. New York: NYU Press.

Lopata, Helena Z., and Barrie Thorne. 1978. "On the Term 'Sex Roles.'" *Signs: Journal of Women in Culture and Society* 3(3):718–21.

Maccoby, Eleanor E., and Carol Nagy Jacklin. 1975. *The Psychology of Sex Differences*. Stanford, CA: Stanford University Press.

Mitchell, Juliet. 1974. *Psychoanalysis and Feminism*. New York: Pantheon Books.

Parsons, Talcott, and Robert Bales. 1956. *Family Socialization and Interaction Process*. London: Routledge & Kegan Paul.

Rubin, Gayle. 1975. "The Traffic in Women: Notes on the 'Political Economy' of Sex." Pp. 157–210 in *Toward an Anthropology of Woman*, edited by R. R. Reiter. New York: Monthly Review.

Thorne, Barrie. 1993. *Gender Play: Girls and Boys in School*. New Brunswick, NJ: Rutgers University Press.

2

With Love and Respect for Young People

Learning with and from Barrie Thorne in the Ethnography of Childhood

MARJORIE ELAINE FAULSTICH ORELLANA

In the spring of 1993, around the time when *Gender Play* was published, I was the mother of a five-year-old, a teacher by day, and a doctoral student in education at the University of Southern California at night. Required to take cognate courses outside my department, I stumbled onto a class, The Sociology of Sex and Gender, taught by Barrie Thorne. I remember walking across campus into a classroom that looked and felt different from any I had ever learned in. There was food to share, a circle of chairs to sit in, and a stack of books (not just a reader) that we would devour that semester. One was *Gender Play*.

Meeting Barrie changed my life. So, too, did reading her book. I was introduced to the idea that both gender and childhood were social constructs. I learned grounded ethnographic approaches to study *how* they are constructed, and how those constructions matter in the social world. And I was mentored into a way of doing/being academia that was profoundly humanizing: for myself and for the young "subjects" of our research.

In this essay, I discuss Barrie's influence on how I came to study aspects of social life that are so often hidden from view by the "adult ideological viewpoint" (Speier 1976) that prevails in the research world. I show Barrie's influence on my own pathway into and through academia, and on future generations, as I, like many others, have tried to "pay forward" the support and guidance we received from her. Barrie's influence has been broad and generative, both through her scholarship and through the hearts and minds she touched as a teacher, mentor, feminist, scholar, and human being.

Conceptualizing Gender, Children, and Childhoods

Beyond Binaries

Barrie's ways of conceptualizing gender and educational research with young people profoundly shaped my dissertation research. As a classroom teacher and doctoral student in education, I had been planning to study literacy practices in two primary-grade bilingual public-school classrooms. I was interested in how young children become bilingual and biliterate, and how teachers and schools could support them.

When I initially proposed to include attention to gender within this inquiry—as required by the certificate program I decided to complete, offered by the Center for the Study of Women and Men in Society (a program that Barrie helped forge)—faculty in the school of education suggested a kind of chi-square analysis. Put the two classrooms on one side of the square; boys and girls on the other, and analyze the "results" inside each box: a neat double binary leading to some kind of proof of differences within and across the cells.

Under Barrie's tutelage, I took a different approach. Eschewing gender as a duality, a variable, or a trait, located only in the bodies of readers and writers, I did not ask about *differences* between girls and boys on literacy performance measures. Instead, I asked *how* gender mattered in relation to young people's literacy learning. Connecting Barrie's work and other germinal texts in the sociology of gender that Barrie introduced to me (including, especially, *Gender and Power* by R. W. Connell, author of the preceding chapter in this volume) with the ideas of feminist literacy researchers (e.g., Davies 1997), I asked how literacy shaped children's ideas about what it means to be a boy or a girl. And how did the ideas about gender that young people brought to their literacy learning shape their engagement with and take-up of literacy *tasks, texts,* and *talk*?

Viewing literacy as a social practice, enacted by people in social and cultural contexts, I considered the *many* ways it became gendered: in different activities, practices, relationships, texts, and contexts. I showed how gender *became salient* in relation to literacy practices within and across the two classrooms, and what this meant for literacy learning. Barrie's notion of "borderwork" was key. I probed where and how borders between gender binaries were reinforced in relation to literacy, and where and how they sometimes blurred, with differences fading from significance.

I found that borderwork was done in various ways within and across the two classrooms. For example, one teacher used the boy/girl binary to structure almost all of her classroom practices, as part of her classroom-management strategies: pairing boys and girls to read, and setting up carefully gender-balanced groups for other activities. The texts she selected further structured gender, both in their content (with many reinforcing traditional gender roles) and in their *language* (especially because Spanish is an overtly gender-marked language). Children in the second classroom had considerable free choice over how they organized themselves for literacy tasks. In this project-based, "free-choice" setting, literacy was largely supported through the writing of student-authored books. Young authors workshopped drafts that were eventually typed, bound, and shelved in the classroom library. The teacher *never* used gender as an organizing variable, or even as an identity marker; she referred to kids as authors rather than "boys and girls." But, perhaps not surprisingly, kids organized themselves largely by gender, with few mixed-sex authorship teams. They also depicted largely gender-separate worlds in their stories, with girls almost completely absent in stories written by boys. Love, romance, and jealousy were central themes in many of the girls' stories, which were often seemingly "still life" sketches of life at home. Many boys, in contrast, wrote action-filled adventures about superheroes of all kinds, depicted as bold, daring, and powerful. Characters seemed to reveal the authors' understandings of what girls and boys should or should not be allowed or expected to do, with girls, for the most part, presented as cheerful, kind, obedient, and helpful, while boys were adventurous, powerful, and sometimes, daringly "bad" (Orellana 1999).

Children as Actors and Agents

With Barrie's voice in my head—as a gender theorist and an ethnographer—I tried to stay alert to disconfirming evidence. This helped me to notice a small group of students whose writing defied the dominant narratives of the classroom, with characters in their stories that transgressed stereotypically gendered social norms. I looked at the risks these authors took in their writing, and how their texts were received. This helped me to contemplate how *ideas* about gendered differences take hold and become solidified; and how they can be challenged. Adults—especially teachers like the one in the first classroom—were powerful socializing agents, but children both conformed to and resisted the socialization in different ways.

In doing these things I was countering the dominant approaches in my field (education).[1] Seeing young people as creative actors in their own learning is surprisingly lacking in educational research and practice, especially in school-based research with young children. Indeed, as Cindy Dell Clark (2011) has pointed out, educational research is one of the fields in which children are *least* visible as actors and agents. With a few important exceptions by educational ethnographers who have been shaped by the new social study of childhoods (e.g., García-Sánchez 2014; Lewis 2003) and participatory action research with older youth, educational research treats children mostly as "adults in the making." It has been my honor and pleasure to bring to the field of education what I learned from Barrie: an orientation to viewing young children as actors and agents in the here-and-now who contribute to social processes and make their own sense of the world.

Childhoods as Social Constructions

Barrie's influence on my thinking, and my life, grew even greater after I finished my doctoral studies in 1994. Around that time, Barrie was invited to participate in an interdisciplinary network of scholars charged by the MacArthur Foundation to study "successful pathways through middle childhood." Barrie offered me a position as postdoctoral researcher on a project she was about to launch: a study of different kinds of childhoods in California.

Barrie was a bit of an outlier in the MacArthur Foundation network, which was dominated by developmental psychologists. In the meetings that I attended, Barrie continually questioned implicit assumptions, such as the idea that childhood was something to be traversed on teleological pathways to adulthood, or that children were the objects of adults' socialization efforts. She pushed her colleagues to consider how children experienced "middle childhood" in the here and now, and how their actions mattered not just for their futures but for their present contributions to the social world. She further questioned the meanings of success: Who decides what counts as successful? Do children get to have a say?

Like all of the ideas I learned with and from Barrie, the notion that childhood was not a transparent thing was new to me at the time. Certainly, from both personal and professional experience, I knew that there were many variations in cultural norms, values, practices, and beliefs about what children should or should not be expected to do, both within and across cultures, and over time. My partner had grown up in Guatemala, wielding a machete at the age of three and crossing the border to the United States on his own at the age of sixteen. I knew his childhood had been very different from mine in a large, Catholic, working-class New England community. I knew, too, that my mother's ideas that her eight children "should be seen but not heard" contrasted with the child-centered parenting I saw modeled by my contemporaries. But I did not really question the idea that *some* kind of clear distinction could be made between children and adults. Barrie helped me to see that age-based distinctions were not unlike other categories that humans have created to reduce the complexity of the social world: slippery, evasive, political, and variable across place and time—and yet believed, by most people, to be transparent, universal, and true.

Barrie was moving to UC–Berkeley at the time that I graduated, and she invited me into a multisited ethnography to study *ideas* about successful childhoods, and to examine how institutions structured opportunities for young people. The "California Childhoods" project would probe how children participated in everyday activities, and what sense they made of them, as well as how they imagined their own futures. I would conduct fieldwork in the community around the school in which I had taught for the previous decade, while Barrie would develop a comparative field site in Oakland, California. Catherine Cooper would lead a team at UC–Santa Cruz as a third site. I leaped at the opportunity to work closely with Barrie in a community that was dear to my own heart.

And so over the course of three transformative years (1995–1998), I "hung out" with children in homes, schools, and community programs in this densely populated, central Los Angeles community that was home to new immigrants, mostly from Mexico and Central America.

Barrie led a team doing fieldwork in a mixed-income, mixed-ethnic community that was undergoing rapid demographic change. We observed children working and playing, conducted focus groups with children and parents, interviewed teachers and community members. We elicited children's views of the world via writing, drawing, "maps," timelines (in which they projected their own lives into the future), and photographs.

Comparing notes across sites, Barrie and I, and other students who joined us along the way, including Eréndira Rueda and Allison Pugh (other contributors to this volume), examined the unequal distribution of resources in each community and how they were taken up. We considered how this shaped individual pathways as well as experiences of childhood itself. At the same time, we attended to how children resisted, reshaped, transformed, and created their own present lives and imagined, possible futures.

Extending from Barrie's theorizing about the construction of gender, we considered how gender intersected with race/ethnicity, language, national origin, and age in children's daily lives and experiences, and children's understanding of these categories (Garcia Coll, Thorne, Cooper, and Orellana 2004). We looked at how diverse borders were marked and/or muted, with some differences *made* to make a difference and others evaporating from view (Duster 2001). We probed constructions of gender, race/ethnicity, and other forms of difference in and through social practices, and vice versa, revealing how practices were shaped by ideas about who should or should not engage in them, and how ideas about who typically participates in these practices (in different ways) shaped how people understood the practices.

One personally meaningful line of analysis that I developed with Barrie involved examining *temporal* construction of children's daily life experiences in the multitrack, year-round school community I was working in, and where I had taught for ten years (Orellana and Thorne 1998). In this school that served twenty-seven hundred children in kindergarten through fifth grade, students were placed onto three different color-coded tracks, with two tracks in school at any one time for two-month stints followed by one month of "off-track" vacation time. This temporal reconfiguration—an attempt to deal with overcrowded schools—allowed three classes to share classroom spaces, with the "roving" track moving each month between two rooms. As a teacher I had *lived* through the enormous monthly shuffling of bodies and materials that this arrangement required. With Barrie I got to *theorize* about schools' futile, time-based attempts to provide "equity" in instruction.

In addition to its temporal nature, Barrie helped me to think about childhood's *transnational* nature: again theorizing about things I had witnessed (as a teacher) and to some extent lived (as the mother of two "Guategringa" children who had extended family in Guatemala, Canada, and the United States). As always, Barrie empowered me and others from our team to draw on what we knew from our own life experiences and personal connections while *expanding* our understandings by situating our experiences in relation to those that others recounted to us. Anna Chee, Wan Shun Eva Lam, Barrie, and I interviewed families that were split across national borders, comparing different forms these transnational arrangements took. We theorized how children of different ages, national origins, legal statuses, cultural groupings, and social positionings were defined and positioned by national and state laws and cultural beliefs that varied across national and cultural contexts. Cross-case comparisons helped us to see variations in the transnational imaginaries that served as foils to shape childhood experiences here, and to reveal how children participated in families' migration trajectories (Thorne, Orellana, Lam, and Chee 2003). Children were not just "baggage" to be brought along or left behind, as so much of the migration literature treated them.

Seeing Kids' Worlds

As I have suggested already, Barrie's influence was methodological as well as conceptual. I had taken the requisite course on ethnography in graduate school, but it takes a long time to really learn the art and science of this craft. Working closely with Barrie was a priceless course of study. I learned the power of using theory to understand social processes, and using fieldwork to build, deepen, complexify, and extend existing theory. I got extensive practice in "making the familiar strange," the hallmark of ethnography. And I saw how enjoyable this work could be. Barrie was like a child in an ethnographic playground: approaching the social world with enthusiasm, curiosity, interest, and delight.

The core aim of ethnography is, arguably, to see and understand others on their own terms, without imposing our own preformed ideas. This requires stepping out of our own viewpoints, and many treatises counsel researchers to check our positionality. Too often, however, ethnographers give fleeting nods to the influence of our life experiences. But with Barrie I learned to probe deeply into the fact that as ethnographers we *are* the instruments of seeing. Our social locations, relational positionalities, phenotypes, physical features, and self-presentations shape who others assume us to be, and thus how they interact with us. And our histories of experiences in the world have led us to interpret what we see in particular ways. No matter how much of a relative "insider" we may be to the populations and places we study, when we work with children, we are *always* outsiders to their social worlds. Most significantly, I learned with and from Barrie ways of *striving* to see the world from the viewpoints of children.

Following the ideas laid out in *Gender Play*, I minimized my authority, getting down on children's level both literally and metaphorically as best I could. In classrooms, I sat on small chairs or on the floor, following the gaze of children toward their teachers at the front of the room. I noticed what was positioned at children's eye level in their classrooms, homes, and community centers, which were invariably decorated by adults—who, at least on average, are taller than children. Barrie helped me to see how very adult-centric most of the world is, since children are given little input into the design of institutional spaces.

In order to quite literally try to see from children's perspectives, I went on several community walks with young children, noticing what they noticed. As a literacy researcher, I was curious what environmental print was available at children's eye level, and what print drew their interest and attention (Orellana and Hernández 1999). I also gave kids cameras, to document what they considered photo-worthy. Their attention was drawn to things I had not noticed: the flowers behind the gates (where my attention stopped at the gates); the people on their balconies above our eye level (perhaps because children are used to having to look up); and places that held history for them that was invisible to my eye (such as a storefront that had suffered from a fire several years back). Years later, I would do this again with children from the same community, seeing both commonalities and differences in how children saw their worlds over this span of time (Orellana 2016), and how my own views had changed, or not, as well.

Barrie and I also gathered kids' writings and drawings to elicit their viewpoints on the world. We invited kids to map places they go, sketch timelines of their lives, and represent themselves in self-portraits. We delighted in seeing how they chose to represent their social worlds, and how they imagined them otherwise. All of these experiments with viewing the world through the eyes of others—and especially from the vantage point of children—made me a better ethnographer. I learned to question my own deeply engrained ideas about the social world, and to see in fresher ways. I asked how young people living in *this* time and place forge their understandings of social processes—and how we could all learn from this to imagine how things *could* be.

Seeing the Work of Kids

It was during my postdoctoral research on the California Childhoods project that I began to attend to the work children do in households and communities as informal translators/interpreters: a practice that was just beginning to be recognized as "language brokering" (Tse 1995). Most of the scant body of research on the practice was framed by developmental theories that presumed language brokering involved "parentification" or "adultification," with kids taking on roles "beyond their years." It was focused on developmental outcomes, in the normative press to determine how childhoods matter for adulthood, and much attention went to the presumed *negative* effects of language brokering on psychological measures. Most research was done with adults, not children, in the form of interviews with former language brokers. There was virtually *no* ethnographic research on the practice, and no interviews with elementary-school-aged youth themselves.

With three years of training with Barrie under my belt, I questioned assumptions that were layered into research on language brokering about what counts as "proper" adult-child relationships, what children should or should not be allowed or expected to do, their agency, and the locus of attention on the future. The California Childhoods project had given me practice in a multisited ethnography, and made me fearless about gathering copious amounts and multiple kinds of data to develop grounded theory about questions that had never really been asked before. And so I set out to understand the practice of language brokering in all its complexity, and especially from the perspective of brokers themselves. I observed in diverse contexts, conducted interviews and focus groups with children (and some adults), followed a set of active language brokers across the contexts of their daily lives, invited kids to keep journals about their brokering experiences, and gathered hours of audiotaped data documenting actual language-brokering events. I mapped the range and kind of brokering that kids engaged in: at home, at school, and in public settings. I used discourse analysis to unpack just *how* brokering happened in relation to particular contexts, activities, and purposes, set within different relationships, and the strategies that youth deployed. I asked how children perceived their experiences as brokers and how they felt about different types of brokering events, contrasting this with the views of their parents, teachers, and other adults. I considered how kids' *own* ideas about the practice changed over time, seemingly shaped by how those adults responded to their work. And indeed, I framed it as work.

I wonder now: Would I even have recognized children's contributions as language and culture brokers without Barrie's influence on my thinking? Or would children's active collaboration in family and social life have remained as invisible as it was in the literature at the time—or as unremarkable as it seems to be to many teachers? Dominant ideologies of childhood treated children's activities as *play*, not as work; their work may literally not be seen. But Barrie had introduced me to the work of Viviana Zelizer (1994), who documented historical shifts in the ways the Western world views children: from active contributors to family economies to beings that are "economically useless but emotionally priceless." She also introduced me to feminist sociologists who probed the invisible labor of women in households (e.g., Fishman 1983). This helped me to see that language brokering mattered not just for families but for the larger society. The costs and contributions of adult immigrants are often considered in policy debates, but the general assumption is that children are only a drain, "taking" from educational and health systems without giving anything back. Thanks to Barrie, I was alert to ethnographic evidence that made clear that immigrant children's work is "only as invisible as we allow it to be" (Orellana 2001:387). Simply naming it as work shifted the frame. I am indebted to Barrie for that shift.

Pathways through Academia

Playing in the Academy

I am not sure I would have pursued a career in academia had I not met Barrie. Her offer of a postdoctoral fellowship came at a critical time when I was trying to figure out what one does with a PhD. I deepened and extended my methodological skills and conceptual understandings in the ways I have detailed above; I was apprenticed into the art of writing scholarly work in engaging, enjoyable, and accessible ways; and I realized that I could live my life and be a scholar too! All of these things matter for the way I built an academic career, and for what I impart to and model for future generations.

Just as Barrie helped me to reconceptualize children's activities as *work*, she helped me rethink academic work as *play*. Typing up thousands of pages of fieldnotes was a pleasure, because I got to vet and share them with Barrie. Transcribing hours of interviews and focus groups was delightful, because Barrie took genuine interest with me in what young people had to say; her scribbles fill the margins of the hundreds of pages of fieldnotes and countless analytical memos I wrote during those years. Barrie encouraged my sociological and ethnographic imagination, evincing true *delight* in the pursuit of interesting ideas. With Barrie I learned that academic writing did not have to be boring or tedious, and theorizing did not have to be bland. There was no pressure just to "reduce" and process data, propelled by the pressure to "publish or perish," as I have seen in too much other social science research. Writing was an art form, as we sculpted words and ideas into shape on the page.

Balancing Work and Life

Looking back now, I know I did not understand what it meant to be an academic at the time. I had no idea how to balance being a professor and living my life. I had not really gotten to know my professors in college or even in graduate school, perhaps because I was afraid to approach them. They did not really get to know me, either. Throughout graduate school, I had never mentioned that I had a child at home. But Barrie asked about my children, always seeming to delight in their being-ness (not just their accomplishments, growth, and development). She shared from her own experiences as a mother and daughter. With Barrie, I did not feel the need to bifurcate my identity as a parent and an academic. She provided an important model of how to be a mother-scholar—and daughter, sister, auntie, friend: valuing all aspects of my identity, not hiding one behind another, and not letting the academy determine *how* to be a female scholar and a mother in a field still dominated by men.

Paying It Forward

Barrie's influence echoes through my training of new generations of ethnographers, both graduate students and the undergraduates that I have had the pleasure to introduce to fieldwork through participant-observation in an after-school program. For research for what would become my book *Immigrant Children in Transcultural Spaces: Language, Learning, and Love* (Orellana 2016), I encouraged these budding ethnographers to see children not as "students" but as multidimensional beings. As they reflected on their experiences, I asked them to notice what parts of kids' identities are most salient to them, and when. Where, when, and how do they name participants in their fieldnotes as students, young people, boys, girls . . . or people of particular ages, races/ethnicities, or national origins?

Barrie's voice reverberates through my feedback as I invite student ethnographers to notice the categorical labels they choose to describe young people. Her voice gets picked up as students internalize this way of thinking themselves, as for example in this student's reflection:

> Looking back at my notes I tried to pay attention to the words that I used to describe the students or specific situations. First of all, when describing the type of students . . . I failed to mention that 7 out of 8 of them were girls. . . . Did I just say students to remain neutral or in by doing so did I fail to provide detail that may have otherwise been helpful? Now aware of the fact that I referred to them as students, it makes me wonder if that affected the way I chose to describe the kids that arrived to the group and were talking and moving a lot. I referred to them as "energetic" but in my mind, I knew it was girls who I was referring to, would I perhaps have used the word "rowdy or loud" if the majority were boys instead? This is definitely something that I think about a lot because I know that words carry weight and meaning, not only in field notes but in real life too.

Most importantly, I encourage students to consider the labels that participants in our research might use to describe themselves. *Gender Play* made it okay for researchers to talk about kids as kids, precisely because that is the word that young people often choose for themselves.

Barrie's influence on me extends to new generations of educational researchers I have mentored over the years. These educational researchers center young people in their analyses and are taking a deep respect for young people into diverse sectors of educational research, where a genuine valuing of young people's perspectives is sorely needed. See for example the work of Jacqueline D'warte (2014), Lisa Dorner (2012), Janelle Franco (Franco, Orellana, and Franke 2019), Antero Garcia (2017), Inmaculada Garcia-Sánchez (2014), Danny C. Martinez (2015), Krissia Martinez (Martinez, Orellana, Murillo, and Rodriguez 2017), Ramón Martínez (2018), and Lilia Rodriguez (2019).

With Love and Respect for People of All Ages

What I most learned with and from Barrie was to conduct research from a place of deep respect and love for people of all ages: including and especially young people, who are *not* generally accorded full personhood rights in society. I learned to honor and value the perspectives of those who are not different from adults in categorical ways (since age is a continuum, and age categories are somewhat arbitrary and socially constructed), but who have had fewer years on the planet, and thus a bit less socialization into society's dominant ways. This helped me to see in *new* ways, and to imagine new possibilities, including for my own pathway through academia, and life. As we navigate the precarious times we are living, the world would benefit from such imagination, and from seeing from the perspectives of young people.

NOTE

1 In an earlier draft of this chapter, I wrote "dominant thrusts" of the field. Eréndira Rueda (author of the next chapter in this volume) read it—in a delightful, collaborative exchange in the way we learned to do working with Barrie—and commented, "I can hear Barrie's voice in my head right now telling us that this sounds so masculine and suggesting a less implicitly gendered word." We laughed together about how she had taught us to substitute "germinal" for "seminal" and to make other consciously feminist word choices.

REFERENCES

Clark, Cindy Dell. 2011. *In a Younger Voice: Doing Child-Centered Qualitative Research.* New York: Oxford University Press.

Connell, R. W. 2013. *Gender and Power: Society, the Person, and Sexual Politics.* Hoboken, NJ: Wiley.

Davies, Bronwyn. 1997. "Constructing and Deconstructing Masculinities through Critical Literacy." *Gender and Education* 9(1):9–30.

Dorner, Lisa M. 2012. "The Life Course and Sense-Making: Immigrant Families' Journeys toward Understanding Educational Policies and Choosing Bilingual Programs." *American Educational Research Journal* 49(3):461–86.

Duster, Troy. 2001. "The 'Morphing' Properties of Whiteness." Pp. 113–37 in *The Making and Unmaking of Whiteness*, edited by B. Rasmussen, E. Klinenberg, I. J. Nexica, and M. Wray. Durham, NC: Duke University Press.

D'warte, Jacqueline. 2014. "Exploring Linguistic Repertoires: Multiple Language Use, and Multimodal Literacy Activity in Five Classrooms." *Australian Journal of Language and Literacy* 37(1):21–30.

Fishman, Pamela. 1983. "Interaction: The Work Women Do." Pp. 89–102 in *Language, Gender, and Society*, edited by B. Thorne, C. Kramarae, and N. M. Henley. New York: Newbury House.

Franco, Janelle, Marjorie Faulstich Orellana, and Megan L. Franke. 2019. "'Castillo Blueprint': How Young Children in Multilingual Contexts Demonstrate and Extend Literacy and Numeracy Practices in Play." *Journal of Early Childhood Literacy* 21(3):1–27.

Garcia, Antero. 2017. *Good Reception: Teens, Teachers, and Mobile Media in a Los Angeles High School.* Cambridge, MA: MIT Press.

García Coll, Cynthia, Barrie Thorne, Catherine Cooper, and Marjorie Faulstich Orellana. 2004. "From Social Categories to Social Process: 'Race' and Ethnicity in School-Based Research with Children of Immigrants." Pp. 241–62 in *Hills of Gold: Rethinking Diversity and Contexts as Resources for Children's Developmental Pathways*, edited by C. R Cooper, C. G. Coll, T. Bartko, H. Davis, and C. Chapman. Chicago: University of Chicago Press.

Garcia-Sánchez, Inmaculada. 2014. *Language and Muslim Immigrant Childhoods: The Politics of Belonging.* Hoboken, NJ: Wiley-Blackwell.

Lewis, Amanda E. 2003. *Race in the Schoolyard: Negotiating the Color Line in Classrooms and Communities.* New Brunswick, NJ: Rutgers University Press.

Martinez, Danny C. 2015. "Black and Latina/o Youth Communicative Repertoires in Urban English Language Arts Classrooms." Pp. 59–80 in *New Directions in Teaching English: Reimagining Teaching, Teacher Education, and Research*, edited by E. Morell and L. Scherff. Lanham, MD: Rowman and Littlefield.

Martinez, Krissia, Marjorie Faulstich Orellana, Marco A. Murillo, and Michael A. Rodriguez. 2017. "Health Insurance, from a Child Language Broker's Perspective." *International Migration* 55(5):31–43.

Martínez, Ramón A. 2018. "Beyond the English Learner Label: Recognizing the Richness of Bi/Multilingual Students' Linguistic Repertoires." *Reading Teacher* 71:515–22.

Orellana, Marjorie Faulstich. 1995. "Texts, Tasks, Talk, and Take-Up: Literacy as a Gendered Social Practice in Two Bilingual Classrooms." *Reading Research Quarterly* 30(4):674–708.

———. 1999. "Good Guys, 'Bad' Girls: Identity Construction by Latina and Latino Student Writers." Pp. 582–92 in *Reinventing Identities: Social Categories in Language and Gender Research*, edited by M. Bucholtz, A. C. Liang, and L. Sutton. New York: Oxford University Press

———. 2001. "The Work Kids Do: Mexican and Central American Immigrant Children's Contributions to Households and Schools in California." *Harvard Educational Review* 71(3):366–89.

———. 2009. *Translating Childhoods: Immigrant Youth, Language, and Culture*. New Brunswick, NJ: Rutgers University Press.

———. 2016. *Immigrant Children in Transcultural Spaces: Language, Learning, and Love*. New York: Routledge.

———. 2019. *Mindful Ethnography: Mind, Heart, and Activity for Transformative Social Research*. New York: Routledge.

Orellana, Marjorie Faulstich, and Arcelia Hernández. 1999. "Talking the Walk: Children Reading Environmental Print." *Reading Teacher* 52(6):612–19.

Orellana, Marjorie Faulstich, and Barrie Thorne. 1998. "Year-Round Schools and the Politics of Time." *Anthropology and Education Quarterly* 29(4):1–27.

Rodriguez, Gloria Beatríz. 2016. "Writing Names, Reading Hip Hop: Children (Re) Mixing and (Re) Making Language, Literacy, and Learning through the Hip Hop Cultural Naming Practices and Pedagogies of StyleWriting." PhD dissertation, UCLA.

Rodriguez, Lilia. 2019. "Power to Imagination: An Ethnography of Imaginary Play between Children and Adults at an Afterschool Program." PhD dissertation, UCLA.

Speier, Matthew. 1976. "The Adult Ideological Viewpoint in Studies of Childhood." Pp. 168–86 in *Rethinking Childhood: Perspectives on Development and Society*, edited by A. Skolnick. New York: Little, Brown.

Thorne, Barrie. 1993. *Gender Play: Girls and Boys in School*. New Brunswick, NJ: Rutgers University Press.

Thorne, Barrie, Marjorie Faulstich Orellana, Wan Shun Eva Lam, and Anna Chee. 2003. "Raising Children—and Growing Up—in Transnational Contexts: Comparative Perspectives on Generation and Gender." Pp. 241–62 in *Gender and U.S. Immigration: Contemporary Trends*, edited by P. Hondagneu-Sotelo. Berkeley: University of California Press.

Tse, Lucy. 1995. "Language Brokering among Latino Adolescents: Prevalence, Attitudes, and School Performance." *Hispanic Journal of Behavioral Sciences* 17(2):180–93.

Zelizer, Viviana A. 1994. *Pricing the Priceless Child: The Changing Social Value of Children*. Princeton, NJ: Princeton University Press.

3

From Classrooms to Bathrooms

(Un)Learning How to Do Grounded Ethnography with Kids

ERÉNDIRA RUEDA

A choreographed frenzy of squeaky sneakers, trailing backpacks, crumpled homework, and visually arresting artwork came to typify my sensory experiences in the hallways and classrooms of Oakdale Elementary School from the moment I gained access to the school as a graduate student research assistant in the spring of 1999.[1] In my first year of graduate school at Berkeley, I took a job transcribing interviews for Barrie Thorne. That small job quickly grew into a multiyear collaboration on the California Childhoods Project, which provided an auspicious entry into the primary field site for my master's and dissertation projects, and marked the beginning of a relationship that has profoundly shaped my thinking as a sociologist of education, immigration, and childhoods.[2]

In writing this chapter, I struggled to distill all that I learned with Barrie. Her influence has been so far reaching—personally and professionally—that I kept crafting narratives that went beyond what I learned from her work in *Gender Play*. In an effort to retrace her impact on my thinking, I found myself going back to old emails, her commentary on my fieldnotes and writing, drafts of articles and chapters that she was working on and sent to me for commentary, fieldnotes that she wrote up while working on the California Childhoods Project, and even a video interview that a classmate and I conducted with Barrie as part of a public sociology course taught by Michael Burawoy (UCB 2005).

Preparing to write this chapter was not unlike the first few months of fieldwork at Oakdale Elementary, when I found myself taking notes about *everything* that was happening in classrooms and on playgrounds. Barrie referred to this stage in data collection as akin to being a baleen whale, when the researcher takes huge gulps of data before she is able to sift through information and settle on what seems most important.[3] In the initial stages of writing this chapter, my list of "Things I Learned from Barrie" kept growing longer and longer. In later stages, as we exchanged drafts of our chapter contributions to this volume, Raewyn Connell and Marjorie Faulstich Orellana can attest to my struggle in drafting a chapter with a clear overarching theme, framed by a vivid metaphor (something Barrie has always been so good at), that could yield a cohesive narrative about the ways in which Barrie shaped my scholarship. Ultimately, I kept returning to two key lessons that I learned from Barrie that have shaped my thinking in the spaces where the sociology of education, immigration, and childhoods overlap. From the moment I began working with Barrie, she skillfully nudged me to trust the insights I had gained from my own lived experiences. From Barrie I learned how to use what I knew to be true in my world to ask questions of and locate omissions in existing scholarship. She also pushed me to rethink what it meant to do research with kids, and to take seriously the notion that there is much to be learned *from* and *with* kids, rather than *about* kids.

Learning from Experience

In Barrie I found an exemplary mentor, someone whose approach within sociology felt intuitive and validating. As a feminist scholar, Barrie mentored and conducted scholarship in a way that emphasized the notion that our life experiences and what we observe in the world around us can yield fruitful insights. It was inspiring to discover that the fact of becoming a mother had encouraged her to explore how kids participate collectively in shared social practices that reproduce, challenge, and reconstitute gender. Her curiosity as a parent of a preschooler is what initially led her to examine how kids cocreate the world around them. Her observations as a first-time mother and experience as a feminist scholar led to the realization that the same analog for women was present for kids: both were omitted from processes of knowledge creation (Thorne 2002). Barrie's approach provided a different model for how to articulate my emerging research interests within the sociology of education.

As the first person in my family to complete more than an eighth-grade education, I have rarely found the academic world intuitive, and that feeling was particularly acute in the early stages of my graduate training. The idea that what we experience and observe—that our particular positionality in the world—can yield insights that help identify omissions in existing scholarship and articulate critiques of sociological approaches to the study of social life was a game-changing realization. I had encountered so much disdain for what was pejoratively referred to as "me-search" that my early sense of how to craft a "valid and rigorous" research agenda was so bogged down by existing scholarship and convention that I struggled early on to heed Barrie's advice. Her notes on my earliest project proposals are filled with comments like "this is highly abstract and reified"; "too reified and singular; be more grounded"; "keep school stuff situated in real life cases . . . the literature is driving the depictions of students and their experiences, you start with actual experiences and don't be bound by conventions of analysis"; and "don't be trapped by the literature!" Her commentary always emphasized inductive discovery and the value of staying close to the meaning of experience and interaction to particular actors because those meanings might reveal omissions in existing scholarship. It was that validation and encouragement to trust my insights and not feel so bogged down by convention that ultimately led to my dissertation work.

As the oldest of four children from a Mexican immigrant family, I was drawn to the study of what was then referred to as "minority" student achievement. In high school I puzzled over the absence of low-income Latinx peers in my AP and honors classes, an absence that was magnified when I reached the University of California system. As a sociology major at UC–San Diego, I was drawn to scholarship that highlighted the agency of working-class, urban, and minoritized racial/ethnic high school youth. Richly detailed ethnographic accounts provided compelling narratives that cast academic underachievement as grounded in a critique and rejection of the behavioral norms and expectations of formal schooling. Having read scholarship focused on cultural and linguistic deprivation, as well as culture-of-poverty arguments, I found it exhilarating to read vivid accounts of the strategies that young people pursued as they defended their sense of identity, culture, and dignity in the face of institutional messages and behavioral norms that felt threatening. I eagerly read accounts of the complex peer pressures exerted against "acting white" among Black youth (Fordham 1996; Fordham and

Ogbu 1986). I savored poignant critiques by Latinx youth who felt that it was pointless to care about school when teachers did not care about *them* (Valenzuela 1999). And I marveled at the nascent structural critiques articulated by working-class youth who questioned the point of staying in school when it was clear that a high school diploma was not going to improve their occupational or life chances (MacLeod 1987; Willis 1977).

However, by the time I got to graduate school and started working with Barrie, I felt that what I had been reading about youth "resistance" to schooling was missing something. I kept thinking about the elementary school kids I had worked with as a teaching assistant in San Diego public schools.[4] I had not seen resistance to schooling of the kind documented in my favorite ethnographies in any of the classrooms, whether I was at a predominantly Latinx immigrant and low-income school or whether I was at an affluent, predominantly white suburban school. The sense that kids in the primary grades are generally eager to learn regardless of social class or racial/ethnic background was reinforced by the years that I spent doing fieldwork at Oakdale Elementary as part of the California Childhoods Project.[5] I witnessed a general enthusiasm for school as I sat in classrooms, observed at recess, and chatted daily with a cluster of ethnically and economically diverse kids as they went from first to second grade. As I finished up the final year of fieldwork for Barrie and the fieldwork for my master's thesis, I had not yet figured out what to make of the disconnect I felt between the scholarship that I found so compelling and the daily lives of elementary school kids. However, in the year that followed, Barrie's guidance through the master's thesis and my return to *Gender Play* as I prepared for qualifying exams helped me articulate the mismatch between existing scholarship and my observations in the field.

I was drawn to the perspective that Barrie articulated in *Gender Play*, one that posited kids as full social actors in their own right. My thinking was also guided by the drafts of articles and chapters that Barrie shared based on the California Childhoods data gathered in Oakland and the Pico Union neighborhood in Los Angeles (see Orellana, this volume). As Barrie and colleagues examined converging lines of difference marked by racialized ethnicity, immigration, social class, age, and gender, they continued to challenge the notion that kids were passive recipients of adult and institutional interventions (e.g., Orellana, Thorne, Chee, and Lam 2001; Thorne 2001; Thorne, Orellana, Lam, and Chee 2003; Thorne 2005). Their work acknowledged the unequal power dynamics that exist between kids and adults, while remaining attuned to how kids shape interactions with the adults in their lives and the institutions around them. As I grew up in areas of Los Angeles County that were heavily populated by families like my own from all over Latin America (and Asia), the reality that I had experienced throughout my life was that kids' contributions to the material, logistical, and emotional well-being of families were in many ways *necessary*. I had also seen this dynamic in evidence as a teaching assistant in San Diego public schools and again during my time at Oakdale Elementary—kids served as invaluable conduits of information between schools and their families. The focus on the experiences and agency of elementary school kids in all of this work, and Barrie's encouragement for me to consider how trajectories unfold in a particular time and place, solidified my interest in examining how and why kids' feelings about school—that general love for learning, schooling, and teachers that I had so often observed in the early grades—might wax and wane over time and place (Rueda 2008).

After being away from Oakdale Elementary for a couple of years, I returned in the fall of 2002 to pursue an ethnographic project of my own.[6] I spent the next two years doing research in Oakland public schools, drawing on a framework that centered the perspectives of kids, focused on group life, and cast kids as active coconstructors of their social worlds.[7] Barrie's grounded and kid-centered approach to ethnography felt intuitive in many respects, though it was not without its challenges, which brings me to a discussion of the second key lesson from Barrie: "Learn from kids."

Learning from Kids

A key message reflected in *Gender Play*, and throughout Barrie's scholarship, is the recognition of power as central in all relationships. The approach to working with kids that came across in our conversations and all that I read as I prepared to return to Oakdale is distilled in the concept of ethical symmetry. The core tenet of this approach is that researchers should "employ the same ethical principles whether they are researching children or adults" (Christensen and Prout 2002:482). While recognizing the reality of social life is necessary—namely, that children and adults lack *social* symmetry in most contexts—it remains important to use the same ethical standards whether working with children or adults. I summarized key reminders on a sticky note that I attached to the inside flap of my field notebooks:

- question assumptions/render the familiar strange!
- ethics: same as adults
- curiosity/respectful discovery
- kids = competent, experts, cocreators
- focus = kids' POV

I was reminded of kids' agency and the need to take their feelings seriously on my very first day back in an Oakdale classroom. I walked into a classroom in full swing that morning and after a few minutes, Ms. Hoffman paused the lesson to introduce me. She explained that I would be there throughout the school year to observe and interview them, to which a girl promptly responded, "I'm not a science experiment!" I was mortified by her reaction; I had not been in the classroom for more than ten minutes and someone was already objecting to my presence and my purpose. Sydney's objection was an early reminder of just how much kids actively negotiate and challenge the parameters of classroom dynamics that are set by adults, and of the need to maintain an attitude of "respectful discovery," as Barrie often noted.

Barrie's approach to ethnography felt deeply intuitive because I wanted to understand what made kids' feelings about school shift over time and across contexts. I was familiar with what the literature on "engagement" and "resistance" had to say, and with teachers' opinions of what caused those fluctuations, but I wanted to hear directly from kids about what made them love and hate school. Throughout my time in Oakland schools, I found myself engaged in a constant process of recalibration as I worked to step away from conventional understandings and adult-centered perspectives that so often crept into the process of observing, recording, and interpreting kids' daily lives in school.[8] I entered the field expecting to document the variety of ways that kids actively shaped daily life in schools, yet I had not given equal thought to how they might actively shape the ethnographic process itself. As the following discussion illustrates, in addition to shaping my reentry at Oakdale, kids actively shaped the process of data collection, my role in the classroom, and my position vis-à-vis adult authority, oftentimes strategically and to their advantage.

"Write This!": Kids' Impact on Data Collection

How kids responded to my presence in the first months of fieldwork put my methodological training to the test. Practicing ethical symmetry in ethnographic research with fifth graders meant taking their objections, desires, and feelings seriously. Doing so meant carefully reacting to the array of responses that they had toward me as I tried to establish my presence in their school lives.

Kids' influence on my data collection was apparent in the information and interactions that I documented in my fieldnotes. Throughout the year, kids explicitly expressed their desire to influence what I was writing about. Their curiosity about what I was writing in the five-by-four-inch notebooks that I carried everywhere routinely turned into insistence that I document things that mattered to them, such as what they thought about their teachers, how they felt about each other, and what they were proud of. I obliged kids whenever they approached me to ask, "Did you write about what just happened?" and with instructions to "write this!"

Zach says Mr. Beattie tries to be cool when he really isn't. Zach thinks Tanesha and Jada are stuck up. Oscar comes up to us and asks what I write about. He asks if I write that Mr. Beattie says things like "hecka," "fresh," and "tight." He seems amused by that.

Kemi wants to know what I wrote about her and James says, "She don't write about you because you're boring!" Kemi looks hurt and asks me to write that down.

Corey is really happy and excited today because he's going on the GATE fieldtrip to Chabot. He wants me to write that in my notebook. He stands over me, watching me write, to make sure that I get it all down correctly.

At recess I ask the kids to help me think of questions to ask when I interview them. Danika thinks I should ask, "Do people treat you wrong at school? Do people call you names?"

Taking seriously their requests to document things that they wanted me to write about was an obvious way to learn from kids. Their insistence that I document particular moments in their relationships and school days provided much-needed context for my understanding and analysis of how their love of or frustration with schooling evolved over time.

"Come Look": Kids Reshaping My Role in the Classroom

Within the first month of observations, it was clear that kids were redirecting my approach to fieldwork in many ways. One of the most important modifications had to do with my role in the classroom. Originally, I thought it best to participate as little as possible in classroom settings and avoid becoming the teacher's aide. I felt that doing so would place me squarely in the kind of adult role that would make it difficult to gain the kids' trust. One of my main concerns about serving as a classroom aide was that I might be expected to enforce rules and discipline kids. In addition, on the basis of my experiences volunteering in Mrs. Fiore's second grade classroom two years prior, I knew that taking on the role of classroom aide made it difficult to observe and take notes. I wanted a broader sense of classroom dynamics this time around, and I worried that I would be called upon consistently to help only a particular subset of kids.

However, after a few weeks of rotating among Oakdale's three fifth grade classrooms, I realized that the role of detached observer was counterproductive. In those first few weeks of observations, when kids called me over to their desks and I declined, they gave me looks of confusion, frustration, and disappointment. I had underestimated how much their feelings would affect me and how much the desire to maintain strong, positive relationships with them would shape my approach to fieldwork. When I began to modify my approach to requests for help during lessons, I realized that doing so produced a much better sense of how they were doing academically. I was able to see what was giving them trouble and how their understanding of lessons improved over time (or didn't).

Had I remained off to the side in the classrooms, doing my best imitation of impartial observer, I would not have been privy to the *process* of learning, to the joys and frustrations that kids were willing to share with me. At best, I would have been able to log "outcomes" whenever kids and teachers were willing to share information about grades, test scores, or the number of homework packets completed.

These instances also made me question the arbitrary line I was drawing between helping in the classroom and other forms of help that I was happily offering to Latinx immigrant families at Oakdale. I routinely provided free after-school tutoring, translated at parent-teacher conferences and school events, and helped parents navigate the district bureaucracy. The notion of remaining aloof in the classroom became increasingly difficult to justify the more I thought about the help I provided outside of school and the value I placed on my ability to give something in return to the families (and teachers) who were helping me finish my graduate degree.

Of equal importance was the realization that when kids motioned for me to come to their desks, they were not always doing so because they needed help. Oftentimes they were proud of their work and wanted to show me what they had accomplished. In these moments, they either requested that I document what they were showing me or they happily obliged when I asked if I could copy down their work into my notebook. I then wondered whether the earlier looks of confusion also indicated that they did not understand why I was passing up an opportunity to document something important about them. After all, if I was there to learn about what it was like to be a fifth grader at Oakdale and I wanted to learn about being in school from their perspective, as I explained whenever they asked what I was doing there, why wouldn't I write down things that they were telling me mattered to them and that they were proud of?

There were many moments like these in the course of doing fieldwork, when really paying attention to what the kids were telling me and understanding the character of the interactions they were trying to engage me in forced a reexamination of the role I was taking at the school, the perspective that role allowed me, and the kind of information I had access to. I learned that letting kids lead allowed me to make good on the idea that I would take them seriously and that I would treat them as experts on their lives.

Observer, Helper, Confidant, Witness: Kids Shaping My Relationship to Adult Authority

Following kids' leads and paying closer attention to how they were shaping the research process also yielded insights about how they shaped my ability to navigate the different social worlds of kids and adults. My concerns over what my relationship to adult authority should be loomed large as I tried to figure out what kind of adult I was going to be at the school.[9] I knew that establishing strong relationships with Oakdale teachers was of paramount importance since their perspectives and assessments of their students were important factors in kids' daily lives at school. Those relationships were also important because my ability to learn from kids relied on the access I was granted by adults. However, Sydney's first-day reaction to my plan was a reminder that gaining access to kids' feelings and experiences required more than the access to the school site granted by adults. Figuring out how to position myself so that I could learn about kid and adult perspectives was a challenge given the relational complexities of moving between those different social worlds.

Despite numerous conversations with Barrie and careful rereading of the methodological discussion in *Gender Play* and other favorite ethnographies, my role at the school was far less consistent than I had planned.[10] Learning from kids and gaining their trust entailed creating a certain amount of distance between myself and school adults. I had a list of "don'ts" as I reentered the school site, including don't play the role of teacher's aide; don't scold kids or dispense disciplinary sanctions; don't intervene or tell on the kids when they break rules. However, I was surprised to discover that it was rarely interactions with adults that made that list of "don'ts" difficult to avoid. It was often interactions with kids that nudged me into the realm of adult authority. Kids strategically called on my adult authority when it was to their benefit. Depending on the situation, they made different social calculations about the value of my adult power.

As much as I tried to avoid being called as a witness, there were times when kids pulled me into the process of resolving disputes. At recess one afternoon, I sat chatting on a bench with Angela, one of the focal kids in my study, when Aisha came over and sat down hard on her leg. Aisha refused to get up, despite Angela's increasingly frustrated pleas and a failed attempt to scoot out from under her, which left Angela partially hanging off the bench, awkwardly trying to hold herself up with one arm against the slope of the blacktop while trying to unpin her leg from under Aisha's weight. Angela's frustrated pleas—"Get off! Get off! You're hurting me!"—became increasingly frantic. She eventually lost patience and hit Aisha hard on the back. When Aisha finally got up and walked away, and another friend went to console her, Angela started sobbing. As tears rolled down her cheeks, Angela explained that she was upset because "Aisha doesn't tell the whole story" and "always makes it sound like she's the victim." In between sobs Angela complained, "She changes the story and lies! And they believe her!" The next fifteen minutes of recess unfolded as Angela had predicted:

> Aisha tells Mr. Beattie that Angela hit her. He calls Angela over and she motions for me to come. I hang back and give them space to talk first. I can see and hear that Aisha is changing the story, even when Mr. Beattie confronts her version with Angela's. Aisha makes it sound like she's not the one to blame and was unjustly hurt by Angela. This makes Angela really flustered. She cries harder and tries to tell her side. But their versions are so different that Mr. Beattie calls me over to settle the score. "Miss Eren, it seems like you're the only witness." I ask Aisha to explain; I want to give her a chance to tell the truth. But she sticks to her version and says that she merely sat between us. She makes it sound like she sweetly and politely asked to sit with us. She denies sitting on Angela and making her fall over. Then she says that she did listen to Angela and was trying to get off her leg when Angela hit her. Mr. Beattie looks at me and I shake my head.

Moments like these reinstated the conventional child-adult power dynamics that I tried to avoid, though such moments provided clear examples of how kids "act, resist, rework, and create" and how much they influence adults, in addition to being influenced by them (Thorne 1993:3). Most of the time I managed to avoid being drawn into playground drama, but in moments when kids felt as though the stakes were particularly high, whether because there were punishments they wanted to avoid or because their honor was at stake, they did not seem to hesitate to draw on my adult authority. Angela drew me into the exchange expecting that I would be a credible witness, someone Mr. Beattie would believe, in anticipation that Aisha would lie about what happened.

Over time, my role at the school became far more fluid and context specific than I had originally imagined, and that had everything to do with the ways that kids shaped and redirected my role in the classroom and on the playground. Though I worried about taking on an inconsistent role at the school and about how that might undermine the social ties I was trying to establish with kids and adults, eventually I realized that the fluidity of my role did not threaten the relationships I was building.[11] The kids did not seem to mind that I crossed back and forth between different social worlds and social roles. They seemed to accept that in some moments I was just hanging out with them, asking them questions about how school worked and without intervening as other school adults might, and that in other moments I might play a traditional adult role, usually at their behest.

The time I spent with Inez one afternoon in February during lunch recess was typical of the context-specific nature of my position at Oakdale. As we walked out of the cafeteria and passed the lunch tables where kids left their backpacks and lunch bags while they played, Inez stopped to look through a friend's lunch bag. Though she felt the need to explain—"I want to see if she has any good food left over!"—she did not hesitate to root through her friend's bag in my presence. Disappointed with the empty lunch bag, Inez shrugged and asked if I would go to the bathroom with her. During our bathroom excursion, I was able to ask why her best friend had detention that day and got a sense of her perspective regarding the disciplinary system at Oakdale.

Inez explains that Gaby got two recess academy assignments, which equals a detention. I ask why kids get recess academy. Inez explains: they get punished that way if they talk in line, are out of line, or if there is a gap in the line. Gaps indicate to teachers that students aren't paying attention because they're talking to each other. Inez thinks the assumption is unfair because sometimes it's not their fault that there is a gap in the line, and sometimes a gap doesn't mean that they weren't paying attention or talking. E.g. once she twisted her ankle playing during recess and had to walk slowly in line. She got recess academy because there was a gap in front of her in line. She tried to explain to the teacher, to no avail because adults at the school "don't listen to little kids."

From the bathroom we meandered back toward the playground. As we approached, the "yard duty lady" asked if I would take over for a few minutes. She needed to use the bathroom but could not leave the yard unattended. I had never supervised recess before and had never paid much attention to what the adults on the yard were doing—unless they were yelling at kids—but I agreed. "I joke with Inez about being strict with the kids and being able to yell at them because I have so much power over them now. She giggles and tells me that I should yell at Sydney for bouncing a ball on the slope and I should yell at the boys across the yard who are playing in the ditch behind the baseball diamond."

By the middle of the school year, the kids, adults, and I had reached an implicit understanding about the multifaceted role I played at Oakdale. I was able to move between kid and adult spaces—e.g., from the girls' bathroom to classrooms to the teachers' lounge—and slip into different roles as the situation required. Most of the time, my role at recess and lunch was that of confidant and playmate, someone who might not participate in what the kids were doing (e.g., throwing paper towels at the ceiling in the girls' bathroom or rooting through other kids' lunch bags) but also someone who was not going to give the kids "recess academy" or detention. It was precisely because I tried to exercise as little power as possible over kids that Inez found it amusing to consider what I might do with my temporary power over the schoolyard. Even in moments of make-believe, kids' agency was in full view. Inez's understanding of the relatively less hierarchical relationship between us was reflected in her impulse to *direct* how I might use my temporary position of authority. In that moment of pretend, she imagined colluding to rule over the schoolyard together, rather than assuming that she, too, would have to adhere to my authority.

Barrie's attention to the fluid, highly contextual, and variable processes at work in social interactions can be seen in the framing of the work that I produced after following kids around Oakland schools for nearly four years. Paying attention to the interpersonal aspects of what was happening in classrooms and on the playground and learning to listen to kids helped shape my thinking about their relationships to schooling across time and place. The scholarship that emerged from the Oakdale years highlighted key themes that reflect the impact of Barrie's guidance: situating kids' feelings about school within a close analysis of local contexts; attending to how key players (kids and teachers) understand the "fields of difference" that exist in different classrooms and schools; attending to the ways that school cultures, racial demographics, institutional practices, and student-teacher relationships affect kids' academic trajectories; and recognizing the profound impact that cultivating a sense of belonging at school can have on kids' daily lives and long-term school success (Rueda 2008, 2013, 2015, 2018).

It Could Be Otherwise

Valuing commonly overlooked ways of knowing and seeing the world is at the heart of what I learned from Barrie. Learning to trust my own insight and experiences, as well as the insights and experiences of the kids I spent several years shadowing through Oakland public schools, profoundly reshaped my approach to scholarship and my understanding of what it means to learn from and with kids. By encouraging me to value these ways of knowing, Barrie mentored me into one of the most important insights she had learned from sociology, anthropology, and history, which is that "it could be otherwise. It has been otherwise" (UCB 2005). *Gender Play* demonstrates that although gendered forms of comportment have persisted over time—and are therefore treated as "natural" and inherent—kids are remaking gender daily. A key lesson that Barrie took from the time she spent learning with kids is that it is possible to remake the world. The fact that kids resist, rework, and create gender in daily life suggests that adults can engage in the same kind of reimagining when it comes to rethinking and building a more equitable world.

These insights are what endeared me to sociology and to Barrie from the start. In sociology I found a vocabulary and a framework that helped me make sense of the inequalities I had observed and experienced from an early age growing up in a low-income immigrant family. In Barrie I found a mentor who introduced me to the more critical traditions within sociology, perspectives that emphasized the potential of sociology to function as a science of social critique *and* social change. Thanks to the time I spent learning from kids, my interests shifted away from pinpointing early signs of resistance to schooling toward focusing on how kids develop a sense of belonging in school. It has felt more gratifying to work from an asset-based framework and imagine how schools might do things differently in order to support and maintain the early love of learning that so many kids express in elementary school.

As my interests were coming into focus, Barrie recommended that I look up the definition of key concepts in the dictionary. She shared that she had looked up the definition of "play" in the *Oxford English Dictionary* when she was writing *Gender Play*. She found that there were sixteen columns of meaning, but the definition that stood out to her the most was the one that characterized play as a plenitude of possibilities. "It's imagination, it's seeing that there are multiple framings and ways of doing things" (UCB 2005). She continued: "We should have that attitude toward social forms and realize how they're deep in our unconscious, they're built into institutions, they're laden with power, but they still can be altered and they *have* been altered" (UCB 2005). That message—that there is a plenitude of possibilities—is at the core of Barrie's work as a sociologist, a mentor, and the author of *Gender Play*.

NOTES

1 The names of all people and places have been changed in order to ensure confidentiality.

2 The California Childhoods project was funded by the John D. and Catherine T. MacArthur Foundation Research Network on Successful Pathways Through Middle Childhood in a grant to Barrie Thorne and Catherine Cooper.

3 For an honest and compelling discussion of the challenges of doing grounded ethnography, see Allison Pugh's chapter in this volume.

4 At UCSD I completed coursework for the Teacher Education Program, which included a teaching practicum every quarter. During my junior year, I was a teaching assistant in three elementary schools, each one located in a different part of the district, serving markedly different student demographics.

5 As I prepared for qualifying exams, I began reading the scholarship on "attitudes toward schooling" among elementary school kids, which noted that regardless of social class or racial/ethnic background, all kids start school with a desire to learn and achieve, and tend to form emotional attachments to their teachers (e.g., Entwisle and Alexander 1989; Gallas 1998; Suarez-Orozco and Suarez-Orozco 1995; Tyson 2002).

6 Though my formal research involvement in Oakland schools spanned four academic years, my relationships with Latinx immigrant families spanned well beyond that, for the better part of my time as a graduate student at Berkeley.

7 In the second year of my dissertation fieldwork, I followed ten Latinx students from Oakdale Elementary into four middle schools throughout Oakland.

8 See the chapter by Christo Sims in this volume for a frank discussion of how difficult it is to retrain ourselves to take young people seriously, to avoid discounting what they say and do, and to reassure ourselves that what we are documenting during our time with young people is worthwhile.

9 See Mandell (1988) for a discussion of the "least adult role" and Christensen and Prout (2002) for "another kind" of adult, as well as the work of Atkinson (2019), Mayeza (2017), and Randall (2012) for more recent discussions that revisit those concepts. The chapter in this volume by Margaret Hagerman and Amanda Lewis also provides a candid discussion of the insights provided by *Gender Play* on the question of how to navigate adult authority.

10 Guadalupe Valdes's *Con Respeto* and Anne Ferguson's *Bad Boys* remain two of my favorite K–6 ethnographies.

11 However, at the end of the school year, I met with the Oakdale principal to ask for tips on how to approach the principals at the four middle schools that the focal students in my study would attend in the fall. At one point she noted, "I wondered what you were up to at first because you didn't take more of an authority position with the kids. But then I realized that you probably had to take a more neutral position with them so they'd trust you." That discussion suggested that while teachers had not said anything to me, they likely had a similar reaction.

REFERENCES

Atkinson, Catherine. 2019. "Ethical Complexities in Participatory Childhood Research: Rethinking the 'Least Adult Role.'" *Childhood* 26(2):186–201.

Christensen, Pia, and Alan Prout. 2002. "Working with Ethical Symmetry in Social Research with Children." *Childhood* 9(4):477–97.

Entwisle, Doris R., and Karl L. Alexander. 1989. "Children's Transition into Full-Time Schooling: Black/White Comparisons." *Early Education and Development* 1(2):85–103.

Ferguson, Anne. 2000. *Bad Boys: Public Schools in the Making of Black Masculinity.* Ann Arbor: University of Michigan Press.

Fordham, Signithia. 1996. *Blacked Out: Dilemmas of Race, Identity, and Success at Capital High.* Chicago: University of Chicago Press.

Fordham, Signithia, and John U. Ogbu. 1986. "Black Students' School Success: Coping with the Burden of 'Acting White.'" *Urban Review* 18(3):176–206.

Gallas, Karen. 1998. *"Sometimes I Can Be Anything": Power, Gender, and Identity in a Primary Classroom.* New York: Teachers College Press.

MacLeod, Jay. 1987. *Ain't No Makin' It: Aspirations and Attainment in a Low-Income Neighborhood.* Boulder, CO: Westview Press.

Mandell, Nancy. 1988. "The Least Adult Role in Studying Children." *Journal of Contemporary Ethnography* 16(4):433–67.

Mayeza, Emmanuel. 2017. "Doing Child-Centered Ethnography: Unraveling the Complexities of Reducing the Perceptions of Adult Male Power during Fieldwork." *International Journal of Qualitative Methods* 16:1–10.

Orellana, Marjorie F., Barrie Thorne, Anne Chee, and Wan Shun Eva Lam. 2001. "Transnational Childhoods: The Participation of Children in Processes of Family Migration." *Social Problems* 48(4):572–91.

Randall, Duncan. 2012. "Revisiting Mandell's 'Least Adult' Role and Engaging with Children's Voices in Research." *Nurse Researcher* 19(3):39–43.

Rueda, Eréndira. 2008. "Navigating School Transitions: Changing Patterns of Academic Engagement among Children from Low-Income, Latino Immigrant Families." PhD dissertation, Department of Sociology, University of California–Berkeley.

———. 2013. "Navigating Middle School Transitions: The Role of Track Placement, Peer Networks, and Teacher Support in Shaping a Sense of Belonging to School." Pp. 69–85 in *The Education of the Hispanic Population*, vol. 2, edited by B. Gastic and R. Verdugo. Charlotte, NC: Information Age Publishing.

———. 2015. "The Benefits of Being Latino: Differential Interpretations of Student Behavior and the Social Construction of Being Well Behaved." *Journal of Latinos and Education* 14(4):275–90.

———. 2018. "The Power of Schools to Redirect Pathways: Shaping and Supporting Students' Love of Learning across Time and Place." Pp. 77–92 in *Why Kids Love (and Hate) School: Reflections on Difference*, edited by S. P. Jones and E. C. Sheffield. Gorham, ME: Myers Education Press.

Suárez-Orozco, Carola, and Marcelo Suárez-Orozco. 1995. *Transformations: Migration, Family Life, and Achievement Motivation among Latino Adolescents*. Stanford, CA: Stanford University Press.

Thorne, Barrie. 1993. *Gender Play: Girls and Boys in School*. New Brunswick, NJ: Rutgers University Press.

———. 2001. "Pick-Up Time at Oakdale Elementary School." Pp. 354–76 in *Working Families: The Transformation of the American Home*, edited by R. Hertz and N. Marshall. Berkeley: University of California Press.

———. 2002. "From Silence to Voice: Bringing Children More Fully into Knowledge." *Childhood* 9(3):251–54.

———. 2005. "Unpacking School Lunch Time: Contexts, Interaction, and the Negotiation of Differences." Pp. 63–87 in *Developmental Pathways through Middle Childhood: Rethinking Contexts and Diversity as Resources*, edited by C. R. Cooper, C. G. Coll, T. Bartko, H. Davis, and C. Chapman. Hillsdale, NJ: Lawrence Erlbaum.

Thorne, Barrie, Marjorie F. Orellana, Wan Shun Eva Lam, and Anna Chee. 2003. "Raising Children, and Growing Up, across National Borders: Comparative Perspectives on Age, Gender, and Migration." Pp. 241–62 in *Gender and U.S. Immigration: Contemporary Trends*, edited by P. Hondagneu-Sotelo. Berkeley: University of California Press.

Tyson, Karolyn. 2002. "Weighing In: Elementary-Age Students and the Debate on Attitudes toward School among Black Students." *Social Forces* 80(4):1157–89.

University of California at Berkeley (UCB). 2005. "Public Sociology at Berkeley: Faculty Interview with Barrie Thorne." Retrieved January 25, 2021 (https://publicsociology.berkeley.edu).

Valdés, Guadalupe. 1996. *Con Respeto: Bridging the Distances between Culturally Diverse Families and Schools.* New York: Teachers College Press.

Valenzuela, Angela. 1999. *Subtractive Schooling: U.S.-Mexican Youth and the Politics of Caring.* Albany: State University of New York Press.

Willis, Paul. 1977. *Learning to Labor: How Working-Class Kids Get Working-Class Jobs.* New York: Columbia University Press.

PART II

Racial and Ethnic Borderwork and Play

4

Playing to Resist

Youth Challenging Racial Oppression

JESSICA S. COBB

Play is powerful. It contains possibilities for both conformity and sub-version, for maintaining boundaries and transgressing them. As *Gender Play* poignantly reveals, play is one of the few sites where children are free to exercise power, and they do so with relish. Kids (to use Barrie's term) participate in the "underground economy of food and objects"; they engage in pollution rituals (like cooties); they chase one another, invade others' spaces, and organize into troupes (Thorne 1993:20). All of these activities are structured by differentials in power—between adults and kids and among kids of different genders, classes, and racial-ethnic groups—and they also involve direct negotiations of power—who can do what to whom. The "play" frame that brackets these activities from "more serious life" allows kids room to adopt powerful positions and relinquish them in ways that are fluid and imaginative (Thorne 1993:79).

Not all kids have equal access to uninhibited play. The playgrounds of Oceanside and Ashton appeared as areas of bounded and supported freedom, "where adults exert minimal control and kids [we]re relatively free to choose their own activities and companions" (Thorne 1993:44). Though playground activities at Oceanside and Ashton were sometimes regulated by school staff, students had the leeway to construct their own social worlds, and they seemed to trust school adults to intervene when needed. These conditions of freedom and trust are less available to many young students of color in the United States. Teachers, especially white teachers, tend to exert tighter disciplinary controls over students of color in their classrooms. Playgrounds, hallways, and other student spaces have been securitized since the 1980s, with the addition of metal detec-tors, surveillance cameras, and armed police on campus. These measures are more prevalent in urban schools serving low-income students of color, and the invasions of privacy, physical assaults, and criminal-legal consequences that result from securitization fall especially heavily on students of color in general and on Black students in particular (see Hirschfeld 2008).

In *Bad Boys: Public Schools in the Making of Black Masculinity*, Ann Ferguson (2000) observes that Black children's behavior is "refracted" through two cultural images: the endangered species (animalistic, maladaptive) and the criminal (threatening to self and society). Through these lenses, Black children are "adultified" such that "their transgressions are made to take on a sinister, intentional, fully conscious tone that is stripped of any element of childish naivete. The discourse of childhood as an unfolding developmental stage in the life cycle is displaced in this mode of framing school trouble" (Ferguson 2000:83). Under the logic of white supremacy, Ferguson suggests, Black children and other children and youth of color who are subjected to criminalizing practices are denied their existence *as children* and are punished for their activities of play.[1]

If curtailing play is an enactment of power in service of white supremacy, engagement in play by children and youth of color can also serve as a form of resistance to racist oppression. In *Punished: Policing the Lives of Black and Latino Boys*, Victor Rios (2011) observes that Oakland youth in the early 2000s used the language of "going dumb" associated with the Bay Area hyphy subculture to describe actions that were consciously oppositional to the "youth control complex" of family, police, probation, and schools that subjected youth to hypersurveillance and punishment. Oppositional actions included petty crimes (e.g., stealing a twenty-five-cent bag of chips), and they included code switching between deliberately silly classroom outbursts and sanctioned school behavior. These actions enabled boys to expose the inefficacy and absurdity of hypersurveillance and claim agency in systems that labeled them as maladaptive and threatening. Through these actions, youth "played a game and flipped on its head the very stigma which had been imposed on them from a very young age" (Rios 2011:118).

Rios describes these actions as part of a dissident culture with the potential to contribute to more organized resistance. Citing Robin Kelley's reflections on the "hidden history of the unorganized, everyday conflict of African American working people" (1993:76), he notes that the shared quotidian practices of resistance constitute an unseen politics that at times provides a basis and tactics for more mainstream political movements.[2] Though Rios did not study formal organizing work in *Punished*, he concludes the book by suggesting that the playful resistance he observed can provide alternative pathways to dignity and empowerment that have the potential to support more organized challenges to systems of oppression.

Indeed, children and youth of color *do* mount highly organized and successful challenges to the oppression of criminalizing policies and practices. Local social movements across the country are working to dismantle the racist apparatus known as the "school-to-prison-pipeline" by reinvesting in the flourishing of youth through mental health services, academic supports, arts education, and extracurricular programming. Recent victories to eliminate police from school budgets in Columbus, Ohio, Oakland, California, and Pomona, California, were achieved through years of diligent organizing by youth, families, and communities. Even in an environment of racial terror where everyday acts of disobedience to unreasonable commands from police officers can and do lead to violent assaults and arrests of BIPOC youth, students are acting collectively to make their voices heard.

In this chapter, I will reflect on the action of *play* as a crucial component of youth of color social movements to challenge criminalizing policies and practices. Through my policy research, I have had the opportunity to observe from the sidelines the actions of Students Deserve in Los Angeles: a powerful, intersectional youth social movement that prioritizes Black leadership and Black liberation to advocate for schools to invest in "us as Black, Muslim, undocumented, indigenous, and queer youth in poor and working class communities of color," as the organization's website proclaims. Students Deserve members employ traditional movement tactics in their campaigns to change the structure of schooling from punitive to supportive and to shift adult priorities from youth control to youth development. These tactics include grassroots organizing, coalition building, rallies, and speeches. As the campaign case study in the next section will show, Students Deserve members also engage in playful tactics. Though perhaps less immediately recognizable to adults as "activism," playful tactics stand in direct opposition to the school apparatuses designed to constrain their opportunities and restrict their freedom. Through play, youth resist racial domination by altering labels, subverting authority, crossing into forbidden spaces, and upholding their right to exuberant joy.

Case Study: Students, Not Suspects

In June of 2019, a youth-led coalition of students, teachers, and formal organizational activists called "Students, Not Suspects" succeeded in their campaign to abolish the "random" metal-detector search policy of the Los Angeles United School District (LAUSD). The policy mandated that all middle and high schools in the district engage in the daily practice of interrupting learning time, removing a group of students from the classroom, sweeping their bodies with metal-detector wands, and rifling through their backpacks in an ostensible search for weapons. The logic behind the policy followed what Paul Hirschfeld (2008:82) calls the "prevailing rationale of contemporary criminal justice practice—deterrence and incapacitation." Though the district previously allowed principals to determine the timing of such searches, in 2011 the school board adopted a policy mandating these daily exhibitions of the district's power to search with the explicit intent of deterring students from bringing weapons to campus.

As written, the policy was "random." Every classroom and student in grades six through twelve in the district should have had a roughly equal chance of being subjected to this intrusive surveillance. In practice, students reported, higher-income schools and high-track classrooms avoided the practice, and school staff intentionally selected students they deemed suspicious: Queer, Muslim, Latine, and especially Black students. Though the stated rationale for the policy was to locate and deter dangerous weapons, the policy also allowed school staff to confiscate any "contraband" they located, with no guidance as to what student possessions constituted contraband.

I became involved in the campaign to end LAUSD's metal-detector search policy as a law student extern with UCLA's Civil Rights Project and the ACLU of Southern California. As members of the Students, Not Suspects coalition, these adult civil rights organizations offered to provide empirical research and policy analysis to support the youth-led social movement to end the search policy. Alongside lawyers and other researchers, I conducted an analysis of search logs for the 2013–14 and 2014–15 school years (Leung, Mendoza, and Cobb 2018). The results illustrated a total disconnect between the stated rationale for the policy and its application. Fewer than 0.1 percent of the searches produced a weapon of any sort, and none produced a gun. Instead, the items confiscated by school staff as "contraband" were the normal contents of student backpacks: school supplies including markers, white-out, and highlighters accounted for 61 percent of confiscated items, and personal hygiene items such as lotion, hand sanitizer, and Midol, another 10 percent. The searches also resulted in the confiscation of items that are allowed for adults but prohibited for school-aged youth: lighters, rolling papers, e-cigarettes, cell phones. Especially poignant in the search logs were confiscated items indicating the small pleasures of childhood: chips, candy, gum, notebooks with art in a tagging style, a photo of a tattoo, a balloon, a golf ball, and lots of ketchup packets.

The policy was emblematic of the way that school systems throughout the United States racialize Black, Indigenous, Latine, Pacific Islander, and Muslim children as threatening, requiring surveillance and discipline, rather than as developing, meriting leeway and support. Under a search policy that regarded every student as a potential source of deadly violence, school staff felt justified in violating children's privacy and bodily autonomy and in treating innocuous childhood possessions as "contraband." The policy sent a clear message that students were not to be trusted, and in so doing, eroded students' trust in school adults to provide for their education and to ensure their personal safety.

Organized under the social media tag #StudentsNotSuspects, the campaign to end random metal-detector searches employed a wide array of social-justice organizing techniques. Policy organizations analyzed data and prepared reports. A major teachers' union made abolition of the policy part of its collective bargaining process. A Black-led, multiracial, primarily low-income student grassroots organization—Students Deserve—raised awareness among students, created protest art, and cultivated new chapters. Coalition members of various ages and social statuses created picket signs and demonstrated outside district offices. Parents, teachers, and especially students delivered thoughtful, carefully prepared speeches during the public comment periods of school board meetings.

While adult actors in this social movement largely employed formal tactics, the Students Deserve members were imaginative in their organizing. The May 2017 mass mobilization at the LAUSD school board meeting provided a clear example of this tactical creativity. Students Deserve members delivered some of the most powerful public comments to the school board. They also playfully crossed boundaries with those comments. Black and Latina teen girls delivered their comments in rapid-fire fashion, challenging board members to keep up intellectually as they demonstrated the insufficiency of the allotted time. When notified that their time had run out, these students continued, unabated, and celebrated triumphantly by slapping the podium, grinning, and embracing other students when their comments were complete.

After the board meeting, students moved from the school board offices to a grassy parkway a block away to hold a mass rally. The use of the parkway was an appropriation by the public of private space that served as an advertisement for and entryway to one of the monstrous gated "multi-use" apartment compounds that dot downtown LA. Students chanted racial-justice chants, held up signs, cheered, and hollered. Students who had provided public comments and others who were not granted a chance to speak read their prepared remarks. A group of students performed a dramatization of metal-detector searches—a brief play—with one youth taking on the role of school staff selecting students, demanding their backpacks, and accusing them of using markers, highlighters, and hand sanitizers to "get high." Other teens took the roles of students, rationally pointing out the injustice of the searches and confiscations to no avail. The dramatization served an outward-facing purpose—illustrating to adult attendees the criminalization processes that students undergo in their own schools—and it also served an inward-facing one, enabling students to subvert the authority of school staff by rendering their actions absurd.

After these performances, the rally entered a celebratory phase. Students played hip hop and reggaeton music through a loudspeaker and formed a dance circle, pushing each other to enter the center and perform unique dance moves. They good-naturedly teased and celebrated one another as they danced. The music shifted into pop dance songs, and students fell into a slide-style line dance. When the rally ended, students left in a joyous fashion, pushing each other, grabbing others' bags, laughing, and joking. Adult parents, teachers, and activists attending the rally were witnesses to the dramatization, dance, and joking, and some even joined in, but their participation was peripheral. The students created a space for their own joy.

In subsequent creative actions recorded and shared on YouTube, Students Deserve youth joined with Black Lives Matter LA to stage a dramatization of metal-detector searches in Santa Monica's Third Street Promenade retail district and to confront LAUSD superintendent Austin Beutner at a fundraiser at an extravagant private residence in the Pacific Palisades. In both actions, low-income youth of color crossed boundaries into spaces distinctly marked as adult, white, and moneyed. In the Santa Monica action, Black youth stood at the forefront of the dramatization while Latine students played supporting roles, enabling students to enact a form of multiracial solidarity that uplifts Black leadership and acknowledges that schools' criminalizing practices are enacted especially acutely upon Black youth.

In the Pacific Palisades action, student activists put their own subjectivity on the line to speak against injustice. In a room full of wealthy, mostly white donors, four Black and Latine teens read speeches demanding that Superintendent Beutner commit to ending metal-detector searches, to reducing class sizes in underresourced schools, and to funding community schools. He fled from the students to a private room while donors remained in the dining area and the students continued to speak, arguing that their communities, too, were deserving of resource investments. The donors interrupted the speeches with condescending and passive-aggressive commentary; at one point during the students' speeches, the owner of the residence called them "threatening," though his tone was snide and he displayed no fear. At another point, a donor loudly stated, "I'm so sad for them." But the donors did not remove the youth from the party or stop them from speaking. The students' status as paying attendees and as children allowed them to continue to command the room. This action did not end with exuberant celebration, as the onslaught of hostility and indifference from the adult attendees took its emotional toll. Instead, it ended with tears, hugs, and a chant of solidarity among the youth activists: "It is our duty to fight. It is our duty to win. We must love and protect one another. We have nothing to lose but our chains."

After years of active campaigning, Students Deserve and the other members of the Students, Not Suspects coalition achieved a victory with the LAUSD school board's June 2019 decision to end the mandatory metal-detector search policy. Another victory in the youth-led social movement against student criminalization in LAUSD was achieved in February of 2021, when the school board agreed to ban the use of pepper spray by police against students, to stop stationing police officers on school campuses, and to redirect $25 million from the Los Angeles School Police Department budget to the Black Student Achievement Plan. This decision followed similar decisions in other California school districts, most prominently, Oakland USD's decision to eliminate its school police department in response to a nearly decade-long campaign by the Black Organizing Project. Similar campaigns continue as youth of color, their families, their teachers, and other adult allies refuse to accept the status quo of criminalization and demand support and nurturance from their schools.

Conclusions: Play, Power, and Antiracist Activism

In *Gender Play*, Barrie revealed multiple aspects of play that are significant to understanding how kids exercise power:

1. Play is collective, involving the negotiation and renegotiation of meaning among participants.
2. Play is context specific, responding to immediate social and physical dynamics.
3. Play is emotionally charged, involving joy and laughter but also frustration, anger, and hurt.
4. Play involves "boundary work" to either instantiate or cross meaning-laden social divisions.
5. Because of the other aspects of play outlined above, play promotes social change.

Gender Play focuses closely on the social worlds that kids construct together and on how kids enact power in relation to one another by doing—playing at—gender. Barrie's careful participant observation shows that the meanings associated with gender categories are never entirely predetermined but instead are negotiated through games and rituals. While adults often speak of gender as totalizing, Barrie shows that the salience of gender varies for kids according to the circumstances of their play. Though play is indeed bracketed from more "serious" pursuits, play also forms a major part of the emotional life of kids and has real consequences for their gendered sense of self. Kids in the schools Barrie studied typically engaged in play that acknowledged and reinforced traditional boundaries of gender, but they also sometimes crossed those boundaries to explore activities and relationships typically reserved for other groups. As they accumulate, these actions of crossing boundaries create the potential for change in the meanings of gender.

The case study of the Students, Not Suspects campaign focuses not on power dynamics among kids but on the ways in which kids cultivated solidarity with one another and resisted powerful adults. The poor and working-class, BIPOC youth in Students Deserve employed playful tactics that opposed their criminalization through random metal-detector searches. Through demonstrations and speeches, youth undermined the stated rationale for the searches (student safety) and exposed its real effects (violation of dignity, punishment). Their tactics took different forms in different settings (inside the school board meeting, outside on the parkway, in a wealthy shopping area, in a high-dollar political fundraiser) but always contained elements of play: of delight in other youth, of crossing boundaries by taking up times and spaces where powerful adults intended their exclusion. Their boundary work could be emotionally difficult, especially when confronting hostility from the moneyed, white adults whose power they challenged. But when they celebrated one another as low-income youth of color, exuberance and joy marked their activities.

The use of play by Students Deserve youth strengthened their advocacy for policy change. It also served another purpose: it enabled low-income youth of color to assert their right to *be kids* and to *enjoy childhood* even in the face of criminalizing racial regimes that deny them the status of child through adultification (Ferguson 2000). Their tactics reflected Hava Rachel Gordon's observations in her excellent chapter in this volume that youth use play to socialize one another to act, to "get around" adult authority, and to create impactful social change.

These playful, imaginative forms of activism are not limited to youth activists; rather, they are part of a broader tradition of protest tactics that defy oppression by celebrating marginalized identities. Teresa Gonzales worked alongside women of color activists in land-use campaigns who practiced "ratchet-rasquache" activism by "playfully subverting negative narratives of their often-vilified communities" and celebrating "working-class Black and Chicano/a/x cultures, aesthetics, and sensibilities" (Gonzales 2020:3). Indeed, Students Deserve youth intentionally grounded their work in a larger social movement to celebrate Black joy as a "site with which to operate outside of white supremacy" (Johnson 2015:180). Claiming their right to and enjoyment of play is something that youth activists did with their subjectivities as young people and as people belonging to intersecting racial-ethnic, class, religious, gender, and sexuality categories. They did so in direct opposition to those who refuse to recognize the fullness and beauty of their being.

A Personal Note: Barrie and the Joy of Resistance

I first met Barrie in 2006 at a café in Berkeley. I was working as a youth care counselor at Sunny Hills, a residential treatment facility for adolescents with serious emotional disorders, and I had just been accepted into UC–Berkeley's Sociology PhD program. I had applied on the encouragement of my college professors, but I knew nothing about doctoral programs or about careers in sociology. Like many other first-generation college graduates, I wanted formal training in sociology because I wanted the ability to name social injustices and the authority to transform social institutions.

After I received my acceptance letter, my undergraduate advisor put me in touch with a Berkeley PhD recently hired by my alma mater. He spent twenty minutes waxing rhapsodic about his own years at Berkeley, the training I would receive, and how the program would set me up for a top academic job. When I told him that I wasn't planning to become a professor, he was audibly irritated. "Don't tell anyone at Berkeley that," he said. "At least not for your first four years." He quickly ended the call.

I left the conversation with the (mistaken) impression that Berkeley Sociology would be a department obsessed with the markers of elite status. Not a good fit for the daughter of a carpenter. I met with Barrie the following week as her prospective advisee. Over lemonade and sandwiches, I relayed the conversation and my own motivations for attending graduate school. She looked me straight in the eye and asked, "Is that something you would do? Would you hide your political commitments to fit in?" When I responded that I would not, she laughed. With delight, she told me that throughout her early career, she was repeatedly told that feminist research and research on children would make her unemployable, "but I refuse to step on the bones of the women who came before me."

Barrie's scholarship—like her mentorship—locates power in social spaces and actors that are overlooked by much of mainstream sociology. Barrie is intensely interested in how people in marginalized positions make, unmake, and remake the social world. Hers is not the detached interest of the supposedly objective social scientist. Barrie takes great personal joy in the ways that people explore liminality, create bonds of care, and transgress social boundaries. The emotional contours of social life—joy, but also frustration, anger, and sadness—are central to Barrie's work. Her ability to feel with others gives her great insight into her research participants as well as her students.

My path since completing my PhD under Barrie's mentorship looks different from the normative academic career path. I have been beside my family in difficult times, worked in college access and in higher education in prison, earned a law degree, and conducted policy research and advocacy to support marginalized youth with the ACLU SoCal and in my current position with the National Center for Youth Law. Along the way, I have incorporated so many lessons from Barrie into my life and my work. Barrie taught me to be precise in my writing and to pay careful attention to meaning. She taught me to be skeptical of ideas that others hold in reverence (especially those attributed to "dead white men") and to trust my own insights. She taught me to research alongside other social actors (not to study from "above" or "below") and to take seriously people's experiences and emotions. Above all, she taught me the importance of cultivating a caring, intellectually and politically engaged community that sustains me and challenges me to grow.

NOTES

1 While Ann Ferguson's (2000) work focused specifically on Black boys in elementary school, other research shows that teachers similarly constrain the behavior

and self-expression of Black girls and Latine children. For example, Edward Morris (2005) found that teachers in a Texas middle school treated Black girls' assertiveness as un-ladylike and regarded Latino boys' behaviors as threatening. Angela Valenzuela (1999) found that adults at a Texas high school believed that Chicano/a students who adopted street-style fashion choices indicated a disinterest in school and divested from their education accordingly.

2 Kelley, in turn, draws from James Scott's concept of "infrapolitics," or "the circumspect struggle waged daily by subordinate groups," which is "like infrared rays, beyond the visible edge of the spectrum" (1990:183).

REFERENCES

Ferguson, Ann. 2000. *Bad Boys: Public Schools in the Making of Black Masculinity*. Ann Arbor: University of Michigan Press.

Gonzales, Teresa. 2020. "Ratchet-Rasquache Activism: Aesthetic and Discursive Frames within Chicago-Based Women of Color Activism." *Social Problems* 69(2):380–97.

Hirschfeld, Paul. 2008. "Preparing for Prison? The Criminalization of School Discipline in the USA." *Theoretical Criminology* 12(1):79–101.

Johnson, Javon. 2015. "Black Joy in the Time of Ferguson." *QED: A Journal in GLBTQ Worldmaking* 2(2):177–83.

Kelley, Robin D. G. 1993. "'We Are Not What We Seem': Rethinking Black Working Class Opposition in the Jim Crow South." *Journal of American History* 80(1):75–112.

Leung, Victor, Anna Mendoza, and Jessica S. Cobb. 2018. *Here to Learn: Creating Safe and Supportive Schools in Los Angeles Unified School District*. Los Angeles: ACLU Foundation of Southern California, Youth Justice Coalition, Public Counsel, Black Lives Matter, Students Deserve, and United Teachers of Los Angeles.

Morris, Edward. 2005. "'Tuck in That Shirt!': Race, Class, Gender, and Discipline in an Urban School." *Sociological Perspectives* 48(1):25–48.

Rios, Victor. 2011. *Punished: Policing the Lives of Black and Latino Boys*. New York: NYU Press.

Scott, James C. 1990. *Domination and the Arts of Resistance: Hidden Transcripts*. New Haven, CT: Yale University Press.

Thorne, Barrie. 1993. *Gender Play: Girls and Boys in School*. New Brunswick, NJ: Rutgers University Press.

Valenzuela, Angela. 1999. *Subtractive Schooling: U.S.-Mexican Youth and the Politics of Caring*. Albany: State University of New York Press.

5

Learning from Kids

Race and Racism in the Lives of Youth

MARGARET A. HAGERMAN AND AMANDA E. LEWIS

Since it was published in 1993, Barrie Thorne's masterful book, *Gender Play*, has provided a model for scholars seeking to write ethnographic accounts of how, together, children navigate, create, and challenge social categories like gender and race. As scholars of race and children, we have found Thorne's work to be a critical contribution in guiding an orientation to scholarship that seeks to understand children on their own terms, and to recognize their ongoing work not just to "learn" the rules of race but to question, reconfigure, or transform them. Thorne's work has informed a wide range of scholars as they examined the messages about race that kids interpret at school (Blume Oeur 2018; Fine 1991; López 2003; Perry 2002; Pollock 2009). Her work has also shaped Van Ausdale and Feagin's (2001) exploration of how children as young as three years old express racist ideas at a day care center as well as Moore's (2002) examination of how kids negotiate race at summer camp. Her insights have informed the work of Dreby (2015) and Patel (2012), who have studied how young people interpret messages about race and immigration in the context of public policies, and her influence can be seen in the work of Lacy (2007) and Warikoo (2011) and Winkler (2012), who have studied how kids navigate racial meanings and racial structures in their neighborhoods and communities. From this body of scholarship, it is clear that Thorne's foundational research has extended beyond the study of kids and gender and has also shaped the study of how children come to understand race and racism.

We have drawn directly on Thorne's research and insights in our own scholarship on kids and race. Amanda's book, *Race in the*

Schoolyard: Negotiating the Color Line in Classrooms and Communities (Lewis 2003), is an ethnographic look at the lessons children learn (and teach) at school about race and how schools themselves are race-making institutions. Maggie's book, *White Kids: Growing Up with Privilege in a Racially Divided America* (Hagerman 2018), takes an ethnographic approach to understanding how white, affluent kids learn about race and racism through their families as well as their interactions in and observations of their everyday lives. In this chapter, we will briefly explore why Thorne's scholarly work is theoretically and methodologically useful to research with kids about race in general and how Thorne's scholarship has influenced our own thinking and research on the topic in particular.

Theorizing Kids as Active Participants in Learning Race

The New Sociology of Childhood

One important influence Thorne's work has had on the study of how children learn race is connected to larger shifts in the field of the sociology of childhood that emerged in the 1990s. Rather than viewing children as passive recipients of socialization, scholars like William Corsaro (2014) advocated for what became known as "the new sociology of childhood." Corsaro and others embraced the notion that kids are active participants in the social world, and in particular, that theories of childhood social learning must account for children's agency. Instead of thinking of kids as a "blank slate" to be written upon, Corsaro instead argued that kids interpret messages and patterns that they observe around them and reproduce or rework those ideas, sometimes in ways that challenge the ideas of adults in their lives. He described this learning process as "interpretive reproduction." As Heather Johnson writes in an overview of the field of the sociology of children and childhood, "By accentuating children's agency and focusing on children's social interactions (especially with their own peer groups), Corsaro in particular made major theoretical contributions to the sociology of children and childhood. Contemporaries, including Eder, Fine, Goodwin, and Thorne, among others, have shared Corsaro's structure-agency perspective and have contributed significantly to the expansion and reconceptualization of socialization theory" (Johnson 2001:70). *Gender*

Play shows that rather than being socialized, kids have agency and free will and participate in the process of constructing knowledge about gender. Thorne's work illustrates how kids are creative in this process and how children are "competent social actors who take an active role in shaping their daily experiences" rather than being passively "managed or controlled" by adults (1993:12). Thorne also emphasizes that kids are not just future adults; rather, their lives as kids are important to study because children are social actors in their own right. As Thorne puts it, "Children's interactions are not preparation for life; they are life itself" (1993:3). Moving away from adult-centered ways of seeing the world, Thorne and others urge sociologists to take seriously the unique contributions of kids to social life in general.

Applying Thorne's Theories to Research on Kids and Race

When it comes to understanding how kids learn about race, these lessons from Thorne and others are very important. Historically, most studies of "racial socialization" do not center kids' perspectives and experiences but instead focus on those of family members like parents. Much of this work involves interviews with adults about what they observe among children. Many studies, even to this day, ask parents to report how many times they talk about race with their children in a given time frame, or ask parents to describe how they approached discussions about racial violence with their children, or ask teachers to report incidents of racial harassment at schools. Though studying the sources of messages about race received by children is important, in order to access how children themselves actually perceive these messages, researchers are required to talk directly with kids, observing their interactions with others and listening to them. In short, as Thorne argues, we cannot rely exclusively on adult reports of what they think kids think. We must talk to kids themselves and hear their voices and views.

Black Studies scholar Erin Winkler addresses this point in the introduction to her excellent book, *Learning Race, Learning Place: Shaping Racial Identities and Ideas in African American Childhoods* (2012). Drawing on Thorne's work explicitly, Winkler introduces a new way of thinking about how kids learn about race, which she labels "comprehensive racial learning":

As Barrie Thorne (1993, 13) reminds us, children don't necessarily see themselves as "'being socialized,'" and research on children should "move beyond adult-centered" models. In this book, I address this issue . . . by introducing a new framework. . . . Comprehensive racial learning is the process through which children negotiate, interpret, and make meaning of the various and conflicting message they receive about race, ultimately forming their own understandings of how race works in society and their lives. . . . Using the terms learning (as opposed to a passive term like socialization) suggests the centrality of the active, ongoing role of the child in developing his or her ideas about race. (Winkler 2012:6–7)

This new way of understanding racial learning processes paves the way for research that takes into account the role children play in not only interpreting the social world but also reproducing and contesting ideas about it. As Winkler depicts in her research, kids interpret messages about race from a range of sources, including from where they live, and these kids' interpretations are not always what their parents expect them to be. For example, Winkler shows the complexities of how growing up in Detroit specifically shapes Black children's understandings of race and racism. And, as she emphasizes, "Children's and mothers' assertions of what the children think or experience or feel do not always match. Indeed, the story would have been quite different if only parental perspectives were included." As Winkler concludes, this finding illustrates the importance of "not just studying children, but listening to their voices and letting them tell us where to look" (2012:179).

In *White Kids*, Maggie draws on Winkler's framework and applies the idea of comprehensive racial learning to white, affluent children. She argues that in order to understand how dominant racial ideologies that serve to maintain the unequal racial status quo are produced and socially reproduced, sociologists must learn more about how white children make meaning about race and racism. And this work, Maggie argues, begins with listening to white children, taking their words seriously, and as Thorne puts it, "learning from kids." In addition, because many white people, including white children, are uncomfortable talking openly about race and racism, observing kids in their everyday lives as they navigate a racialized society offers important insight into not only what these kids think about race but why they reach the conclusions they do. As Maggie finds, often parents' ideas about what their kids think about race are inaccurate. For example, when many of the white parents in this research were asked to participate, they made comments like, "My kids don't know anything about race! They don't even see race. Maybe I could put you in touch with my Black colleague who has kids? She might be more helpful." And yet, it only took Maggie a few moments of speaking with white children from these families to learn all kinds of things about their ideas about race.

It was not simply the case that white parents misunderstood what their kids knew about race. Kids and their parents also disagreed on fundamental issues such as whether something was, in fact, "racist." Here is a brief excerpt from *White Kids* that makes this point clear:

One Saturday morning, I sit in a coffee shop with Meredith (13, Sheridan) and her mother, Veronica Chablis. Veronica and I are drinking coffee while Meredith stirs the whipped cream on top of her hot chocolate with her pointer finger, periodically licking her finger and sticking it back in the cup. I ask Meredith if she has ever witnessed an act of racism first-hand. Given the strong, resounding, "No" that I typically hear from kids growing up in Sheridan, I am taken aback when she says, "Yes." Meredith goes on to tell me a story: "I remember one time I was at [a liquor store in Petersfield] with my mom about a year ago and there was a bunch of black guys in front of us and only two of them out of the three or four I think, had an ID but they were obviously like 45. But the guy wouldn't let them buy the one bottle of liquor. So they were like, 'Oh fine man' and then they left. And then my mom and I were there, and she was getting her bottle of Merlot or whatever, and [the cashier] didn't even ask her for an ID. He was just like, 'Okay, you're done.' And we went outside and I heard [the black men] talking near their car about white trash and saying all this stuff [about the cashier]."

Meredith's mother suddenly interrupts Meredith's story. "Um, but I think when you buy something at the liquor store, all the people that are in your party need to show—." Meredith interrupts her mother in return, angrily. "Those guys were N O T even standing near the register! And I was with you! And I'm not 21!" Her mother rolls her eyes, and replies in a condescending tone, "Okay honey. If you say so." This sets Meredith off emotionally; she grabs her cell phone and stomps off to the bathroom. She is gone for the next ten minutes. Her mother goes on to tell me that this is just one of her most recent "teenage antics" and that "god only know what I have in store for the future." With a look in her eye that seems to suggest that she believes we certainly agree on the matter of Meredith's story, and trying to smooth things over, Veronica says, "Of course the cashier wasn't being racist! I mean, come on, you know? How ridiculous."

Later, when her mom is not around, Meredith insists that her version of the story is accurate; something "was not right" in that interaction, she tells me. "It was racism. And sometimes my mom is racist and tries to pretend like she isn't. . . . My mom just hates talking about that stuff," she confides in me with frustration. (Hagerman 2018:161–62)

Children like Meredith challenge their parents' perspectives and at other times, parents challenge their kids' perspectives. These moments of family conflict around whether something is racist or not make it clear that children are active participants in their own racial meaning-making processes. They are not "being socialized" or "being managed" by adults, as Thorne helps us see. Rather, they argue and disagree with adult authority figures.

Amanda also embraces the notion of kids who are active rather than passive participants in the social construction of race in her book, *Race in the Schoolyard*. Through ethnographic research in three school communities, she shows children who are working to make sense of the world around them. This includes navigating racial structures and meanings related to identity (theirs and others') but also related to power. For example, she describes a conversation while driving a group of African American boys to see a basketball game at a private school out in the suburbs. Amanda reports explaining to the boys that she has never been to the school before but has heard that it is "fancy." The response that follows from the boys provides layers of understanding about race and class. "Don't worry, Ms. Lewis, Darnell knows how to talk white," says Malik reassuringly. Darnell follows with a series of impersonations of stereotypical white male characters including, "Give me my slippers, Geoffrey"; "All right, son"; "Whaddya say, Billy."

Here and elsewhere in the book we see children working to generalize the things they have experienced and "know" to new contexts, new people, and new situations. Malik was also the child who almost got into a fight with his friend Jose one day in class. When Malik read aloud an essay he had written for the MLK holiday, he said he was grateful to King for making it possible for him to have "white" friends like Jose. Yet Jose was angry at being seen as white. Here, the book shows children contesting racial boundaries and meanings quite vigorously as they argued about their quite different understandings of where this Latino boy fit in the racial landscape.

The book offers a view of how children are ascribing categories and meanings to one another, testing things out, and asserting their own authority to name themselves and to name others.

> Lily and Kate, two fourth-grade girls, stand on the schoolyard talking. As part of a class presentation that morning, Lily had described her ethnic heritage as "Mexican American and European American." She is asking Kate about her own background—"just Caucasian." Seeing Benjamin (a biracial/bicultural Colombian and Indonesian fifth grader) sitting nearby eating his morning snack, Lily turns to him and asks, "What are you?" He looks at the two girls for several moments without replying. Eventually he responds that he would "rather not say." Trying to be helpful, one of the girls offers, "You're Chinese, right?" When he does not respond to either confirm or deny their suggestion, the girls turn away. (Lewis 2003:128)

Children also describe their experiences with racism and with coming to understand the ways that others in the world are making assessments of them based on racial stereotypes. In *Race in the Schoolyard*, a nine-year-old describes being yelled at in a store as a moment when he understood that someone was treating him differently because of his color. He does not have a deep analysis of the situation but knows what it "sounded like."

Moving with children across social contexts, we see them navigating a range of social spaces that have distinct rules: where meanings, boundaries, and norms shift, where their exact location in the racial landscape can move. We see children taking in what is being offered (both explicit and implicit lessons) and actively working to make sense of themselves and others and to figure out how to chart a course through the complex hierarchies and fields of meaning. We see race "at play" and in play, being played with and played out and played on. *Race in the Schoolyard* does not suggest that children can remake the world anew every day. The book is clear about the constraints kids operate under, the force of racial structures on their access to a high-quality education, and the impact of racism on their developing sense of their place in the world. Here, Lewis's work is directly in conversation with Thorne's writing on gender as she argues that children are "becoming and emerging" and that "race does not exist inert and separate from us" (Lewis 2003:190).

Methods of Learning from Kids

Theorizing kids as agentic and meaning-making social actors rather than passive recipients of knowledge means that research methods must adapt so that children's perspectives can be accurately accessed. Moving away from research *on* kids, Thorne and others urge researchers to embrace methods that allow for research in which we learn *from* kids: "To learn from children, adults have to challenge the deep assumption that they already know what children are 'like' both because as former children, adults have been there, and because, as adults, they regard children as less complete versions of themselves. When adults seek to learn about and from children, the challenge is to take the closely familiar and to render it strange" (Thorne 1993:12).

Scholarly work that situates children and children's perspectives at the center takes into account the power dynamics between adults and children, how to gain consent/assent from young people adequately, how to navigate institutional gatekeepers and IRBs, as well as how to design interview guides and use other creative methods to make kids feel comfortable and build rapport ethically. Since the publication of *Gender Play*, a number of resources have offered guidance for how to conduct child-centered research (e.g., Best 2007; Biklen 2007; Clark 2010; Freeman and Mathiston 2008; Thomson 2008). And it is important to note that this methodological progress is the result of reframing theories of childhood, which are in part due to Thorne's contributions.

In *White Kids*, Maggie drew upon child-centered methods with particular attention paid to building rapport and trust with children and their families over a period of time. Spending two years in the field with this group of families allowed her to build solid relationships with kids and their parents that encouraged more open and honest dialogue about race, a topic many white people actively avoid, especially in survey research (Alexander 2018). Building these relationships over time also made follow-up interviews conducted a few years later when the children were in high school more successful as the youth remembered Maggie and enjoyed "catching up." As with the research in *Race in the Schoolyard*, the lesson here is about the advantages of longer-term ethnographic projects that facilitate observing not just what people say but what they do, of building trust over time, of seeing relationships unfold.

In addition to well-established methods of participant observation, other kinds of research strategies can help us access young people's "knowledge" about the world. For example, Maggie developed an approach to use in interviews and focus groups that the kids came to refer to as "the Celebrity Thing." This visual method involved showing children images of various celebrities and using these images as a starting place to talk about racial identity. Most of the children enjoyed this part of the interview process because they liked particular celebrities, such as Beyoncé, Selena Gomez, and Justin Bieber. Creating a comfortable space in which kids were having fun discussing things and people they had ideas about, this strategy revealed many powerful and often otherwise implicit logics that kids were operating with. For example, many of the white kids believed it was racist to say aloud that Beyoncé is Black because to them, identifying anyone's race, or even talking about race whatsoever, was understood as offensive behavior. In developing this visual method, Maggie drew on other children (who were not part of the study) as experts about which celebrities were popular and of interest to kids their age. Without other kids informing this part of the larger ethnography, the data gathered from children would not have been as rich or informative; and the children would likely have been less excited about being interviewed.

As Thorne has argued, it is critical when doing research with young people to embed ourselves in kids' social environments, spaces where kids actually play and interact and spend their time. Whereas Amanda embedded herself in classrooms, lunchrooms, and on four-square courts, Maggie positioned herself in everyday places outside of school where kids spend their time, watching them observe patterns around them and interact with people. She picked kids up from school, attended their school events, and drove to and attended many soccer practices. She listened to kids talk to each other in the back seat of the car on the way to hockey practice or ballet, and she spent time with kids at private country clubs and community pools. She did homework with kids and observed family dynamics between siblings or with other kids as they played video games or did craft projects. She attended political rallies with kids and their parents and observed families in public spaces like farmer's markets, coffee shops, and community celebrations. Collecting observational data in these everyday kid- and family-centered spaces was especially important to this study because many of the white kids lived with parents who refused to even talk with them about race. "It is rude to talk about race" was often the sentiment parents expressed to their children. Parents avoided these conversations with their children because they thought it was best to not address race or racism directly as a result of their color-blind perspectives on the world. Given this, kids were often left to their own devices to figure out the contradictory and confusing messages about what race is and how it matters or not in American society.

For example, in these everyday moments Maggie observed kids arguing with each other about whether Black NBA players had extra muscles in their legs that allowed them to jump higher than white players, or if Rihanna's skin was white like their skin, just with a little bronzer applied, or if she was Black. Children constantly navigated tricky ideas about race, often in spaces where adults were absent or not paying attention. When kids played games, much like the children in Thorne's research, they negotiated ideas about race and what constitutes racism. Is picking the black chess piece racist? Is wearing the white pinney during gym class racist? Can you "just joke around" about racism, or is that racist? Much like the children Thorne observed in her work, Maggie observed these white kids regularly engaging in conversations about race and related social routines as they navigated the racialized society in which they lived.

As both books highlight, children produce ideas about race, racism, inequality, and privilege through interacting within and observing patterns and dynamics in their "racial context of childhood"—in their schools, neighborhoods and wider social environment. As *White Kids* argues, these "contexts of childhood" are often more important than adults' explicit lessons about race in helping us to understand children's evolving understandings. In this sense, parents and the other adults in their lives shaped—but did not determine—children's ideas about race. For example, when parents in *White Kids* opted to send their kids to an exclusive, predominantly white private school, and when kids who attended this school were consistently told they are smarter than the public school kids and more likely to be leaders in the future, kids interpreted these messages to mean that white kids are most suited to be leaders and have more academic promise than the Black and brown kids at the public school. Although parents told Maggie that they wanted to raise antiracist kids, the message that their white kids interpreted as a result of their social environment was that they were superior to their peers of color. These findings never would have emerged if Maggie had simply interviewed parents about their white kids' ideas about race.

Another key insight that *Gender Play* offers is how to navigate adult authority and being associated with adult authority. This was a similar challenge that Amanda faced when conducting fieldwork for *Race in the Schoolyard*. In many ways, children and adults in schools operate in different social milieus, and maintaining good relations with both groups over the long course of an ethnographic study can be tricky. Children, for example, regularly test out whether you are going to be another authority figure in their lives. Whereas some childhood-studies scholars argue strongly that building trust and rapport with children is about trying to get them to see you as one of them (e.g., meaning such things as no enforcing of rules), Amanda found that that was not always the case. In some spaces, being an adult but not acting like one functioned more to convey a lack of care and respect. As she writes,

> If I allowed children to run past me down the hallway without asking them to slow down, they would assume either that I did not care or that I was unable to assert authority (a justification for lack of respect). In this way I found that for children at West City to see me as someone who was "on their side" . . . did not mean entering their world by subverting my adult position. Rather it meant having genuine conversations about their lives, listening to them carefully when they spoke, helping them when they were confused, and expressing care. (Lewis 2003:202)

As Blume Oeur (2018) and other scholars of children and youth have also found, for young people who struggle with having their full humanity honored and embraced in the world and who regularly experience disrespect and adult hypocrisy, respect for adults and institutions is not necessarily automatic. Adults, like everyone else (and perhaps especially adults, since they can easily breach trust by abusing power), have to earn respect. Thus, Amanda was working to be seen not as a "big kid" but as a different kind of adult. Similarly to what other childhood scholars have strategized, this involved striving to be seen, as Christensen (2004:174) describes, "as an unusual type of adult, one who is seriously interested in understanding how the social world looks from children's perspective but without making a dubious attempt to be a child." It is important to stress, however, that this is not just a choice we make as researchers but involves ongoing processes of negotiation. As Thorne (1993:25) writes of her own process, our relationships with young people shift and evolve, with our capacity to "feel more deeply inside their world" bounded by our own capacity for empathy and ability to identify with them. In Amanda's research, tensions arose when kids would recognize that the other adults in their space were behaving badly and would ask Amanda if she was properly bearing witness: asking her, in reference to her taking fieldnotes on classroom dynamics, for instance, "Are you getting this down?" This was another moment when children signaled that they were not looking for a playmate but for an adult who would see the world from their perspective and act as an advocate.

Conclusion

Barrie Thorne has advanced the sociological study of children and youth both theoretically and methodologically. Her contributions can be seen across and well beyond the discipline, especially in studies of gender and school environments. But as we describe here, her work has also made a positive impact on research involving how kids learn about race, racism, racial inequality, and racial privilege inside and outside of schools. Thorne's work has inspired many scholars studying children's racialized worlds and experiences to approach this research in child-centered ways and to listen to kids as they talk about their ideas and their experiences. Certainly, Thorne's work has inspired both of us.

Overall, we can learn a great deal from kids if we as adults take young people's words and social worlds seriously. This means theorizing children and childhood in ways that account for kids' agency and developing research methods that place kids at the center—and this includes theories of childhood racial-learning processes. We hope that scholars in the future turn back to the lessons from Barrie Thorne as they build on her work in new ways. And we hope that overall, the discipline of sociology recognizes the importance of children's perspectives and the lessons kids can teach the rest of us.

REFERENCES

Alexander, Elizabeth. 2018. "Don't Know or Won't Say? Exploring How Colorblind Norms Shape Item Nonresponse in Social Surveys." *Sociology of Race and Ethnicity* 4(3):417–33.

Best, Amy L., ed. 2007. *Representing Youth: Methodological Issues in Critical Youth Studies*. New York: NYU Press.

Biklen, Sari Knopp. 2007. "Trouble on Memory Lane: Adults and Self-Retrospection in Researching Youth." Pp. 251–68 in *Representing Youth: Methodological Issues in Critical Youth Studies*, edited by A. L. Best. New York: NYU Press.

Blume Oeur, Freeden. 2018. *Black Boys Apart: Racial Uplift and Respectability in All-Male Public Schools*. Minneapolis: University of Minnesota Press.

Christensen, Pia Haudrup. 2004. "Children's Participation in Ethnographic Research: Issues of Power and Representation." *Children & Society* 18(2):165–76.

Clark, Cindy Dell. 2010. *In a Younger Voice: Doing Child-Centered Qualitative Research*. New York: Oxford University Press.

Corsaro, William A. 2014. *The Sociology of Childhood*. 4th edition. Los Angeles: Sage.

Dreby, Joanna. 2015. *Everyday Illegal: When Policies Undermine Immigrant Families*. Berkeley: University of California Press.

Fine, Michelle. 1991. *Framing Dropouts: Notes on the Politics of an Urban Public High School*. Albany: State University of New York Press.

Freeman, Melissa, and Sandra Mathiston. 2008. *Researching Children's Experiences*. New York: Guilford Press.

Hagerman, Margaret A. 2018. *White Kids: Growing Up with Privilege in a Racially Divided America*. New York: NYU Press.

Johnson, Heather Beth. 2001. "From the Chicago School to the New Sociology of Children: The Sociology of Children and Childhood in the United States, 1900–1999." *Advances in Life Course Research* 6:53–93.

Lacy, Karyn R. 2007. *Blue-Chip Black: Race, Class, and Status in the New Black Middle Class*. Berkeley: University of California Press.

Lewis, Amanda E. 2003. *Race in the Schoolyard: Negotiating the Color Line in Classrooms and Communities*. New Brunswick, NJ: Rutgers University Press.

López, Nancy. 2003. *Hopeful Girls, Troubled Boys: Race and Gender Disparity in Urban Education*. New York: Routledge.

Moore, Valerie Ann. 2002. "The Collaborative Emergence of Race in Children's Play: A Case Study of Two Summer Camps." *Social Problems* 49(1):58–78.

Patel, Lisa (Leigh). 2012. *Youth Held at the Border: Immigration, Education, and the Politics of Inclusion*. New York: Teachers College Press.

Perry, Pamela. 2002. *Shades of White: White Kids and Racial Identities in High School*. Durham, NC: Duke University Press.

Pollock, Mica. 2009. *Colormute: Race Talk Dilemmas in an American School*. Princeton, NJ: Princeton University Press.

Thomson, Pat. 2008. "Children and Young People: Voices in Visual Research." Pp. 1–19 in *Doing Visual Research with Children and Young People*, edited by P. Thomson. New York: Routledge.

Thorne, Barrie. 1993. *Gender Play: Girls and Boys in School*. New Brunswick, NJ: Rutgers University Press.

Van Ausdale, Debra, and Joe R. Feagin. 2001. *The First R: How Children Learn Race and Racism*. Lanham, MD: Rowman & Littlefield.

Warikoo, Natasha Kumar. 2011. *Balancing Acts: Youth Culture in the Global City*. Berkeley: University of California Press.

Winkler, Erin N. 2012. *Learning Race, Learning Place: Shaping Racial Identities and Ideas in African American Childhoods*. New Brunswick, NJ: Rutgers University Press.

6

From Gendered Borderwork to Ethnic Boundaries

The Case of Two Norwegian Schools

INGRID SMETTE AND INGUNN MARIE ERIKSEN

Barrie Thorne drew in *Gender Play* (1993) attention to forms of interaction through which children establish gender separation as well as enable interaction across gender boundaries.[1] Barrie took inspiration from Barth's landmark text *Ethnic Groups and Boundaries* (1969) and created a new concept, borderwork, to explore how gender boundaries are reproduced by children in schools. Inspired by *Gender Play's* analysis of gender relations, researchers on children and youth have taken the borderwork concept and transported it back, so to speak, to the field of ethnicity, more specifically to ethnic borderwork in schools (Nukaga 2008; Peltola 2021; Seele 2012). In this chapter, we engage in a critical discussion of this reencounter between the borderwork concept and ethnicity.

Our empirical cases come from two ethnographic school studies. Some years ago, Ingrid conducted ethnographic fieldwork in a junior high school in Oslo, the capital of Norway. Around the same time, Ingunn conducted similar fieldwork in a high school (ages sixteen to nineteen) in another part of the city. Both schools were located in suburban areas where a majority of people had immigrant and working-class backgrounds, and both localities were commonly agreed to be places with a substantial degree of territorial stigmatization (Wacquant 2008). Both schools had a majority of ethnic-minority students. And at the schools, we noted that *ethnicity* was a significant identity marker. "Ethnicity" in this context refers to the attribution of people to categories on the basis of an assumption of shared cultural background and phenotype, or race.[2] We focus on a specific expression of ethnic ascription, that is, the students' colloquial distinction between "Norwegians" and "foreigners." "Foreigner" has explicit meanings related to immigration background, but as we will show, it also connotes specific cultural forms as well as skin color. While we in the following write foreigner/foreign and Norwegian (rather than "foreigner"/"foreign" and "Norwegian") we emphasize that we use and explore these as emic terms, not as juridical designations of citizenship or immigrant status.

After writing up our respective analyses (Eriksen 2013; Smette 2015), we discovered some puzzling differences: the division between foreigners and Norwegians was stricter at the high school, and the room for maneuvering identities seemed narrower than in the junior high school. The connotations were also different: whereas foreigners in the junior high were seen as the high achievers, it was the other way around in the high school. These differences, why they occurred and what they meant for the students in the two schools, are the focus of this chapter.

Only a year separated the students' age in our two studies: Ingrid's participants were fifteen years old and in their last year of junior high school, while Ingunn's participants were sixteen and had only just started high school. However, their everyday interactions were taking place in different contexts. For the junior high school students, it was the last of ten years of undifferentiated, comprehensive schooling in which many of the same students had accompanied each other through the entire trajectory. For the high school students, the context was a school with low rank in the high school admission hierarchy, and Ingunn followed the initial phase of establishing social relationships among mostly unknown peers. Our quasi-longitudinal approach facilitates the chapter's main questions: Under which conditions are ethnic boundaries accentuated in school settings? What does the accentuation of ethnic boundaries in school entail for young people's educational opportunities and sense of belonging as they approach adulthood? In answering these questions, we explore what a shift from the field of gender to the field of ethnicity may entail for the conceptualization of specific forms of social interaction as borderwork.

Borderwork and Boundaries

In *Gender Play*, "borderwork" refers to interaction across gender boundaries. Barrie advanced the idea of borderwork, but she attributes the notion to Barth, who suggested approaching ethnicity by investigating "the boundary that defines the group, not the cultural stuff that it encloses" (Barth 1969:15). Drawing on Barth's argument about boundaries as enabling of interaction between groups, Barrie argued as one of her main points that contact may both create and reduce a sense of difference between gender groups.

We are interested in the differences between gender borderwork and ethnic borderwork. To understand *borderwork*—which ultimately refers to an action done on and beyond boundaries—we first need to clarify what *boundaries* are. To start, there are important differences between gendered and ethnic boundaries. In contrast to the careful explanation of borderwork both theoretically and empirically in *Gender Play*, there is less elaboration of the concept of *boundaries* in Barrie's writings. A reason why she does not allocate more space to the notion of boundaries may be that gender boundaries, though not the same as the categorical distinction between boys and girls, nevertheless overlap with them. There is more often agreement as to who belongs to which gender category, and thus where the boundary should be drawn in situations where they become relevant.

Ethnic boundaries, however, are less straightforward. In an elaboration of his concept of boundaries, Barth (2000) defined boundaries as conceptual constructs that become particularly salient in situations where categorical distinctions are not clear. To illustrate, Barth explains categorical differences as being like the difference between sea and land, where the drawing of a boundary is not required for us to note the difference. Boundaries, in contrast, are constructs that Barth, with reference to Lakoff (1987), defines as *image schema*: patterns that constantly recur in our everyday bodily experience and that therefore emerge as generalizations because we experience constantly repeated and compelling connections. Boundaries thus reflect, in a different manner than categorical distinctions, something that is important to and revealing of specific groups' experiences of living in a social world. Consequently, an important concern is the kinds of experiences and connections that lead people to draw boundaries.

Investigating the origins of gender boundaries and their consequences was not Barrie's main interest: one of her main contributions was to develop the borderwork concept, which is highly fruitful as a concept that draws attention to specific forms of interaction. However, when adapting the borderwork concept to the analyses of ethnic boundaries, we argue, it is necessary to go beyond the border*work*, or the drawing and marking of boundaries in any given situation, to see where boundaries come from and what they do.

Interlinked with the presuppositions and connections people make when they draw boundaries are the *affordances* of boundaries (Barth 2000): in other words, what people can do with boundaries and what boundaries do. The act of drawing boundaries may have consequences on different levels: for the formation of children's friendships at the micro-level and for people's access to legal rights and resources on a macro-level. This emphasis on the consequences of boundaries ties in with the distinction between symbolic and social boundaries: symbolic boundaries are discursive and conceptual categorizations and identifications with groups, whereas social boundaries relate to the distribution of resources and social opportunities. Symbolic and social boundaries are equally real in the sense that both are consequential (Lamont and Molnár 2002).

In this chapter, we focus on how young people activate ethnic boundaries in schools. We argue that analyses of ethnic boundaries require that we move beyond situational analyses and carefully investigate how contexts—such as a local school as well as broader institutional structures—shape both the form and the intensity of young people's boundary drawings.

Encountering the Schools

When we brought our two fieldworks together, we recognized that they provided an opportunity for a comparative case study of ethnic boundary drawing in different schools. From the start, our intentions for the studies were similar: both grew out of an interest in how pupils' experiences of schooling and their educational choices were informed by gender, ethnicity, and social class. Both fieldworks were situated in schools in Oslo suburbs that were similar in terms of demographic composition, with a comparatively high minority population. Ingrid's fieldwork at Lakeside Junior High School encompassed around sixty students.[3] They were in the tenth grade, the last year of lower secondary, and around the age of fifteen (Smette 2015).[4] Ingunn's fieldwork in the first year of Forestfield High School encompassed sixty-four students who were around sixteen years old (Eriksen 2013, 2017). Both Ingrid and Ingunn participated in classroom activities and breaks throughout the school year and interviewed many of the students.[5]

In Norway, junior high schools, like Lakeside, are as a rule public, nonselective, neighborhood schools. The private sector is minimal at the elementary and lower secondary level (Wiborg 2013), and students usually attend the school closest to where they live. As Oslo is a significantly segregated city in terms of ethnicity and social class (Wessel, Turner, and Nordvik 2018), there is a distinct selection bias in the student composition of schools. Lakeside's student body reflected the population in its school district: a mix of families of immigrant origin, most of them living in apartment buildings, and Norwegian families who had lived in the area for generations, many of them in an old villa housing area.

In contrast to the nonselective admission to junior high school, admission to high school is competitive, based on the grade point average achieved at graduation from junior high. Hence, while some high schools attract and admit high-achieving students from across the city, other high schools have no admission threshold and gain a reputation for catering to low-achieving students. This was the case for Forestfield High.

The reputation of schools was a topic that students at both schools brought up. In conversations Ingrid had with students at Lakeside Junior High, the young people would refer to their school as the best school among the three schools in their proximity: it was neither a "foreigner school" nor a "snob school." In Oslo, "foreigner school" is a colloquial term that people occasionally use about schools with a high percentage of minority-language students and a reputation for trouble and low achievement.

In contrast, students at Forestfield High had been selected and accepted to one of the lowest-ranked schools in the city, a school that commonly was defined as the kind of "foreigner school" to which the Lakeside students alluded. Some of the students who lived close by, mainly ethnic-minority students, had chosen the school for social and practical reasons. Quite a few of the students, however, likened enrolling in this school to failure. Iselin, an ethnic Norwegian girl, explained her reaction when she learned that she had been admitted only to this school—and none of the schools she hoped for: "Yes, or it was just that . . . well, I don't know about bad, but . . . I don't fit in there, it just won't work! You see? So I remember that I got that answer, and I remember that I just sat down and cried! And I cried! And I cried and I cried and I thought that this is the end of the world!" The horror Iselin says she felt was closely connected with her estrangement from the places she mentioned. These places had a majority ethnic-minority and working-class population, and the high school's reputation as a "foreigner school" was as such closely linked to who lived in its proximity as well as to the ethnicity and academic merit of the majority of its students. Moreover, not only do high schools become associated with the academic qualifications of their student body; they also become an important signifier of a person's style and identity (Pedersen and Eriksen 2021). Hence, our fieldwork enabled us to compare how the character of ethnic boundary drawing may differ between a nonselective neighborhood school and a high school at the bottom of the admission hierarchy, and what consequences boundary drawings have for the students.

"It's Always the Foreigners Who Get the Best Grades": Achievement in the Junior High School

As Barrie, among others, has stressed, the meaning of boundaries shifts according to context. The categories foreigner and Norwegian were associated with different levels of achievement, but as mentioned above, the connections the students made were quite the opposite in the two schools. In the junior high school, students would sometimes say that it was mainly the foreigners who were hard-working and high-achieving students. In the high school, in contrast, being a foreigner was associated with being disruptive and displaying lack of concern with school. However, what first came across as a puzzling contradiction turned out to reveal how boundaries may be constituted in ways that afford possibilities for inversion and resistance.

At the junior high school, the connection students were making between foreigners and high achievement was not unreasonable, as several ethnic-minority students were regarded as the most ambitious and diligent students in class. In addition, some of the most disruptive students belonged to a group of ethnic Norwegian boys, whereas many of the ethnic-minority boys, both high and low achievers, were among the quiet and less active students. The teachers, however, would stress that there were high and low achievers among ethnic-minority and ethnic-Norwegian students alike.

Although students would sometimes refer to this perception in regular conversations, activation of the distinction between foreigners and Norwegians as a boundary between high- and low-achieving students occurred in a few very specific situations when some low-achieving students, mostly ethnic-Norwegian boys, were taken into a different room than the rest of the class to receive extra help. To Ingrid, the teachers explained that this temporary division was a measure aimed partly to relieve the other students of the disturbances of which these students tended to be the instigators.

Some of the students in the special group attempted to make this an opportunity for playing with, and thus highlighting, the ethnic boundary that the school had a policy of playing down. One situation occurred when a few of the students were taken out from a class in Norwegian language. Returning essays to the group, the young teacher praised one essay without mentioning the name of the author. One student, a boy named Jon, immediately tried to involve the other students in guessing who it could be, looking in the direction of the adjacent classroom and saying loudly, "I am sure it was a foreigner. They are always the ones who get the good grades." In another lesson where the same boys had been taken out of the classroom for a basic course in mathematics, Jon insisted on practicing mathematics by calculating the percentage of ethnic-minority students among the ten boys in the small group. Teachers would rebuff this kind of boundary drawing whenever it occurred within their earshot. Hence, Jon's allegation about who would get the best grades as well as his conclusion that 20 percent of the group was foreigners was instantly rebutted by the teacher. He challenged Jon's labeling of people who were born and bred in Norway, suggesting that they were just as Norwegian as he.

It is significant that the elicitation of the foreigner/Norwegian boundary came from a student like Jon, who held a position at the margins of the class community. He earned neither high grades nor prestige in sports, nor did he excel in the many music and dance performances organized by the school in which other low-achieving students thrived and received recognition. The activation of an illegitimate ethnic boundary that the teachers inadvertently had made visible through the classroom setup provided opportunities for resistance against the school and the teachers, but also against the definition of community as culturally diverse and inclusive. While such attempts at disruption were not very successful—neither in terms of affecting the social center nor in terms of improving the instigators' social status—they reminded everyone of the salience of the ethnic boundary in the broader context of the students' lives.

"It's Always Me Who Is Put in the Troublemaker Class": Achievement in the High School

In contrast to the situation at Lakeside Junior High, the common understanding between the students at Forestfield High was that the foreigners were low achievers and Norwegians were high achievers. This understanding persisted even if logically, the achievement-based admission system would have admitted students with similar grade point averages, regardless of their background. Moreover, statistically, ethnic-minority young people in general fare better in the Norwegian school system than their disadvantage in terms of socioeconomic background predicts, visible for instance in the high level of participation in higher education compared with majority young people (Reisel, Hermansen, and Kindt 2019). How did the connection between low achievers and foreigners and high achievers and Norwegians come about in Forestfield High?

The high school students' use of terms such as "foreigner" about themselves was ubiquitous already from the beginning of the school year, when they met their new classmates for the first time. In rapid progression, the first few weeks of school witnessed an almost total split in the students' social groups between the ethnic-minority students and the ethnic-Norwegian students. Hanne explained how a white, ethnic-Norwegian girl like herself, starting a few weeks into the school year, had become part of Hanne's group of friends:

> HANNE: And then came Marianne from [area close to the school]. Um, she came after a while. So . . . She came, and was placed right into our group, so that was fine.

INGUNN: She was? By the teacher?

HANNE: Yes. So . . . then it wasn't a choice, so to speak. Well, it was, but . . . [laughter]. I don't think I would have ended up with anybody else in the class, so to speak.

INGUNN: Why not?

HANNE: So, not to, to be discriminating or anything, but like, she is white in a way. And it is like, she is used to Norwegian culture. Like perhaps she doesn't speak Kebab Norwegian or *walla* and that whole package, you see?[6] So it's like, she has a whole other approach, or a different attitude.

Hanne signals that talking about the difference between the social groupings in class is awkward, prefacing these racialized connotations with the phrase "not to be discriminating or anything." Although it was a teacher who had introduced the two ethnic-Norwegian girls to each other, Hanne suggests that the racialized segregation in class is almost naturalized and due to her and her friend's shared whiteness. Other than her new friend being white, however, Hanne defined her friend's similarity to herself in terms of her familiarity with "Norwegian culture," as well as in terms of what she is *not*: her friend *didn't* speak Kebab Norwegian—a multilect that is spoken in ethnic-minority social milieus in Oslo—and she *didn't* have "that whole package" of behavior and ways of speaking that came with it.

The ethnic split between the students manifested as a spatial segregation, mostly organized by the students. This was particularly visible in lessons when the students chose their own work groups: ethnic-minority students, who made up the majority of the class, mostly formed one large group, while ethnic-Norwegian students made up a smaller group. The contrast between the groups' approaches to schoolwork was blatant. In a typical lesson, Ingunn was first with the group consisting of ethnic-minority students. Here, everybody was talking loudly, and it seemed that nobody talked about the task they were given. Inside a small room next door, Ingunn found five ethnic-Norwegian students. Here, the mood was completely different: concentration on the assignment with sprinklings of calm conversation. One of the girls giggled and said that she was totally fed up with the noise in the room next door. Another girl said drily, "In this class, people just waltz in and out. They never get told off!"

To return to the question that motivates this section: How did low achievement come to be associated with foreigners, and high achievement with Norwegians? One answer is that the students drew on image schemas that then formed into boundaries (cf. Barth 2000). An indication of the schemas the students drew on may be seen in a conversation between two ethnic-minority girls, Inas and Elif, who were Muslim and wore headscarves (also quoted in Eriksen 2019).

> INAS: Mum said to me, she says, every class I'm in, it's always me who's put in the black class, you know?
> ELIF: Me too! Troublemaker class!
> INAS: Me too.
> ELIF: No, not my last school. We had troublemakers, but they worked. We had Norwegians too, you know?
> INAS: We had troublemakers in my class. We had Norwegians too. Half of the class were Norwegians, the other half foreigners, *noisy* foreigners!
> ELIF: Here, there are *only* foreigners, nothing else!
> INAS: There are two, in all, *two* Norwegians in our class.

What is particularly striking about this interview excerpt is the portrayal of the inflexible boundaries between foreigners and Norwegians, as well as equally rigid connections the girls make between foreigners being "noisy" and "troublemakers," and Norwegians being those who "work." As we noted above, these connotations were not the only possible ones. But in the context of a low-ranking school framed as a "foreigner school," this image schema became consolidated, giving it the quality of a boundary. The foreigner/Norwegian boundary was further strengthened by what came across as a shared experience of not being fit for, or entitled to, success in a Norwegian school system. This became clear when Inas, in protest of a teacher's academic demands, exclaimed, "She doesn't understand that we're foreigners. You see? I want to tell her: Don't you understand that we're foreigners? For fuck's sake, do you think I speak Norwegian at home?" They interpreted the school as adapted to the needs of Norwegians, but not to their needs.

Being an "Almost Norwegian Foreigner" in the Junior High School

In the junior high school, the relationship between ethnic categorization and the foreigner/Norwegian boundary was shifting and therefore rather confusing. This was illustrated during a lesson in which a journalist visited the class. Her purpose was to learn more about youth language in the suburbs, the so-called Kebab Norwegian. At the beginning of the lesson, sensitized to others'/the journalist's view of the students as potential speakers of Kebab Norwegian, Huy, a child of Vietnamese refugee parents, exclaimed as he looked across the classroom, "Look, there are no Norwegians here!" The journalist proceeded to present the students with a list of words to discuss in small groups. During the discussion, many students seemed to conclude that they knew very few of these words, and that the journalist should have visited a different school if she wanted to meet students who were familiar with them. At the end of the lesson, as a comment on their lack of familiarity with language associated with foreigners, Huy exclaimed, "We are almost Norwegian!"

Huy's two claims—there are "almost no Norwegians here" and "we are almost Norwegian"—may appear as two slightly different ways of stating that the students were not categorically Norwegian. There is, however, an additional layer of meaning that is relevant to understanding how the foreigner/Norwegian boundary afforded possibilities for identification at the junior high school. Huy's point was that while the majority of the students in class did not belong to the category of Norwegians, they were *almost Norwegian* in their way of speaking and being. Thus, the boundary is drawn between the foreigners speaking Kebab Norwegian and those who may be categorically non-Norwegian, yet still are Norwegian. This point is also made by Vassenden (2010) in his analysis of how people use concepts such as Norwegian and Norwegianness and foreigner and foreign with different referents in different (discursive) contexts.

That Huy said "*almost* Norwegian" (our emphasis) is significant here, as it suggests not only affordances but also limitations embedded in the boundary: namely, that identification as Norwegian is conditional (Aarset 2018) and must be ascribed and acknowledged by gatekeepers. At Lakeside Junior High, gender norms made it more complicated—and risky—for ethnic-minority girls to opt for a self-definition as Norwegian than it was for ethnic-minority boys. This was illustrated in separate individual interviews with a boy, Nuganathan, and a girl, Meena, both of Tamil family background. In the interviews, both made a point of distancing themselves from a group of girls they both referred to as "the foreign girls." While these girls also had Tamil backgrounds, they came across as shy and kept mostly to themselves, and spoke Tamil with each other. Nuganathan and Meena both socialized with students from different backgrounds and rarely or never spoke Tamil with other students. For Nuganathan, the foreigner/Norwegian boundary afforded him with a situational self-definition as Norwegian that he could draw on to emphasize his difference from the girls of Tamil origin: "I am with the Norwegians; I regard myself as Norwegian."

Nuganathan said that he was irritated with the girls because he felt that they harmed the reputation of Tamils, by sticking together rather than integrating. His concern appeared to be of a generalized kind and not related to an immediate risk that others would confound him with one of them. He was after all a boy. This was different for Meena, who shared with these girls not only the ethnic category—Tamil—but also the gender category. Meena had transferred from a middle school in a different part of town and did not know any of the other students when she started at Lakeside Junior High. In the interview, she talked about how other students had assumed that she, as a girl of Tamil background, was the same kind of girl as "the foreign girls." It thus became important to her to clearly mark a boundary between herself and them. Meena described a situation in which a group of boys (Jon was one of them) had approached her and put their arms around her shoulder. Meena, having observed Jon do this with the other Tamil girls before, knew that he expected that she would express dislike and giggle and that Jon and his friends would enjoy having embarrassed her. To make sure she was perceived as different from them, she was conscious of how to react: "They only do it to annoy them. And then [the girls] go 'ugh' and they think that it is funny. But I did not care. So I just said, 'What do you want?' And then after a short while they understood that I was not like *them*."

Meena's irritation with these girls was not primarily related to a concern with the reputation of Tamils. Her irritation was rather related to her understanding of the "foreign girls" as loyal to some of the strict gender norms in the Tamil community she herself was critical of. She was irritated by the girls' embodiment of the role of "Tamil angels," as she called it. She was also worried that these girls could say things about her that would harm her reputation in the Tamil community.

In contrast to Nuganathan, Meena could not self-identify as Norwegian to demonstrate her difference from "the foreign girls." For her, identification as Norwegian risked connotations of having consumed alcohol and even had sex. Meena thus carefully maneuvered around the foreign/Norwegian boundary in a way that enabled her to avoid accusations both of promiscuity and of lacking ability for sociability. These examples illustrate how a boundary may have gendered implications, and that boys and girls may have unequal room for maneuvering with regard to boundaries.

Becoming a More Foreign Foreigner in the High School

In the previous section, we showed how an ethnic-minority student was not always a foreigner in the junior high school. How and where the boundary between foreigners and Norwegians was drawn was constantly shifting. The situation was different at the high school. There, the boundary between foreigners and Norwegians and the meanings ascribed to it was so rigid that it in some cases spurred a redefinition of people's categorical belonging.

Many of the students expressed that they experienced a change in themselves when they started at the high school. Afsheen, a girl with Indian parents, told Ingunn about a gradual process that culminated with coming to the high school:

> AFSHEEN: I used to live in [small town outside Oslo]. And there I only had Norwegian friends, I didn't have any foreign ones. And when I moved to Oslo in the sixth grade, I came into the foreign environment here. [. . .] And then everything changed a lot. I really became a foreign girl. Like really really. And the language changed and everything. But now that I have come here, it is even worse!
>
> INGUNN: Yes, have you become more and more?
>
> AFSHEEN: There are *only* foreigners here!

Afsheen went on to explain what it entailed to be a foreigner at this high school, a description that was reiterated by many other students: being a foreigner meant a certain way of speaking, as well as being fun, being loud, and having a specific sense of humor. It also entailed a possible status of being at the social center. Consequently, students who came to the school were forced to choose sides and adapt identities and practices toward a shared idea of what constituted foreigner-*ness* or Norwegian-*ness*. Although it was possible to negotiate identities, the opportunities were far more limited than in the junior high school, and not necessarily only positive—as Afsheen indicated when she used the term "worse."

Being a foreigner provided a sense of belonging to the social center. For some of these young people, former experiences of being at the margins were turned upside down, as they now could become part of what here constituted the social center and coolness. However, the organization of friendship groups seemed to fixate students' identities in either/or categories. In-between positions—being neither one nor the other or being both—were almost nonexistent at the high school. With the dichotomous identities came equally dichotomous demands for ways of being a student. At the high school, this led to paradoxical cases of "passing." Marte, for example, had ethnic-Norwegian parents and she was white. Yet since she had grown up in the neighborhood around the school, all her friends were Muslims and had ethnic-minority background, and she had recently converted to Islam. Marte actively identified as a foreigner, and she was also referred to as a foreigner—alternately as Somali, Pakistani, Moroccan, and a few other nationalities—in a fond or joking manner by other students. Similarly, there were two ethnic-minority students who constantly were placed together with the Norwegians: quiet and studious girls who were particularly academically driven. This crossing over of categories and boundaries presented some definition problems, as when Marte tried to tell Ingunn about the group they normally called "the Norwegians":

MARTE: There's the Norw—... the N—... I don't mean the Norwegians, I mean, I'm not, I'm Norwegian but ...
ORRI (interrupting): Just say their names!

MARTE: There's all the Norwegians that usually sit alone. Then all of us,
plus me, or, not the for— . . . [to Orri]: you're not foreigners [to In-
gunn]: they are Norwegians, but, the others, the foreigners, and me.

INGUNN: And the Norwegians, they are . . . ?

ORRI: They are: Marianne, Emma, Hanne . . .

INGUNN: So Emma, you consider her Norwegian?

ORRI: No. . . . But she is part of the Norwegians.

MARTE (emphatically, at the same time): YES! About how she is, how
she is! She is so completely Norwegian! [. . .]

ORRI: They are very different from us, because we—

MARTE: We live at [place], and we live at [place], and we live at
[place],[7] and [all of these places] are completely different than for example . . . what should I say . . . [place] and [place].[8] [. . .] These are
other social environments. [. . .] They don't laugh about the same
things and it isn't the same kind of humor and like same language.

Marte stumbled, not surprisingly, when employing the labels that most
of the pupils used: "the foreigners" and "the Norwegians." The difficul-
ties Marte had when labeling illustrate first how the category of foreigner
did not easily overlap with the category ethnic-minority student. This
excerpt also shows that the label "Norwegian" was equally problematic,
as she herself was ethnic Norwegian, but commonly understood as a
foreigner, and Emma, who had an ethnic-minority background, was
understood as a Norwegian. What Marte conveyed was that belonging
to either the foreigners or the Norwegians was primarily related to different youth cultures, defined in part by language and sense of humor.

As shown above, embedded in being foreign was also being a noisy
student. For the ethnic-minority students, being a "noisy" or a "bad"
student could also be a highly conflicted position, even if it entailed
being in the social center. Elif, who herself was one of the loudest girls,
lamented, "I don't care about them [the rest of the class], if they get a
[bad grade] or—what bothers me, the only thing I care about is whether
it affects me. When they are noisy in class, I can't work. And I have no
role models. So it's like . . . who am I going to look up to? I don't understand how the others do well!" (also quoted in Eriksen 2019). Elif
describes a sense of being locked in a position from which she is forced

to participate in the same practices that upset her because they prevent her from learning.

The ethnic-Norwegian students were also troubled by the noise, but as they were quite literally placed in a different room than the others, they observed and wondered about what seemed like the other students' disengagement with school. As Hanne, one of the quiet ethnic-Norwegian girls, said, "And just where I am now, high school, here it is like: think about how serious it really is! Because this really seems like a junior high, [the others] just eat, don't pay attention in class, skip a class here and there. It is like, for me, it is really just like I'm trying to get through this, with good grades." For Hanne, the consequences of being placed in a group of socially marginalized "good students" meant that she was able to concentrate on schoolwork and take school seriously. Thus, the totality of the foreigner/Norwegian split, where ethnic boundaries and achievement boundaries overlapped, gave momentum to the ethnic-Norwegian students' academic endeavors. While the foreigner/Norwegian boundary thus afforded the acquisition of social status through an otherwise subordinate category for the ethnic-minority students, it also effectively hindered academic opportunities for those identifying as foreigners through limiting the possibilities for assuming an identity as a good student.

The Uneasy Relationship between Categories and Boundaries

We started out by drawing attention to how Barrie's concept of borderwork built on insights from Barth's (1969) groundbreaking perspective on ethnicity as defined by the boundary, rather than by the "cultural stuff that it encloses" (15). For the analyses of gender relations in schools, the borderwork concept offered a way of exploring when gender makes a difference—and when it does not. In our chapter, we wanted to explore what happens when we take the borderwork concept back to the field of ethnicity, and more specifically to the study of ethnic boundaries in schools. We asked, Under which conditions are ethnic boundaries accentuated in school settings? What does the accentuation of ethnic boundaries in school entail for young people's educational opportunities and sense of belonging as they approach adulthood?

Analyzing borderwork, as Barrie showed, means focusing on people activating boundaries through language and the movement or use of space in specific situations. Borderwork situations are, by definition, limited in time and place. A sharp ethnographic eye enables one to interpret borderwork situations in relation to broader social patterns in a specific context. As we have brought Lakeside Junior High and Forestfield High into conversation with each other, we are alerted to how the structural position of each school shapes the conditions for boundary drawings, so that they may provide radically different contexts for ethnic borderwork even when they are demographically similar.

At Lakeside, students alternated between defining themselves as Norwegian, foreigner, or none of these, depending on the context. Even if the possibilities for self-definition could be limited by gender, as illustrated by Meena's case, the ethnic boundaries at Lakeside were fluid and shifting, illustrating how community and its boundaries (cf. Cohen 1985) could be defined across ethnic categories. We linked this situation to the positive reputation of the school in the eyes of the Lakeside students. This flexibility was not present at Forestfield High. There, we observed an intensification of ethnic boundaries, as students seemed to feel that they had to define themselves as either foreigner or Norwegian. The students here found themselves—often involuntarily—in a low-ranking school carrying the "foreigner school" stigma. We observed that students categorized as foreigners came to embody the image of a noisy and disruptive student. We interpret this as a form of reversal of an imposed stigma, through which students also redefined what constituted coolness and the social center of the peer group. While students at both Lakeside Junior High and Forestfield High engaged in symbolic boundary drawing, it was at Forestfield that these boundaries became consolidated by collective agreement on their meanings and how they should be drawn. They thereby assumed the character of *social boundaries*—"identifiable patterns of social exclusion or class and racial segregation" (Lamont and Molnár 2002:168–69).

Barth (2000) pointed out that it is when the categorical distinction is not clear that it becomes necessary to draw boundaries. Our analysis has demonstrated that the relationship between foreigner and Norwegian and the apparently corresponding categories ethnic minority and ethnic Norwegian was unclear, tenuous, and open for adaption, and particularly sensitive to differences in the school context. Therefore, the ethnic boundary could exist independently of the ethnic categories. In *Gender*

Play, Barrie argued that while gender may or may not be a salient aspect of interaction, membership in the category "boy" or "girl" is nevertheless never left aside, and thus the categorization of a child as a "boy" or a "girl" is not changed by people doing borderwork. She saw that the gender boundaries were dependent on gender categories. The discussion about the stability of gender categories has changed since Barrie's work. It is an empirical question whether, how, and in what contexts borderwork may change gender and ethnic categorizations. Consequently, analyses of borderwork in schools must start by identifying boundaries and explore, rather than take for granted, their relationship with categorical distinctions.

NOTES

1 We would like to thank colleagues in the research group Living the Nordic Model at the University of Oslo and DISCO at OsloMet, as well as the editors, for valuable comments on earlier drafts. The time for writing this text was funded by UiO:Nordic and OsloMet.

2 Race is used less frequently in the European (and Norwegian) context compared with in the United States.

3 Names of schools and students are pseudonyms.

4 Ingrid's study also included ethnographic fieldwork in a second, ethnically less diverse school, which is not included in this analysis (Smette 2015, 2019).

5 Permission from the schools and consent from parents and students were obtained. For an elaboration of the process of obtaining consent and ethical dilemmas related to ethnographic fieldwork in school, see Smette 2019.

6 "*Walla*" is ethnolect slang for "I swear" (by Allah).

7 These are places where she and her friends are from, with a high concentration of working-class people and ethnic minorities.

8 This place is mixed but more middle-class, and with "white" neighborhoods nearby.

REFERENCES

Aarset, Monic F. 2018. "Conditional Belonging: Middle-Class Ethnic Minorities in Norway." Pp. 291–311 in *Egalitarianism in Scandinavia*, edited by S. Bendixsen, M. B. Bringsled, and H. Vike. New York: Springer.

Barth, Fredrik. 1969. *Ethnic Groups and Boundaries: The Social Organization of Culture Difference*. Oslo: Universitetsforlaget.

———. 2000. "Boundaries and Connections." Pp. 17–36 in *Signifying Identities: Anthropological Perspectives on Boundaries and Contested Values*, edited by A. Cohen. London: Routledge.

Cohen, Anthony P. 1985. *The Symbolic Construction of Community*. Chichester, UK: Ellis Horwood.

Eriksen, Ingunn M. 2013. "Young Norwegians: Belonging and Becoming in a Multiethnic High School." PhD thesis, University of Oslo, Norway.

———. 2019. "Tough Femininities: Ethnic Minority Girls' Aggressive School Opposition." *British Journal of Sociology of Education* 40(8):1090–1104.

Lakoff, George. 1987. *Women, Fire, and Dangerous Things.* Chicago: University of Chicago Press.

Lamont, Michelle, and Virág Molnár. 2002. "The Study of Boundaries in the Social Sciences." *Annual Review of Sociology* 28(1):167–95.

Nukaga, Misako. 2008. "The Underlife of Kids' School Lunchtime: Negotiating Ethnic Boundaries and Identity in Food Exchange." *Journal of Contemporary Ethnography* 37(3):342–80.

Pedersen, Willy, and Ingunn Eriksen. 2021. "Distribution of Capital and School-Related Stress at Elite High Schools." *Journal of Youth Studies* 24:1–18.

Peltola, Marja. 2021. "Everyday Consequences of Selectiveness: Borderwork in the Informal Sphere of a Lower Secondary School in the Metropolitan Area of Helsinki, Finland." *British Journal of Sociology of Education* 42(1):97–112.

Reisel Liza, Are Skeie Hermansen, and Marianna Takvam Kindt. 2019. "Norway: Ethnic (In)equality in a Social-Democratic Welfare State." Pp. 843–84 in *The Palgrave Handbook of Race and Ethnic Inequalities in Education,* edited by P. Stevens and A. Dworkin. New York: Palgrave Macmillan.

Seele, Claudia. 2012. "Ethnicity and Early Childhood." *International Journal of Early Childhood* 44(3):307–25.

Smette, Ingrid. 2015. "The Final Year: An Anthropological Study of Community in Two Secondary Schools in Oslo, Norway." PhD thesis, University of Oslo, Norway.

———. 2019. "Ethics and Access When Consent Must Come First." Pp. 51–63 in *Implementing Ethics in Educational Ethnography: Regulation and Practice,* edited by H. Busher and A. Fox. New York: Routledge.

Thorne, Barrie 1993. *Gender Play: Girls and Boys in School.* New Brunswick, NJ: Rutgers University Press.

Vassenden, Anders. 2010. "Untangling the Different Components of Norwegianness." *Nations and Nationalism* 16(4):734–52.

Wacquant, Loïc. 2008. *Urban Outcasts: A Comparative Sociology of Advanced Marginality.* Cambridge: Polity Press.

Wessel, Terje, Lena Magnusson Turner, and Viggo Nordvik. 2018 "Population Dynamics and Ethnic Geographies in Oslo: The Impact of Migration and Natural Demographic Change on Ethnic Composition and Segregation." *Journal of Housing and the Built Environment* 33(4):789–805.

Wiborg, Susanne. 2013. "Neo-liberalism and Universal State Education: The Cases of Denmark, Norway, and Sweden, 1980–2011." *Comparative Education* 49(4):407–23.

PART III

Feminist Praxis

7

Breaking Up the Pavement

Barrie Thorne's Feminist Sproutings

MICHAEL A. MESSNER

There is a passage early on in *Gender Play* where Barrie Thorne (1993:20) describes how kids operate within the "official agenda" of elementary schools: "The lessons, the rules, the overtly approved conduct—seemed like cement sidewalk blocks, and the kids' cultural creations like grass and dandelions sprouting through the cracks." Beyond the rare (and to this reader, so welcome) use of metaphor in a sociology text, Thorne accomplished something remarkable here, setting up the reader to understand the apparently immovable constraint of school structures, while also inviting our appreciation of kids as active subjects whose gender play creates meanings. I have taught this book many times, and my students always celebrate these moments of playful resistance, while also noting how these moments rarely if ever challenge, much less change, the structure of adult authority and rules in schools. Sproutings happen; but the concrete remains. Or does it, always?

In this chapter, I will note how Barrie Thorne's work—her research, her teaching and mentoring, and her institutional activism—has always been premised on identifying cracks and fissures in oppressive systems, in which she then strategically plants and nourishes seeds of feminist change. To be sure, Thorne would balk at taking personal credit for much of this. In Laurence Bachman's wonderful 2013 interview with her, Thorne responded typically when asked to reflect on her personal accomplishments in bringing feminist insights into mainstream sociology: "'We' is a more appropriate pronoun than 'you' since bringing feminist insights and practices into sociology has always been and continues to be a collective project" (Bachman 2013:8). Here, I will draw from my reading of Thorne's work, and also from my experiences working as Barrie's junior colleague, coteacher, and grateful mentee at the University of Southern California, between 1987 and 1995, to reflect on her singular contributions to this collective work, and to point to indicators of continuing blooms of change by next generations of scholars who work in fields tilled and seeded by Barrie Thorne.

Constraint, Contexts, Agency

In 1992 Barrie Thorne and I cocreated and team-taught a graduate seminar in the sociology of sex and gender. I had already team-taught a large undergraduate general education course on gender with Barrie, but this would be my first graduate seminar, and the prospect of leading it with Barrie was both thrilling and a bit terrifying. I was certainly worrying more about impressing Barrie than about impressing the students, as I overprepared for each seminar meeting. And I marveled at how effortless it seemed for Barrie to lead discussions, carefully listening to everyone while seamlessly weaving in her deep knowledge of women's studies. That year, my first book came out, and I brought a copy of it with me to the seminar, proudly clutching it to my chest like a newborn. Barrie congratulated me, but uncharacteristically dashed some cold water on my moment, commenting that "so many books come out every year, and most of them drop through the cracks and are quickly forgotten." I realized later that this comment reflected, in part, her ongoing struggles to complete *Gender Play* and get it into print. She wondered aloud if it was even worth finishing the book, since some of the key ideas had already appeared in her articles: "By now everyone knows all of this stuff," she lamented. "It's taken me so long to write this book, the ideas all feel like old hat by now." I was one of many who urged her to complete the book, and of course once it was published, *Gender Play* not only did not "drop through the cracks"; it had a deep and lasting impact, both within academia and among educators. I still teach that sex and gender seminar every other year, and while I regularly update the syllabus with new books, *Gender Play* remains on the reading list. It never became old hat.

In *Gender Play*, Thorne (1993:95–96) bemoans how scholars routinely approach our research on a given topic by falling into common assumptions and themes that "operate like well-worn grooves on a dirt road; when a new study is geared up, the wheels of description and analysis slide into the contrastive themes and move right along." Barrie Thorne's analytic wheels jumped the well-worn grooves of research on kids and gender, as she forged new paths. Nearly three decades later, my PhD students still find fresh insights in the book, and they find delight in seeing how Thorne took first steps on pathways that other scholars have continued to explore, and from which they branch out, forging new paths.

One of Thorne's fresh pathways led to an understanding of kids' creative agency, not simply as individual acts but as part of "group life" (Thorne 1993:4). Thorne described this group agency in schools as routine "borderwork" interactions that constructed and solidified gender boundaries, even when at times it seemed to challenge binary categories. This conceptual contribution echoes in subsequent work, including some of mine on children and sport (Messner 2000; Messner and Musto 2014). More recently, scholars have examined the relative flexibility of sport's institutional gender regimes in the face of transgender and gender-nonconforming youths' disruptive challenge to binary gender boundaries (Travers 2016), or of East African Muslim immigrant girls in Minnesota, who demanded their right to play basketball (Thul, LaVoi, Hazelwood, and Hussein 2016).

Ironically, Thorne's analysis of how kids actively do borderwork has a boundaried limitation of its own. Thorne acknowledges that situating her ethnographic observations within schools limits her at best to speculating about how kids navigate their daily movement through other spaces—families, neighborhoods, the street—each with its own "gender regime" (Connell 1987) that differently constrains and enables gender relations. Thorne hints, for instance, at how the meanings and dynamics of kids' cross-gender friendships can take on wildly different meanings when kids move from neighborhood to school contexts. And she identifies a within-school contextual variation between the relatively unregimented playground, which she sees as a rich source of kids' gender play, compared with the more adult-controlled constraint of the classroom. This idea of variable constraint across contexts has been taken up by other scholars, e.g., Michela Musto's (2013) study of the different ways kids on a coed swim team construct gender during the formal practice time in the pool, versus during their more informal times on the deck.

But ultimately, Thorne's contained focus on what happens inside schools confines her analysis of kids' collective agency mostly to what happens within this context. This limited focus risks creating a view of schools as total institutions within which kids' creative sproutings are, at most, temporary moments of rebellion that make the school day tolerable, actions that at best may enhance a kid's reputation with other kids as a joker or as a disrupter. When kids take these actions too far or perform them too visibly, the school gets out its weed killer and suppresses the sproutings. The bringing down of the hammer of institutional discipline ultimately clarifies the school's behavioral boundaries.

Thorne's empirical focus on the school context also impacts the ways that her conceptual focus on gender relations rarely connects with understanding other forms of inequality—particularly race and class—that are also always at play in schools. Musto's (2019) study of a multiracial middle school shows how school teachers' and administrators' responses to kids' misbehaviors serve to reproduce race, class, and gender boundaries and hierarchies. And Ann Arnett Ferguson's (2000) observation of the ways that schools routinely adultify and criminalize Black boys' actions is conceptually tethered to her analysis of how peer relations in the street offer a wider range of possibilities for these boys to create supportive bonds and to find respect. Of course, though street contexts routinely offer boys (less for girls) more elbow room for self-expression than schools, the streets can also subject youth to higher levels of physical risk and violence (Rios 2011). In his acclaimed memoir, Ta Nehisi Coates (2015:25, 33) contrasts the street and schools as sites of race and gender oppression for Black boys, sharply stating, "If the streets shackled my right leg, the schools shackled my left," and concluding, "I resent the schools more."

In thinking about how kids' school worlds connect with other aspects of their lives, my students often nudge Thorne's cement-blocks metaphor a bit further: while rebellious "sproutings" of creative rule breaking might ultimately help to reproduce the race-class-gender inequality regime (Acker 2006) within a school, we can also ask how, and under what conditions, collective agency might challenge and lead to institutional change—breaking up the pavement, as it were—opening possibilities for new (hopefully more democratic and egalitarian) patterns to emerge. A recent example of collective youth agency that cuts across contexts is the international eruption in 2018 of youth-led #FridaysForFuture "climate strikes," in which children and youth cut school for the day to engage in public protests. Criticizing adults for having dragged their feet on perhaps the most important issue of our time, young activists have taken the lead in demanding green public policies and sustainable lifestyle transformations. In some places, kids have risked school or parental punishments by missing school days to engage in Friday climate strikes. In other places, kids' political protests have been supported by parents, and incorporated by teachers into school curricula on climate change. Whether they are opposed or joined by adults, children and youth are literally in the forefront of social activism around climate change.

Anger, Empathy, Mentoring

If there was one thing Barrie Thorne could get riled up about, it was bemoaning the ways that girls are taught to be "nice"—adopting non-threatening body postures that do not take up much space, affecting sweet smiles and apologetic tones that finish sentences with up-voiced question marks that seem to communicate that "no matter how much I know, or how experienced I am . . . I just may be . . . wrong?" Thorne wrote and edited pioneering books about gendered speech and body politics (Thorne and Henley 1975; Thorne, Kramarae, and Henley 1983), and when she talked about this with women grad students, they would nod in recognition. When she would go on a mini-rant with a large class of first- and second-year undergrads, their eyes would widen in apparent disbelief that anyone would criticize being "nice." (The first year I cotaught with Barrie, some of the undergrads "rewarded" her on their course evaluations with specific suggestions on how she might dress nicer for class.) When members of our gender studies faculty complained about the nasty personality of feminist icon Betty Friedan, who for several years had joined us every spring at USC, Barrie Thorne interjected, "Why don't we look at this like feminist sociologists and historians?"—which is in fact what most of us were. "Betty published *The Feminine Mystique* in 1963," Thorne observed. "That means she was writing at the start of the 1960s, *without the support of any feminist movement!* This was still culturally, for women, the 1950s! We should ask ourselves: 'In that historical context, what sort of woman could do what she did?' Certainly not some 'nice girl.' It took someone who was not only smart but tough as nails to put herself out there and take the kind of heat Betty took" (Messner 2015).

Feminist anger, Barrie Thorne insisted, was necessary and productive—a perspective codified by her longtime partner Peter Lyman, who wrote of the productive use of anger in social movements (Lyman 1981). Running parallel with her aversion to feminine niceness, the Barrie Thorne I experienced was deeply kind, and incredibly generous to those around her. Before I even met her in 1987, I had noted that Barrie Thorne was frequently and glowingly thanked in feminist scholars' acknowledgments in their books and articles. I realized soon enough after meeting her how deep was her generosity; Barrie gave some of my early papers a deep, substantive critical reading that also included the fixes of a skilled copy editor. Part of this kindness, I am sure, was grounded in her commitment to building a feminist field—perhaps modeled by women sociologists of a previous generation, like Jessie Bernard (Messner 2021), perhaps seeded during Thorne's own graduate work at Brandeis, a place she described as a "generative institution" that helped to birth feminist sociology in the United States (Thorne 1997). Thorne's own generativity included mentoring and promoting a next generation of scholars, and the existence of this volume is evidence of the impact of this mentoring. (A couple of years after I received tenure, a prominent feminist sociologist told me that she had written a letter in support of my tenure. "Several years ago," she confided to me, "Barrie told me that you are one of the good guys, doing good feminist work." This tidbit I tucked into my mind like a prized trophy.)

Another source of Barrie Thorne's kindness and generosity is undoubtedly grounded in her deep sense of empathy, which she infused into her research on children. Recognizing kids' agency in schools, in part, came from Thorne's ability and willingness to identify with their experience, empathetically connecting to her own child within. In *Gender Play*, Thorne's moments of empathetic connection with the kids are some of her most insightful moments of critical reflexivity: her experience of having been a marginalized, nonpopular girl led her, at first, to focus her research too much on the high-status girls who resembled the girls she had envied when she was young. Thorne yielded different insights, she found, when she hung out with the marginalized girls, though she confessed too that she was sometimes repulsed by them. And Thorne accessed boys' worlds, in part, through her experience of being, at the time, the mother of a young son. She also viewed the kids through her experience of having been herself a good student, stung once by receiving a rare "C"—"the humiliation softened because it was in gym" (1997:104).

Gathering, Tilling, Planting

A recurrent memory I have from nearly a decade of working as Barrie Thorne's junior colleague in two departments at USC—Sociology and Gender Studies—centers on images of Barrie routinely sliding into department meetings fifteen, twenty, thirty minutes late. Her tardiness occurred not because she was a slacker; quite the opposite. Barrie was often late because she was always coming from some other meeting. As a full professor holding an endowed chair, she felt obligated to have an impact on university policies. I believe she told me once (or it's possible that someone else said this about her, I am not certain) that when she left an organization she had been a part of, she wanted to leave it at least a bit more democratic than the way she had found it. She surely had this impact at USC, on scales small and large. Barrie riled some of the old guard sociology faculty by insisting we sit in a circle in department meetings, instead of all sitting in straight lines facing the department chair at the front of a room. Years after she left for Berkeley, I would smile as our department meetings began with a circling of chairs. As a leader in the gender studies program (then called the Program for the Study of Women and Men in Society—SWMS), Barrie made a project of gathering feminist and women faculty from across the campus, building an expanding group of affiliated faculty and staff to support and enhance our small core of dedicated SWMS faculty.

Barrie Thorne's gatherings of people were about building feminist community, and they were also about consolidating feminist clout through which to create institutional change. When she and I were hired at USC in 1987—Barrie as a full professor holding an endowed chair, me as an entry-level assistant professor—the gender regime of the university retained old patriarchal forms and practices. Barrie suggested that she and I should attend the university president's official greeting dinner for new faculty, held at the San Marino mansion the university provided for him and his wife. When Barrie and I walked in the door of the mansion, some women sitting at a card table invited Barrie to join the USC Faculty Wives Club. She was typically gracious in thanking them for the invitation, but noted that she was not my wife; she was on the faculty.

If the invitation to join the Faculty Wives Club hinted at persistent symbolic and interactional patterns that continued to honor men professors while rendering women professors invisible, USC's organizational gender regime created real structural barriers for women faculty. Lila Karp, a novelist with whom I team-taught several gender studies classes in my early years at USC, once asked me, "Have you noticed that nearly all of the few women tenured professors here do not have children? Why do you think that is?" Women professors, I was to learn, often had faced a choice early on: don't have children so you can complete your research, get your publications, and get tenure; or have children, and opt out of the tenure track, perhaps teaching college part-time, moving to K–12 teaching, or becoming a housewife. A "faculty member," it was tacitly assumed, had a wife at home who cared for the kids.

As the 1990s began, Barrie Thorne went to work on this structural inequity. At this time my wife, Pierrette Hondagneu-Sotelo, and I—then both untenured assistant professors—were having our two children, and the university offered no family leave policy. Barrie Thorne gathered a savvy and energetic faculty and staff feminist alliance. Over the course of two or three years, the alliance studied the sorts of family leave policies that other institutions were adopting, created a proposal, and then pressured USC to adopt a progressive system of family leave for faculty or staff. The alliance shaped the policy wisely so that it applied equally to both women and men, to birth parents or adoptive parents, including also same-sex couples. Today, the university's family leave policy exists as a given part of the structure within which faculty navigate their work and family lives.

Of course, history does not end with the creation of a progressive policy that aims to address gender inequities in work-family relations. Continuing inequities—for BIPOC, women, and queer or transgender faculty and staff workers—persist. But Barrie Thorne's work in the early 1990s stands as an example of how a group of people can come up against an oppressive social structure, identify a fissure in that structure, and act to change it in ways that provide greater and more equitable elbow room for a next generation of workers, who subsequently then will together confront new or different structural barriers.

* * *

I titled this chapter "Breaking up the Pavement" in homage to Barrie Thorne's *Gender Play* analogy of kids' creative agency in schools. But what I have written above belies the violence implied in that title. Barrie Thorne's successes were not achieved by wielding a sledgehammer. The conceptual contributions and ethnographic beauty of *Gender Play* resulted from years of careful research, thoughtful analysis, and collective work in a writing group Thorne belonged to. A next generation of feminist scholars continues to build on Thorne's legacies not because she was an intellectual bully or old-school scholarly patriarch but due to her countless hours and years of devoted teaching and generous mentoring. And the community of feminist faculty and staff she built at USC to confront a sexist gender regime was not a wrecking crew. They identified cracks in the system, collected ideas and concepts, planted new policies, and then fought to institutionalize them. The subsequent sproutings, "like grass and dandelions sprouting through the cracks," opened space for more creative and progressive work that continues today. Ultimately Barrie Thorne's body of work, like the summer blossoming of a verdant garden, can be viewed as a legacy of hard work, commitment to a collective democratic future, and feminist love.

REFERENCES

Acker, Joan. 2006. "Inequality Regimes: Gender, Class, and Race in Organizations." *Gender & Society* 20:441–64.

Bachman, Laurence. 2013. "Water Surrounding Deserts: A Lifetime of Spreading Feminist Insights; An Interview with Barrie Thorne, U.C. Berkeley." Working Paper no. 13, University of Geneva.

Coates, Ta-Nehisi. 2015. *Between the World and Me*. New York: One World.

Connell, Raewyn. 1987. *Gender and Power*. Stanford, CA: Stanford University Press.

Ferguson, Ann Arnett. 2000. *Bad Boys: Public Schools in the Making of Black Masculinity*. Ann Arbor: University of Michigan Press.

Lyman, Peter. 1981. "The Politics of Anger: On Silence, Ressentiment, and Political Speech." *Socialist Review* 57:55–74.

Messner, Michael A. 2000. "Barbie Girls vs. Sea Monsters: Children Constructing Gender." *Gender & Society* 14:765–84.

———. 2015. "My Betty Friedan Moment." *Chronicle Review: Chronicle of Higher Education*, February 22.

———. 2021. "Breaking Up the Stag Party: Jessie Bernard's Pioneering Work on Men." *Sociological Forum* 36:520–23.

Messner, Michael A., and Michela Musto. 2014. "Where Are the Kids?" *Sociology of Sport Journal* 31:102–22.

Musto, Michela. 2013. "Athletes in the Pool, Girls and Boys on the Deck: The Contextual Construction of Gender in Coed Youth Swimming." *Gender & Society* 28:359–80.

———. 2019. "Brilliant or Bad: The Gendered Social Construction of Exceptionalism in Early Adolescence." *American Sociological Review* 84:369–93.

Rios, Victor M. 2011. *Punished: Policing the Lives of Black and Latino Boys*. New York: NYU Press.

Thorne, Barrie. 1993. *Gender Play: Girls and Boys in School*. New Brunswick, NJ: Rutgers University Press.

———. 1997. "Brandeis as a Generative Institution: Critical Perspectives, Marginality, and Feminism." Pp. 103–25 in *Feminist Sociology: Life Histories of a Movement*, edited by B. Laslett and B. Thorne. New Brunswick, NJ: Rutgers University Press.

Thorne, Barrie, and Nancy Henley, eds. 1975. *Language and Sex: Difference and Dominance*. New York: Newbury House.

Thorne, Barrie, Cheris Kramarae, and Nancy Henley, eds. 1983. *Language, Gender, and Society*. New York: Newbury House.

Thul, Chelsey M., Nicole M. LaVoi, Torrie F. Hazelwood, and Fatimah Hussein. 2016. "'A Right to the Gym': Physical Activity Experiences of East African Immigrant Girls." Pp. 165–78 in *Child's Play: Sport in Kids' Worlds*, edited by M. A. Messner and M. Musto. New Brunswick, NJ: Rutgers University Press.

Travers, Ann. 2016. "Transgender and Gender-Nonconforming Kids and the Binary Requirements of Sport Participation in North America." Pp. 179–201 in *Child's Play: Sport in Kids' Worlds*, edited by M. A. Messner and M. Musto. New Brunswick, NJ: Rutgers University Press.

8

The Legacy of Relationship

Meditations on Mentoring

ALLISON J. PUGH

My earliest memories of Barrie Thorne are when, as a first-year graduate student, I went with her as she explored the Oakland elementary school that became the site of her last ethnographic project, a school she ended up calling "Oakdale" (e.g., in Thorne 2001).[1] She had already decided to take me on as part of her research team, and while I was a former journalist, I had little idea of how to be an ethnographer, although I knew I was with one. And yet what was this thing called "ethnography"? We wandered around the school and its neighborhood, the glare of the afternoon sun unrelenting on the pastel sidewalks. Nothing was irrelevant and Barrie made note of it all—from churches to the local parks and recreation outpost to the private schools that dotted the area—keeping up a commentary out loud about the availability of public resources, the structuring of private ones. To me, who lived with my own young kids just a few miles away, it was a thoroughly alien experience, and one with no rules to contain it that I could see. I now understand that I was watching, for the first time, someone making the familiar strange.

Barrie ended up spending years there, and while I was deployed mostly to interview parents as part of a school-choice project, her own pleasure was clearly in observing the kids. She sent long emails punctuated with capitalized themes and observations ("CHILDHOOD IS A TERRAIN WHERE DIFFERENT ORDERS OF TIME COME TOGETHER, SOMETIMES COLLIDE, AND ARE CONTESTED [POWER IS AT STAKE] . . . THERE IS A POLITICS OF TIME") that were like a window into her active and constant theorizing. While I do not think she particularly enjoyed her new role of managing a large fieldwork team, it was clear that she relished coaxing sociological meaning from the chaos of everyday life. At Oakdale, she was in her element.

I was lucky that this consummate ethnographer took it upon herself to induct me into the craft. Barrie took the practice of mentoring seriously, bringing her fierce commitment to it as she did to all of her relationships. When I think back on what I learned from her, much of it is about research: starting from that first day at Oakdale, where she narrated for me her approach to new sites. But some of the most important lessons she had to give, I learned by example: how to guide and shape another person's intellectual journey. In preparing this essay, I consulted my own memory (highly selective, of course), as well as the raft of emails I had saved from our exchanges from 1995 to 2005, that tell a story of wise and generous counsel, collaboration, respect, humor, anxiety, and care.

I have since cultivated my own crop of students, building another community of young scholars spread out over the years and dispersed over the miles. At the University of Virginia, I have served on forty-five-some-odd dissertations so far, chairing eleven of them. While each one is as different as the person who writes it and the connection we forge, I bring to each the lessons I learned from Barrie, lessons in what counts as "data," how to collect it, and how to think about it once we have it—but also lessons in the oft-intense, sometimes-complicated give and take of relationship.

Mentoring as Oral Culture

We do not usually teach "mentoring" in academia. Perhaps this is not much of a surprise, because we rarely teach future professors how to teach, either. Yet there are pedagogical supports at many colleges: teaching resource centers, sometimes small grants for course design or improvement. There is usually nothing about becoming a mentor, barring a brief handout or two. This is not to say there is not scholarship on mentoring, as there is. Most of it is in the fields of education and psychology, proving how doctoral mentors increase a sense of belonging (Curtin, Stewart, and Ostrove 2013), forestall attrition (Golde 2005), and lead to more and better jobs (Eby et al. 2013). Scholars have dug into the details of successful mentoring, identifying different types (e.g., instrumental/technical, sponsorship/networking, and expressive/psychosocial, in Curtin, Malley, and Stewart 2016). Yet that research rarely makes it into explicit guides for mentors in academia.

The silence follows a larger societal pattern about the kind of work that involves connecting to other people in order to bring them along on their journey: an emotional journey, an intellectual or cognitive one, or some combination (Pugh forthcoming). This connecting work is part of a much wider variety of jobs than just that of the mentor: the therapist obviously deploys the same toolkit, their eye on the same journey, but so too do wildly disparate jobs such as that of the funeral home director or the hairdresser. Core lessons for the clinical work of helping someone else move forward are rarely identified or discussed. Some fields—often those in counseling—offer training through an apprenticeship system, in which learners get to watch, and then do, under supervision and discussion. In academia, however, there is no such explicit system of passing down the practical wisdom of mentoring. If graduate students are apprentices, the apprenticeship is for research; the articles and books we ponder, the papers we write, are all in service of honing our research craft. Mentoring is an oral culture trapped in a textual world.

In the absence of training or even much conversation about it, most people probably mentor the way they were mentored, give or take a few refinements—while those with toxic mentors vow to do it differently, motivated by the negative example echoing within. A department can feel like a tower of Babel, the many different versions of mentoring milling about without intersecting or informing each other. I have witnessed faculty who enact an intense and dyadic interpretation, their student a constant figure across their desk, murmurs and queries and chuckles emanating from their office as I walk by. I have seen faculty who seem to have a more competitive vision, where students are not quite sure of where they stand, and worry about not being the one taken to this conference or coauthoring on that project. I have seen faculty who give and withhold their time as if in some behaviorist experiment from the 1950s, refusing to work with their advisees anymore unless they pass this or that milestone. Mentoring is viewed as being as personal, and as idiosyncratic, as parenting; its specifics are rarely articulated, and short of outright abuse, it is rarely monitored or counseled or even discussed. In some fields and some settings, this cloak of privacy—just like in families—can foster exploitation, harassment, and cruelty (Hatton 2020). But even when the circumstances are not as dire, the way to improve the personal, clinical practice of accompanying and shepherding another person through their journey, as teachers and therapists know, is to have regular, routine conversations about it.

One problem is that academia most commonly sets up a system whereby your committee chair stands as your primary, if not lone, mentor. The National Council for Faculty Diversity and Development dubs this "guru mentoring," and—speaking of newly hired faculty—argues that it is not just impractical but impossible for one person to serve all of one other person's needs. Their arguments apply to graduate students as well. We are best served by a variety of mentors, they note, and should seek out a variety of people to fill needs such as professional development (how-tos and tips on how to navigate academia), emotional support, a sense of community, accountability, institutional advocacy, access to networks, and project-specific feedback.

While these are all important, when I look at that list, I see little of what I got from Barrie. From Barrie, and from other mentors (particularly Arlie Hochschild, Christine Williams, and Nancy Chodorow), I learned less of what to do or who to know, and more of how to be—with myself, with them, and in community with others. From these feminist foremothers I learned how to ask particular questions, and how to manage particular tensions, in the reflective guiding of another person.

An Interpretive Sensibility

The most important of these lessons was how to cultivate what we might consider an interpretive sensibility, an awareness of the multiple layers of meaning in a given moment. "The imperative for the investigator," writes the theorist Isaac Reed (2011:106), "is to grasp a world of communicated sociality: the meanings that make up relations, script rituals and performances, inflect messages and gestures, and give weight to social ties; the meanings that constitute the 'space' upon which social action proceeds." Reed argues that this world is made up of "landscapes of meaning," and it is the ethnographer's task to capture and convey these landscapes, and their meanings.

Barrie reveled in this task. She learned how to do this signification and resignification in part from Everett Hughes at Brandeis, and used to cite him in her graduate seminar on field methods, particularly his line about drawing "far-out" comparisons—the doctor and the plumber, the psychiatrist and the sex worker (Strauss 1996). In her own work, of course, she was particularly taken by the landscapes that kids traversed. Her notion of "borderwork," the compelling concept from *Gender Play* for the practice of actively making and remaking gender segregation, is a perfect example of an interpretive sensibility, one that divines the patterns that matter around us. In this case Barrie saw and named the everyday processes that give an intense, powerful salience to some kinds of meaning and not others, e.g., gender as opposed to age, or height, or location. At Oakdale, she would pepper her conversation with references from the kids' lexicon, for example, the "Pokémon kids" and the "Chinese girls," which later became the title of one of her articles (Thorne 2008).

The task of cultivating an interpretive sensibility in another gives rise to a whole series of questions that I have faced as an advisor. First among these is the question, How do you quiet yourself to hear others? Without staking a claim for "objectivity," I would argue that getting out of the way is the qualitative researcher's first task, that we are there to hear what others have to say, to understand their perspective. But while that may sound obvious, doing so is tricky, as the qualitative researcher is both instrument and analyst.

Yet Barrie would probably argue that the task is less getting out of the way than it is simply making room for the other; I can hear her even now advocating for a both/and rather than an either/or. When I worked on the Oakdale field site, part of my discomfort there was that in listening to parents anxious about charting their child's path through the thicket of schools that faced them, the discourse so strongly resembled that of my own neighbors. I had trouble stepping back to see or analyze its contours. Barrie saw my own experience as relevant, however, as much as that of the people we spoke to at Oakdale, and welcomed them both with her characteristic warmth (from one generous email of the time: "Your interviews and insights are fabulous; your thinking is synergistic with my own; and everything you do on this will enhance the rest of the vast [but getting-focused] endeavor."). She excelled at articulating the interweavings of one's emotions and analysis, and at noting and observing the ensuing tensions.

Another key question that arises in cultivating an interpretive sensibility is about the tension of being at once humane and analytical, or how to honor the imperative of care in doing research with integrity. How do we help students keep their compassionate selves and their critical selves engaged simultaneously, to both appreciate the informants' gift of their participation and to think about what it might mean sociologically? Barrie crossed that rickety bridge continually. Her commitment to ferreting out sexism and racism was fierce. One of my favorite pieces of her writing was a beautiful memo, which I still remember, pointing to "the ghosting of Jamal," capturing an African American mother's account of the terrible stages by which her son moved, in the eyes of her white neighbors, from cute to invisible to dangerous. Yet her dedication to understanding kids' perspectives meant that sometimes she discovered their own forms of racism or bullying. She did not shy away from these difficult truths, but also took pains to understand their origins and costs (e.g., Haavind, Thorne, Hollway, and Magnusson 2015). Here Barrie also lived the both/and: at once empathetically deriving and understanding her informants' perspectives, and divining and naming the processes of inequality and hierarchy that they themselves enacted.

A third question comes up frequently in my mentoring of students, and it is one that also bothers me more than it seemed to bother Barrie: How do we tolerate the chaos of the early stages of a project? As in the opening vignette, I never quite got my hands around the Oakdale site in all of its variation, but Barrie seemed to love it. I quote at length from one of her 1998 emails, which can still—almost twenty-five years later!—bring back for me the sense of being inundated by the flood of data, ideas, details. Barrie wrote,

> I keep returning to the broad and starting notion of practices (and processes) through which parents, children, and others construct particular childhoods. Practices grounded in varied fields of knowledge, values, reputation-construction (eg of schools—such amazing disparity in how Oakdale is regarded); beliefs and feelings re class, gender, race, safety/danger; differing beliefs re what kids (of different ages, genders) need, generically, in conjunction with parents' specific "diagnoses" of their chil-

dren's "natures" and "needs" (current and projected); and differing beliefs re what sort of person they are helping to shape (including how much control parents may have in the shaping, vs peers, school, etc.).

"Now all of this is far too complex," she noted blithely, just as my chin slipped below the waves. "The challenge is to articulate a basic focus, a simpler and clarifying starting point or skeleton on which to hang arguments and data. Any ideas you have re that (overly complex) way in to the process of 'musing the data' would be appreciated. Now comes the 'honing ideas in the data,' 'building grounded theory' fun part." Barrie looked forward to surfing the data tsunami.

Barrie's tolerance for chaos might have been unusual, but all qualitative projects, I have found, have a similar moment, and most of my students have had at least one occasion in which they have come into my office a little wild-eyed, overwhelmed by the sheer multitude of meanings. It is a common, even inevitable predicament, especially for qualitative researchers: when it feels as if you could use the data to tell any story a little bit, but no story very well. How to engender calm, when the seas threaten to engulf? I do not have an answer to this perennial question, except—like Barrie—to reassure students of its inevitability, and that this too shall pass, that some larger narrative will bubble up, and they will somehow find the story that they and their data want to tell. But I recognize their panic and dread.

Sometimes, of course, the interpretations do not want to come, which is the source of a fourth question: How do we enable students to give themselves the emotional and cognitive room to think creatively about what might be going on? There may be some innate quality to interpretation, but it can also be taught. To be more precise, actually, I find the interpretive sensibility needs less to be *taught* than it needs to be *freed*.

In my experience, it is not that most students do not have the ability to find novel patterns or plumb the interpretive meaning of a particular practice. It is that their capacity to do so is curtailed. They find themselves pinioned by the demands of the program's normative time pressures, the glares or dismissal of faculty given to hostile pronouncements about "me-search," or perhaps worst of all, the censorious weight of self-doubt. Interpretation is creativity: a powerful metaphor, a felicitous comparison, a concept that folds disparate units together. And like creativity, it needs to be coaxed in deftly, with a light touch; if it deigns to come at all, it will be on its own terms, not dragged in because we want it to be but instead invited with whimsy, or playfulness, or a sense of possibility. The only way, I think, is to approach it with lightness, even a sense of pleasure, or as Barrie put it, "'the honing of ideas in the data,' 'building grounded theory' fun part." Sometimes that has meant approaching it sidelong, rather than with a sense of panic or urgency. Deadlines are deadly here. Like Luker's (2009) invocation of salsa dancing, more than once when a student has been stuck and facing down an impending due date, I have told them to go gardening.

Giving and Receiving: Confidence, Care, and Humor in Feedback

The second domain where Barrie's legacy of relationship pervades is in the interactive dance of feedback, editorial and otherwise. She was one of those rare mentors who offered line edits, who could clean up copy deftly but also react to ideas and respond in the margins. Years as a reporter inured me to tough critique, but also allowed me to recognize when someone was as unusually good an editor as Barrie. Feedback is pretty standard fare for mentors, and included on every list of what a good advisor should do. Less well known and more pertinent for our discussion here, I think, is that good feedback requires good relations behind it, involving practices of giving and receiving. Barrie shows us that we should care not simply *that* feedback is given and received but also *how* it is.

The questions that come up for me around feedback are mostly about independence. How do my mentees find their own voices? When do I let them make mistakes? How much feedback is too much feedback? As I write these questions out, however, I can see that they are the questions of someone who is convinced they have the right answer, who wonders simply how forcefully to communicate it. But Barrie was humbler than that, more open to the give and take of relationship, and in that way she made me feel like a true partner, even when I was a nascent researcher, with very little experience. Just a few months after I arrived at graduate school, she was writing me encouraging emails about fieldnotes and memos ("I love your flairs of language, e.g. Tiffany 'flouncing' even tho in baggy t-shirt and jeans; and re another girl, a 'certain loping gait peculiar on someone of her size.' YOUR NOTES ARE REALLY HELPFUL; PLEASE GIVE THIS PROJECT AS MUCH TIME AS YOU CAN!").

This encouragement meant that I assuredly got ahead of myself more often than not. In one email that I now wince to read, I wrote that there was so much variation in our data that it was hard to find an effective frame for it, and suggested that an article we were working on should instead be a book of case studies, with a particular title ("Getting to School"), conceptual frame ("communal childhoods"), and our article as the lead chapter. My, the confidence! In particular, anyone who knows Barrie would know she would likely hate the phrasing "communal childhoods" because of its rosy eliding of power and inequality. Yet Barrie responded with her characteristic generosity, saying that while she did plan on making a book of this, we should stick with the journal article for now.

"I don't think that 'communal childhoods' is the best overall phrasing," she said delicately, "since it suggests 'communes' and harmony." She continued, "Conflict and avoidance are at work (e.g. in white flight; conflicting views of whether or not it's a good thing that Oakdale school is not officially Title I, or 'low income'). As is bonding (as with the white parents and their pact [to send their kids to the school en masse, instead of opting out], or the Latino mothers getting together to complain about the first-grade teacher and location of the classrooms)." Gently, she said, "Let's keep reaching for a vivid organizing concept." At the end of her reply (which went on for many more screens), she concluded not with "let's not get ahead of ourselves here" or "get back to work" but with "What do you think? Thanks for passing the ball further down the field, Allison." Her generosity was a constant.

Feedback is not worth much if it is only positive, and Barrie did not shy away from giving criticism, but she did so (clearly) within a relationship that built confidence, with her characteristic care and good humor. Some of her wise counsel stays with me to this day, partly because of the way that she shared it. For example, the other members of my longtime writing group have heard Barrie's wisdom about writing introductions so often that we repeat it to each other whenever someone gets too declarative in their opening pages. Here is the story: Consider a book introduction like a dinner party that you are hosting, Barrie once told me.

When someone comes to the door, she said, you invite them in, ask for their coat, show them their way around, introduce them to the other guests. You don't open the door and shout (and here I remember Barrie calling out into the distance, and roaring with laughter while she did so), "WE'RE HAVING STEAK! AND MAYBE DESSERT LATER! YES IT'S STEAK!" I have striven for a greater narrative subtlety in my introductions ever since, while those roars of laughter still reverberate, joyfully.

Weathering Conflict and Disappointment

Like all relationships—and particularly like all intense ones—mentoring relationships will involve disagreements or disappointments. I have been lucky with advisees who are feminist, interpretive, critical, and exceedingly smart, while also being caring contributors to our collective culture of shared wisdom and support. That said, a student or two has tested the waters and decided against signing on with me as an advisor, and I have turned away a student or two for whom the fit was not ideal. Part of avoiding conflict and disappointment is making sure your strengths are what they need, and your weaknesses are what they can manage.

Some of Barrie's legacy of relationship is in how to manage conflict: a domain that I am still learning to navigate. In truth, when I read the emails left in my old inboxes, I am haunted by the ways I disappointed Barrie. She was so encouraging on the Oakdale project, so early in my graduate career, and yet my own involvement petered out, as I became overwhelmed by the demands of my own research, while raising three kids and starting a charter school. I had plenty of excuses for not fulfilling the promise of our early collaborations, but I don't remember ever sitting her down and being straightforward with her about the sense of overwhelm.

In reality, that sense stemmed not only from competing demands but also from issues internal to the project. As is probably evident from the slew of examples throughout this essay, I had trouble with the everything-is-grist approach to ethnography, and if there is a continuum of how to approach an ethnographic field with or without preexisting questions—a continuum represented by everything from grounded theory (Charmaz 2014) to abductive analysis (Tavory and Timmermans 2014) to the extended case method (Burawoy 2009)—I am probably somewhere in the middle. I share with Barrie her dedication to kids, her outrage on their behalf, her feminist commitments, her love for the writing craft. But Barrie's lessons to me are also about how to build and experience a mentoring relationship despite an awkward stylistic mismatch, or perhaps an intellectual one: when our approaches to the world of data do not perfectly align.

I now try to avoid that sense of haunting disappointment in my own relationships with advisees by being direct—and encouraging them to be direct—about expectations and limitations. Yet this directness can certainly be threatening to advisees, given the hierarchical relationship. Thus when I told one advisee she needed to respond to my comments on her draft ("You need to take my comments seriously because they represent my work for you, and when you ignore them it makes me feel like I am wasting my time. I'm sure it was just an oversight on your part, but I'm just letting you know what it feels like."), it took several subsequent interactions before we could move past her apology and my reassurance to an easy exchange again. The incident was undoubtedly smaller than all that emotional work would suggest, but I was indeed thinking about Barrie, and how to avoid that haunting feeling. In retrospect, I suppose, I needed to use a lighter touch in conveying the message; a little more Barrie is what is needed here.

Thanks to this desire for air clearing, however, I actually considered it a win (if a sorrowful one) when another advisee wrote me to say she could not continue on a coauthored article because of her other work ("It is not fair to you, as a collaborator, for me to continue in this way."). At the very least, I viewed the email as testament to her own self-awareness and integrity as a scholar, a combination I could not muster twenty years ago. I did not accept her withdrawal, and when I told her I would be keeping her on as second author anyway in light of the enormous contributions she had made earlier, she was moved ("I'm a little blown away by it."). These can be compelling relationships of mutual care, as long as there is room made for our inevitable limitations.

I am sure that Barrie was more sensitive to power differentials in the mentoring relationship as she withheld her own criticism. One email I have from the end of the Oakdale project, asking me for some last remnants of data analysis, is again, characteristically gentle. "Not guilt-loading, my dear; just a bit of querying and prodding. There's back-up skilled help [another graduate student] if for some reason you can't get to it." These are complex relationships, often extremely rewarding, but sometimes intense and even difficult. Barrie's acute awareness of power suffused her approach to mentoring, so that she was solid in her support, unstinting with her care, and gentle with her regrets.

Despite my failings, Barrie was kind enough to serve on my dissertation committee, and indeed, she was a continual source of support and encouragement even after I graduated, advising me at various junctures, sponsoring me for awards and jobs and other plums of academia. We shared lunches at my infrequent visits to Berkeley or yearly ASA meetings, the periodic moments of connection like pearls on a strand, and in those early years—marooned so far from Berkeley and its environs—I was probably a bit desperate for them. Indeed, I drew even closer to her intellectually then, when I taught sociology of childhood myself, and came to really grapple with and subscribe to her argument that age inequality is akin to other forms of socially constructed structures of power (Pugh 2014). But it is in my relationships with students that I can still hear her voice—musing, probing, in laughter, in sardonic commentary—as I contemplate her legacy of relationship.

Conclusion

As a culture academia does not often articulate the components of what it means to be a strong mentor. While Barrie's care and dedication made her support palpable to me as an insecure graduate student, she also offered a practical demonstration of mentoring skills that were not articulated as such, but instead modeled in a way that I continue to return to today. In three domains—cultivating an interpretive sensibility, giving and receiving feedback, and managing and weathering conflict or disappointment—I find myself thinking about how Barrie did or would respond to similar situations. This essay is to make these internal musings transparent, part of saying out loud what mentoring should be, what it could be, what it ends up being—in the hopes of generating a conversation about relationship.

I became a mother at the same time that I became a graduate student. Both experiences involve massive transformation, a total metamorphosis in self-concept and everyday practice. For many academics, these are separate processes. The fact that they were conjoined for me meant that my mentors served as midwives to the person—and the parent—that emerged.

I know the maternal metaphor is a dangerous one. Barrie was the first to note that we need to make sure the mothering language includes those who are not mothers, and to make room for those who have damaged relationships with their mothers, and to be clear we are not taking for granted the caring labor that mothers do, and to be careful about the power that mothers wield, especially over kids. In short, we must neither essentialize nor underestimate mothers' work and its consequences. Yet my mentoring is nonetheless inextricably entwined with my mothering: I cannot escape what feel like strong similarities in the support and shepherding of someone on their journey. The primary way in which it might be different—the leavening of intellectual and political commitments in PhD advising—seems but to add yet another layer of intensity.

As a graduate student, I felt the same entanglements coming from Barrie, and I mean that in the most complimentary fashion: both fierce and loving, Barrie lives the both/and tensions she interrogates. While her conceptual bequest may be abundant, for me her legacy of relationship abides.

NOTE

1 This essay is dedicated to Barrie, and to all of my advisors and advisees, links in a generational chain of care. I am grateful to Andrea Press and Steve Sellers for feedback on earlier drafts, and to the volume's editors, Freeden Blume Oeur and C. J. Pascoe, for their inspired decision to pursue this project.

REFERENCES

Burawoy, Michael. 2009. *The Extended Case Method: Four Countries, Four Decades, Four Great Transformations, and One Theoretical Tradition.* Berkeley: University of California Press.

Charmaz, Kathy. 2014. *Constructing Grounded Theory.* Thousand Oaks, CA: Sage.

Curtin, Nicola, Janet Malley, and Abigail J. Stewart. 2016. "Mentoring the Next Generation of Faculty: Supporting Academic Career Aspirations among Doctoral Students." *Research in Higher Education* 57(6):714–38.

Curtin, Nicola, Abigail J. Stewart, and Joan M. Ostrove. 2013. "Fostering Academic Self-Concept: Advisor Support and Sense of Belonging among International and Domestic Graduate Students." *American Educational Research Journal* 50(1):108–37.

Eby, Lillian Turner de Tormes, Tammy D. Allen, Brian J. Hoffman, Lisa E. Baranik, Julia B. Sauer, Sean Baldwin, M. Ashley Morrison, Katie M. Kinkade, Charleen P.

Maher, and Sara Curtis. 2013. "An Interdisciplinary Meta-Analysis of the Potential Antecedents, Correlates, and Consequences of Protégé Perceptions of Mentoring." *Psychological Bulletin* 139(2):441.

Golde, Chris M. 2005. "The Role of the Department and Discipline in Doctoral Student Attrition: Lessons from Four Departments." *Journal of Higher Education* 76(6):669–700.

Haavind, Hanne, Barrie Thorne, Wendy Hollway, and Eva Magnusson. 2015. "'Because Nobody Likes Chinese Girls': Intersecting Identities and Emotional Experiences of Subordination and Resistance in School Life." *Childhood* 22(3):300–315.

Hatton, Erin. 2020. *Coerced: Work under Threat of Punishment.* Oakland: University of California Press.

Luker, Kristin. 2009. *Salsa Dancing into the Social Sciences: Research in an Age of Info-glut.* Cambridge, MA: Harvard University Press.

Pugh, Allison J. 2014. "The Theoretical Costs of Ignoring Childhood: Rethinking Independence, Insecurity, and Inequality." *Theory and Society* 43(1):71–89.

———. Forthcoming. "Connective Labor as Emotional Vocabulary: Inequality, Mutuality, and the Politics of Feelings in Care-Work." *Signs: Journal of Women in Culture and Society.*

Reed, Isaac Ariail. 2011. *Interpretation and Social Knowledge: On the Use of Theory in the Human Sciences.* Chicago: University of Chicago Press.

Strauss, Anselm. 1996. "Everett Hughes: Sociology's Mission." *Symbolic Interaction* 19(4):271–83.

Tavory, Iddo, and Stefan Timmermans. 2014. *Abductive Analysis: Theorizing Qualitative Research.* Chicago: University of Chicago Press.

Thorne, Barrie. 1993. *Gender Play: Girls and Boys in School.* New Brunswick, NJ: Rutgers University Press.

———. 2001. "Pick-Up Time at Oakdale Elementary School." Pp. 354–76 in *Working Families: The Transformation of the American Home,* edited by R. Hersh and N. Marshall. Berkeley: University of California Press.

———. 2008. "'The Chinese Girls' and 'The Pokémon Kids': Children Negotiating Differences in Urban California." Pp. 73–97 in *Figuring the Future: Globalization and the Temporalities of Children and Youth,* edited by J. Cole and D. Durham. Santa Fe, NM: School for Advanced Research Press.

9

Living Theory

Gender Play *and Learning to Live a Life Less Ordinary*

CHRISTO SIMS

It is October 16, 2011, and I am standing in Washington Square Park in New York City with a small group of friends. We have gathered to join a march that has been called in support of the Occupy Wall Street protest movement. Activists first established an encampment in Zuccotti Park in lower Manhattan about a month before, and the movement has been gaining steam in recent weeks despite much of the media having initially ignored or mocked the protesters. Today's march has been planned in coordination with activists from around the world who, among other things, are marking the five-month anniversary of the 15-M demonstrations in Spain, the anti-austerity movement that helped pave the way for Occupy Wall Street. It feels like the wind is now at the back of an increasingly global protest movement, and I am beginning to feel hopeful that the political-economic regime that has reigned for my entire lifetime might be losing its grip.

But I am also at the protest because it is the weekend and I need a break from the academic work routines that have commandeered much of my life since I entered graduate school in 2005. Six years later, I am a PhD candidate who is living in New York to conduct ethnographic fieldwork for my dissertation, which is centered on an experimental new public school that opened with much fanfare several years earlier. The school had, in my view, turned out to be a disappointment, and at this point I am grappling with how to square the good intentions of the school's sponsors, designers, and supporters with the troubling ways in which race, class, and gender hierarchies were being remade inside the school. I plan to graduate the following spring, so I am spending most of my days trying to figure out how to transform a messy mass of ethnographic documentation into something resembling a passable thesis. I am also applying to a handful of tenure-track jobs with the anticipation of being rejected. In other words, I am spending much of my life like most other doctoral students: immersed in the often uncertain and unsettling work of trying to learn how to become an academic.

So, it feels especially good to be outside on this day, to be doing something to try to change some of those "structures" that keep showing up as mere words on my laptop screen, to share some collective effervescence with friends and strangers—most of them young adults like me and none of them seeming to care if I have sufficient command of "the literature"—to be, in short, away from academia and work, if only for a moment. I am in this state of joyful reprieve when I see Barrie Thorne approach me and my friends, and, upon seeing her, I feel both surprise and trepidation. I should not be surprised to see Barrie since I had invited her to join us the night before while we were having dinner together. Still, somehow I did not expect Barrie to come, but now she is here, and I do not know quite how to act. Part of my disorientation has to do with the social production of age divisions and hierarchies, something that Barrie had first turned me on to several years prior. I am with a group of friends who are in their twenties and early thirties, and Barrie is about the age of my parents. Will Barrie fit in with my younger friends, and can I be at ease if Barrie is with us? This latter question gets at the trepidation I am feeling. It is not that I do not like Barrie (quite the opposite!) or that I am afraid of her (okay, maybe a little?) but because at this time I still primarily associate Barrie with that other world—academia, work—from which I am trying to get a bit of a break.

Barrie is in New York for a meeting of an academic advisory board for the philanthropic initiative that is sponsoring the school I am studying, and I had made a short presentation on my research to the advisory board the day before. Barrie is also a member of my dissertation committee, a role she generously agreed to take on after my initial doctoral advisor, Barrie's spouse, Peter Lyman, tragically died of brain cancer in 2007. I had first met Barrie several years prior to Peter's death when she visited Peter's research group, of which I was a member. I was barely in graduate school at the time, and my primary memory of first meeting Barrie is one of intimidation. Barrie had visited Peter's research group to help the grad students learn how to study young people's digital media practices ethnographically, and I felt overwhelmed by how much she knew and how little I did.

In subsequent years, those feelings of intimidation lessened but never vanished. They lessened in part because I had managed to learn something about the craft of doing ethnographic research, and because I had learned a lot from Barrie about the history and sociology of childhood, all of which was informing my current work. But they mostly lessened because Barrie and Peter had opened their home in Oakland to me and other grad students on numerous occasions, because I had met their children, eaten their food, and enjoyed jokes and banter with them. But, still, all of this had been in the context of work, which was not the same as what I was planning to do on this day with my friends. Or so I thought.

*　*　*

Gender Play is a remarkable work for the richness of its ethnographic descriptions and for the generativity of its analysis. The book's continued use and relevance testifies to those contributions. But *Gender Play* is also remarkable for the courage it models, a courage that is simultaneously ethical, intellectual, and political; a courage, I want to propose, that productively troubles boundaries between "a work" and "a life." Part of that courage stems from the book's treatment of the social production of gender as a legitimate and worthy subject of sociological inquiry, a stance that appears less risky today but that was quite heterodox at the time when Barrie conducted the fieldwork and wrote the manuscript for *Gender Play.* The same can be said about the ways *Gender Play* treats young people as full and worthy social actors who deserve the attention, respect, and resources of serious social inquiry. We now have subfields dedicated to the sociology of childhood, and there is even an interdisciplinary field focused on childhood studies, but those did not yet exist, at least not in an institutionalized form, when Barrie was crafting *Gender Play.* The book helped make those scholarly worlds possible, and in doing so helped create a slipstream for those of us who followed in its trails to craft our own professional lives.

Even so, strong headwinds remain. One of the things that apprenticing scholars come to learn as they transform into more experienced academics is that topics of social inquiry—and, thus, expertise—are subject to innumerable instances of comparative evaluation—some of which are institutionalized, but many of which are informal—that cumulatively articulate and sustain hierarchies of academic worth. Despite the intellectual clearings made by *Gender Play* and other trailblazing works, both gender and childhood remain low in these hierarchies in the eyes of many, and these assessments inevitably have a bearing on our work and careers. That is one of the reasons why it still takes some courage to build one's work, and thus career, around the sorts of questions and topics that Barrie has long championed. Let me provide an example from my own fieldwork.

When I was crafting my dissertation prospectus, both Barrie and another courageous scholar of approximately the same generation, Jean Lave, encouraged me to center my inquiry on the lives of the students who would be attending the new school where I was planning to conduct fieldwork. I had read Barrie's and Jean's books and was impressed with them, so it did not seem particularly novel or courageous to pursue a similar approach. But it was quite another matter to actually do that work, which in my case meant spending countless hours hanging out with eleven- and twelve-year-olds as they went about their daily routines and then spending countless hours more writing up every detail that I could recall. Part of that challenge will be familiar to experienced ethnographers: a lot of what goes on in the field is mundane and (seemingly) kind of boring. But I also struggled with another, and more subtle, challenge, namely, the habituated tendency to discount what young people say and do as not all that important, the feeling that the serious stuff lay elsewhere, the suspicion, in other words, that this form of knowledge making was not so worthy.

I knew about these biases before I went into the field, but I did not, and probably could not, anticipate how they would surface in practice. Time and again, especially in the early months of fieldwork, I would catch myself worrying about whether it was really worthwhile for me to be documenting in great detail how, say, middle schoolers were fervently exchanging Silly Bandz rubber bracelets with each other. The practice was clearly important to the young people I was hanging out with, but wasn't the phenomenon silly, as the bracelets' name itself suggested? An account of such practices might elicit smiles or even touches of nostalgia in my adult interlocutors, but Silly Bandz did not seem to be the stuff of serious scholarship, or so I worried. This is just one example of how the cudgel of sedimented biases can insinuate itself into the practice of conducting ethnographic fieldwork—an example of how those hierarchies of worth can be self-imposed. It was during moments like this one that I would remember the advice of Barrie and Jean, and those remembrances helped give me confidence to keep documenting and thinking about the young people's seemingly silly practices.[1]

And it wasn't just me who was making these sorts of tacit evaluations at my field site. One of the interesting things about the school where I conducted fieldwork is that it ended up attracting a lot of other observers in addition to me: other researchers, journalists, education reformers, government officials, and many more. Ostensibly, these people were there because they cared about children, and I suspect they were sincere in this regard. Yet nobody else appeared to be practicing the approach that Barrie had advocated to me, that is, to try to understand these young people's practices and experiences on their own terms. Instead, the other observers were focused on what they and many others considered to be the serious matter at hand, something called education, the presumed beneficiaries of which were children, understood in a more abstract and general sense. Let me provide an example of this sort of tacit valuation.

On various occasions during fieldwork, I watched other qualitative researchers diligently documenting how students responded to a particular pedagogic intervention or technique implemented by a teacher. This was understandable because the researchers were trying to figure out if and how the school's pedagogic innovations were effective. Fair enough. But these were the serious concerns of the adults, not the silly concerns of the students, and privileging the former had the effect of rendering youth-driven practices like the exchange of Silly Bandz either invisible or unimportant. What is more, this devaluation of young people's experiences and perspectives ironically thwarted the adults from realizing their serious aims. In part because the young people's experiences and perspectives were largely overlooked, many adults who were involved with the new school had difficulty understanding why their intervention, which had been designed for the presumed interests of a "digital generation," did not enthrall many of the students who had enrolled at the school. Absent such an understanding, educators were eventually pressured into resorting to rather familiar and unsettling disciplinary techniques in order to compel students' participation in the supposedly fun activities that the adults had planned for them. What is more, most of the students who were targeted by these disciplinary techniques were students of color from lower-income households, many of whom subsequently left the school. In this way, a school that had been imagined as egalitarian, playful, and student centered ended up resorting to rather raw exercises of institutionally sanctioned adult power, a process that ended up mostly reinscribing entrenched hierarchies of not just age but also racialized social class and gender. Headwinds remain.

* * *

One of the things Barrie told me over dinner the night before the protest was that I should not let people involved in the philanthropic initiative censor my work. When Barrie made this comment, I did not know what she had in mind, and I did not anticipate any such efforts. But the comment was foreboding, so it stayed with me. I thought about Barrie's comment many times as I was writing my dissertation and then turning my dissertation into a book. Over time I started to realize that I was indeed self-censoring my account. In particular, I was omitting the role that the philanthropic initiative had played in bringing the school into being as well as my involvement in that initiative. Why? Mostly because I was afraid of aggravating influential members of the philanthropic initiative, people who had helped fund my academic career thus far and who still held considerable sway over my future. Eventually, I began to stop censoring myself, and, as it turned out, Barrie's warning proved prescient. When the book finally came out, a couple of people who held considerable power in the philanthropic initiative tried to get my press to stop promoting and distributing the book. They also backchanneled with other senior scholars in an attempt to besmirch my credibility, and they privately shamed and threatened me, including by threatening to file formal charges against me with my employer unless I agreed to accede to their demands and pressure my press to do the same.

This period was one of the most difficult ones of not just my career but also my life. I was an assistant professor at the time, and I worried about my tenure prospects and nascent professional reputation if these senior scholars continued with their discreditation campaign or followed through with their threats. I also experienced severe self-doubt, became disillusioned with academia, and considered leaving it. But throughout those travails, I managed to find some solace and confidence in learning that many of the "old-timers" whom I respected the most in academia had been through similar challenges. During this difficult period, I often wondered how Barrie knew to warn me of possible backlashes to my work by those who held power over me. The more I thought about it, the more convinced I became that her foresight was not only prescient but also a learned quality of her feminist praxis.

As the introductory chapter of this volume describes, Barrie's political and intellectual work has always been informed by her life, and vice versa. Among other things, Barrie's journey as a scholar has been shaped by the complex challenges of growing up in conservative Utah and eventually disentangling herself from the Church of Jesus Christ of Latter-day Saints. It is worth pausing for a moment to reflect on what that sort of disentanglement entails. Leaving a home and a church is not as simple as making a proclamation about what you do and do not believe. It involves a willingness to learn firsthand how power operates in the most intimate and personal of ways, and it involves the necessity of nurturing new intimacies and of fostering new communities.

Much of the feminist intellectual and political work that Barrie has done throughout her career has been in this vein: making new worlds possible by working against the grain with others, often off the page and behind the scenes. She has repeatedly fought to make space in academic institutions for gender studies, for childhood studies, and for other lines of scholarship that challenge entrenched orthodoxies and hierarchies. She has spent countless hours mentoring and caring for students who did not feel they had a legitimate and valued place in the academy. And she has championed and defended junior colleagues whose work was deemed threatening or illegitimate by senior faculty and administrators. I was a beneficiary of this feminist praxis of Barrie's, and many others were too, more than readers of Barrie's works or even this volume are likely to know.

An example. Not long after I began work as an assistant professor, I met an accomplished full professor at my new university who shared with me a story about Barrie. The professor had learned that I had worked with Barrie when I was a graduate student, and she wanted me to know how impactful Barrie had been on her own career. She recalled how she had reached a point during graduate school in the 1980s when she had decided to quit academia. She had been an unorthodox graduate student for her time, she recounted, and she had struggled to find a path through academia that would allow her to do the sort of feminist political and intellectual work that mattered to her. Barrie was not at her university or on her committee, but Barrie knew the graduate student, and when Barrie learned of the student's plans to leave academia, Barrie intervened to help the disillusioned young scholar get through the difficult period. Barrie saved the younger scholar's academic career, this now accomplished faculty member recounted. I am confident she is not the only one.

Yet this essential care work—this labor that sustains academic careers and institutions alike—remains largely overlooked and undervalued in the academy. It does not typically show up on the pages of our finished monographs except in the acknowledgments section, a place spatially and symbolically cordoned off from the manuscript's "serious" intellectual contributions. Much of it is not legible in tenure and promotion cases, and when it is accounted for, its value is discounted. It does not really help scholars gain citations or win a higher standing in their fields. It does not really help with job offers. It often does not put those who practice it in good favor with institutional gatekeepers. It does not, in short, really help the careers of those who perform it, and, if anything, it often hinders career success, as conventionally defined and celebrated in the academy.

The longer I spend in academia, the more fortunate I feel to have found Barrie and a few other especially generous and caring mentors when I was in graduate school. My experience, I have come to learn, was not the norm. Too many of my friends and colleagues who pursued a PhD did not feel supported by their advisors and committee members, or they felt supported in highly conditional ways, ways that often depended on their ability to help their mentors advance their own projects and careers. That such abuses exist in academia is hardly news. And I certainly do not want to suggest that variations in mentorship practices can be reduced to an individual's ethics. But the endurance of such patterns of neglect and abuse does point towards some of the problems that can arise when theory and practice are separated, when a work and a life are treated as distinct entities, when works are valorized and the care work that made those works possible is ignored or demeaned.

There is a nice moment in Sarah Ahmed's (2006) book *Queer Phenomenology* when Ahmed revisits Husserl's reflections on his writing table, a concrete place where Husserl's theories were seemingly made. Ahmed uses Husserl's reflections to queer the phenomenological notion of "the background" and to ask about all the concealed work, much of it domestic, that had to take place in order for Husserl's theories to arrive on the page. To quote Ahmed, "We can think . . . of the background not simply in terms of what is around what we face, as the 'dimly perceived,' but as produced by acts of relegation: some things are relegated to the background in order to sustain a certain direction" (Ahmed 2006:31). Ahmed is drawing on a long history of feminist scholarship on the gendered politics of housework and of care labor more generally. But she is also drawing attention to how so many of our prized theorists tend to relegate to the background much of the work that made their work possible. Put differently, they relegate this necessary work to that vast remainder of activity that we often call life.

Nearly forty years before Ahmed, the feminist artist Mierle Laderman Ukeles made a similar observation about the self-proclaimed revolutionary character of much avant-garde art. In an artwork titled MANIFESTO FOR MAINTENANCE ART, 1969! *Proposal for an Exhibition: "CARE,"* Ukeles wrote (as quoted in Lippard 1973:220–21),

> Two basic systems: *Development and Maintenance.*
> The sourball of every revolution: after the revolution who's going to pick up the garbage on Monday morning?
> *Development*: pure individual creation; the new; change; progress; advance; excitement; flight or fleeing.
> *Maintenance*: Keep the dust off the pure individual creation; preserve the new; sustain the change; protect progress; defend and prolong the advance; renew the excitement; repeat the flight.

Development and maintenance, two systems repeatedly divided but integrally constituted, the former routinely valorized, the latter regularly denigrated. These feminist critiques have been with us for some time, and more recently they have even become fashionable in parts of the social sciences. Yet too often, it seems to me, the insight of the theory does not circle back to account for the care work that made the insight possible. What would it mean to not just make theoretical claims and to win acclaim for doing so but also to live by and for those claims? What would it mean to produce and inhabit a living and livable theory? These are questions of a feminist praxis, questions with answers that predate care becoming an intellectual fashion, questions with answers that Barrie has long practiced and modeled in her work and in her life.

* * *

My misgivings about having invited Barrie to join my friends and me at the Occupy Wall Street protest proved to be misplaced. My friends, it turned out, felt perfectly at ease around Barrie, Barrie seemed perfectly at ease around them, and soon I too began to relax. Those dogged divisions of age and role and of work and life did not seem to matter in this case. This was not an instance of "borderwork," as Barrie described in *Gender Play*, in which the temporary crossing of divisions has the effect of firming up the boundaries. Rather, it was a moment of genuine conviviality. Yes, Barrie was still in a position of authority over me. Yes, Barrie would be one of four people who in a few months' time would decide if I was fit to become a PhD. Yes, Barrie was in the process of writing me letters of recommendation for jobs. I would be lying if I were to say that those power relations did not weigh on me, did not make me worry a bit about doing something stupid or off-putting in Barrie's eyes. But I did not worry that much, as much as I could have, as much as I would have if most other senior colleagues had been the ones to join me and my friends on that day. I did not worry that much because I had come to trust that Barrie cared about me and my future, kindly and unselfishly, and without a tacit expectation of fealty or payback. I had come to trust that she cared about me even though there was little I could do to help her advance her career, even though I was not in sociology or gender studies, and even though I was not in a position to become her intellectual acolyte or proselytizer. I trusted that she cared because that is what she had demonstrated in her interactions with me

Figure 9.1. Barrie (*center left*) and Christo (*center right*) at a march for Occupy Wall Street, October 2011, New York City.

and in her writing, because that is how she had lived her theory and theorized lives.

Since becoming a professor, I have often thought about how I can repay the debts I owe to the advisors and mentors who helped me get through graduate school while also encouraging me to stay true to what I thought mattered. It is a debt that cannot be repaid, not even by volumes such as this one. And even if it were somehow possible to settle these accounts, I doubt that Barrie and the other mentors who cared for me in selfless ways would want a return on their investments. The only way I know to pay tribute to these generous and caring acts is by trying to bring a similar praxis to my own relations with graduate students and others over whom I hold some power. In that regard, perhaps I am an acolyte of Barrie's after all.

NOTE

1   As it turns out, the practice of middle schoolers exchanging Silly Bandz is a serious matter, at least if you care about how gift exchange establishes and sustains
social relations or how the wearing of such gifts displays social hierarchies, which
is why the young people cared so much about the practice.

REFERENCES

Ahmed, Sara. 2006. *Queer Phenomenology: Orientations, Objects, Others*. Durham,
NC: Duke University Press.

Lippard, Lucy R. 1973. *Six Years: The Dematerialization of the Art Object from 1966 to
1972*. New York: Praeger.

Thorne, Barrie. 1993. *Gender Play: Girls and Boys in School*. New Brunswick, NJ: Rutgers University Press.

10

Teaching Education, Talking Childhood, Troubling Gender

A Roundtable Discussion on Gender Play

INGRID E. CASTRO WITH KARISSA M. BARBOSA, BRIDGET M. BROYLES, WHITNEY EASTLAND, AND LESLIE TAYI

I came into possession of Barrie Thorne's *Gender Play* at the American Sociological Association's annual meeting graduate student book giveaway. I remember entering into that large exhibition hall, heaps of books strewn about the room. We ran amidst the bounty hoping to find something eye-catching or, perhaps better yet, relevant to our research. Our piles of paper-gold grew feet tall, we congressed as friends in jealous comparison, and those of us who traveled by plane found boxes and hauled our books to the airport. Obviously, that practice lays bare that I went to graduate school some time ago, as there never used to be such strict limitations placed on checked domestic luggage.

When I look at my copy of *Gender Play* today, it is still riddled with the paper sticky notes I used for my two comprehensive exams in gender and in race and my following dissertation: "A Consequence of Inequality: Women, Race, and Friendship on College Campuses" (Castro 2005a). I see underlined passages and notes in the margins, which (cringeworthy as this may be to some of you) I *always* make in pen. Pencil is so impermanent, and I believe that when an idea strikes as I am reading, it should be an everlasting addition to the text. The pen color changes with the project iteration each time I reread *Gender Play*. Looking through those notes, I see agreements ("Gendered by teacher!"), questions of time ("Still?"), further connections ("Does $ matter?"), criticisms ("Not likely—I take jaded approach!"), and more recent pop-culture connections ("No visual story for Hermione and Horcrux . . .").

My book notes reveal that Barrie Thorne's *Gender Play* remains an influential work for application to the academic and cultural imaginary of yesterday, today, and tomorrow. When contacted to contribute to *Gender Replay*, I was struck by an idea. Spring 2020 I was set to teach Sociology of Education, and coincidentally the class size was quite small. While that course usually has good enrollment (I teach at a college that caps at twenty-five students), it just so happened that it was running in the same time slot as my colleague's very popular course on the Sociology of Happiness. So, with four women on the slate and this project serendipitously falling in my lap, I realized that assigning *Gender Play* for a two-week roundtable discussion was a perfect pairing. I knew the four students well: each had taken multiple courses with me, all majored in sociology (with one a double major in psychology), and all had double or triple minors in combinations of women, gender, and sexuality studies; social work; anthropology; criminal justice; and child and family studies. I was confident we would engender lively discussion and debate out of Thorne's work, making thought-provoking connections to our lives and worlds.

Sometimes it is hard to actually focus in focus groups. During our talks, students meandered and I reeled them back in when we went too far astray. And yet, I did not mind these departures so much since the book is really about how we come to fashion ourselves within a vast interconnected structural and cultural framework that harbors various mechanisms of control. Thematically, we proved that Helga Zeiher's (2003) and Kim Rasmussen's (2004) institutional triangle of home, school, and playground is as important today as it was in the past. Social forces that drive the institutional triangle in children's lives—families, teachers, and peers—consistently arose in our memories, stimulated by Thorne's *Gender Play*, of being a child and being an adult.

A second central thematic component to our talk was the intersection of gender, race, class, and sexuality. The students served as discussion leaders, each for two chapters of the book, wherein they constructed prompts for us to consider based on textual quotations. Questions and conversation zeroed in on book/life elements grounded in our identities and various standpoints as women of color, first-generation college students, queer women, poor women, and/or first-generation Americans. When I was an undergraduate at the University of Delaware in the early 1990s, I had the great privilege of taking Feminist Theory with Sandra Harding. I experienced the single most terrifying and liberating assignment of my academic career in this course. She tasked all students to choose between two assignments: write a paper or present a public testimony. Perhaps not surprisingly, most students opted for the former; I opted for the latter. The classroom had a large raised stage, upon which I stood with several other brave students telling/performing the story of the women in our lives from a grounded feminist perspective to an audience of peers looming in the desks below. Shedding tear after tear, we paid tribute to our mothers, our siblings, our families, ourselves: epistemology at its most raw. In some ways, I think the *Gender Replay* roundtable mimicked that long-ago assignment for my students enrolled in Sociology of Education, providing a safe space for honest knowledge creation and the confluence of ideas and experiences.

Our caucus was important for another reason, within which we remain embroiled as I write this piece. Those March days were the last moments I spent quality time with these women, or any students really, as we never returned from spring break due to COVID-19. A year later I am still teaching remotely, and I feel sad for students who graduated without fanfare and I worry for so many others working through their educational journeys battling life stressors, tech fatigue, and that utmost missing link, oh-so-important at a liberal arts school: the close, personal relationships that are born out of small classes, one-on-one advising and mentorship, and individualized enrichment. I am thankful for our conversations and for this current work, as I am able to revisit our recorded sessions with fondness, hopeful that soon I will find myself in the classroom with a new batch of exceptional students once more. As I state in the acknowledgments section of my recent book, "I too dream of what seems like the impossible becoming more than probable—humanity will embrace once again, and that will be a wonderful day" (Castro 2021:x).

And so, we turn to March 2–March 12, 2020, when we shared a "Gender (re)Play." Our dialogue is situated in the key themes, problems, and solutions we identified in and around the text, with pointed discussion of how Thorne's observations and theories were, or were not, mirrored in our own girlhoods and the world today. In the spirit of Beverly Daniel Tatum's *Why Are All the Black Kids Sitting Together in the Cafeteria?* (1997), I present our excerpted questions and answers as an exchange of ideas, concerns, and evaluations (yes, the students were critical of some of Thorne's work). I only wish I had enough room to print our entire four-day roundtable.

Conversations

BRIDGET: Thorne (1993) says, "Children's interactions are not preparation for life; they are life itself" (7). Why does she say this? What insights can be gained from shifting the way children are viewed to a perspective that respects children at any stage of development as human beings with feelings and autonomy?

LESLIE: She touched on children not just being socialized on how to think, but also being people who control how they move and how they think in accordance to gender being shaped. I definitely feel like everybody has an individual nature and could choose how they want to react to things; for instance, my personal reactions with adults telling me how I should "behave as a lady" and then certain things we would fall into because we just want to be able to cope and move with everyday life, even if we don't necessarily agree. I definitely feel every human has their own ideologies, but it's the same argument of nature versus nurture and understanding that it's both you, yourself, but also the society that you grew up in and how they clash or conform together.

WHITNEY: This reminds me of last semester in Sociology of Childhood, how we talked a lot about the agency of children and how they can make their own decisions. Also thinking about the meaning of the quote itself, "They're not preparation for life." Many adults assume that children are adults in the making and not children in themselves. I thought of that and how they think, "Oh, friendships now will teach them how to socialize with people as they get older."

BRIDGET: I think that it's important, and I think this is what Thorne is pushing for, to understand that children are *people*, first and foremost. They're not objects or property, they're not in transit, they *are*, right there as they are, they're people. I think it's really important to really reconsider the way that we treat children, especially regarding gender and these strict expectations that we have for them. Children should be allowed to explore and experiment. I also think we can learn from children. I think it's important to recognize that they're not just learners, they're also teachers. I think that's another thing that Thorne was getting at.

INGRID: It's interesting you mentioned the word "allow" because I think to myself, children will find a way even when they are not allowed. I don't think it's really going to influence so much how they do or what they do, but it's more about how adults see how they do or what they do. This continual question of being and becoming, current childhood scholars are embracing both because you can't really deny that children are evolving, it's hard to deny that. They grow, they have experiences, and as they have experiences they have maybe new outlooks or their old outlooks are reified. Then also, we need to, very much as you say, Bridget, respect their being. Respect who they are in the moment and in the place, what they think, who they interact with, who they don't. That's actually one of the things about this book that I respect the most is how much attention Thorne pays to intergenerational relationships, not just between the children but also the children and the teachers.

LESLIE: I think it's interesting that you say adults have a lot to learn from children, because I feel like when you're speaking about gender, a lot of adults understand it as sex and only understand it in a sexual nature. I feel like a lot of times adults have to unlearn what they know and be humble enough to learn and understand that everything is not what you were taught or what you think. Now there are better studies that can help elaborate and explain what we know.

BRIDGET: Yes, I also think adults have a tendency to speak on things they don't understand. And this whole argument of "kids don't understand. They're not ready for this." We need to trust that kids know how they feel.

KARISSA: I think that when parents tell kids they're "too young to understand," it just makes kids feel they want to grow up faster. When I was younger, it was like, "You're too young to understand" or "You're too young to decide" or "There's no way a kid can go through this." I think everyone's just fighting against these normative ideas and that's why America's saying, like, "Kids are innocent or kids don't know nothing." Kids do actually know a lot of stuff, you're just not giving them the opportunity to do that because it's not "normal." It's not "normal" for a kid to know a lot or for a kid to know about their body, etcetera.

INGRID: It's actually a good point that telling children they're too young to make decisions on their own, or to understand, may in fact influence their desire to grow up quicker. It actually almost tries to force them to move out of place in their childhood. That's something I don't know if I've ever seen really talked about before: the idea that putting these kinds of limitations on children, in the end, may in fact force them to not appreciate their own childhoods when they are living within them in the moment as much as maybe, perhaps, they should.

BRIDGET: I think that adults are less willing to learn and expand their understanding of the world around us. My parents are pretty ignorant to the social world and what's right and what's not right. I think a lot of adults reach this point of, "All right, I'm an adult now. I don't have anything more to learn. It's now my turn to teach people." I think that's a loss because we should be learning and growing throughout our entire lives. Kids do that all the time but as we reach adulthood, it seems like people do that less and less.

* * *

INGRID: Thorne makes that comment about when children experience adults coming into their school space as surveillants that they're there to somehow write down the bad things that they're doing and get those particular children in trouble. Do you think all children get nervous when visiting adults come in, or only the children who tend to act up and be mean?

WHITNEY: Yes, I definitely think that's true, because when I was younger I never got in trouble, so I didn't care who came in or who didn't, but the kids who were disruptive in class were like, "Oh, well, I'll have to be quiet today." Also, I worked in an after-school program for a couple of years, and I remember every however-many-years you have to get relicensed. And I remember my supervisor came in and she told us, "When she comes, everyone has to be perfect" that day. It's more the adults who want to mold the children into this perfect status. We'd then say to the kids, "If you guys are this good today for this one lady, we'll give you ice cream." We had to bribe them, but as soon as she left, everything went back to completely normal. I think in some situations it's not so much about the kids (it is why they were bribed), but the adults had to maneuver around the situation because *they* were nervous.

KARISSA: I find it interesting you talk about a negative connotation with someone being in the room. I personally thought about the most shy kid who would always try to go hang out with the principal or even just a new person they've never seen, like, "Hey, my name is" kind of thing that Thorne was saying in the book, like, "Write my name, that I'm the perfect person in the classroom." I saw them more of trying to create relationships that either they didn't have in the school or in the classroom.

INGRID: I'm reminded quite a bit of when I was in the fourth grade I had a teacher, Ms. Rose, who was obviously young. This is the very early '80s and she was probably just out of college. So many of us really loved Ms. Rose, and she always tried to include us. She would ask us to stay after school and help her clap off the erasers and clean out the desks, and all these people would volunteer because they wanted to be around her since we all thought she was so nice. I remember the following year, in the fifth grade, I went trick-or-treating around my neighborhood with one of my friends who also had Ms. Rose. We're at this one house, a couple of streets down, we ring the doorbell because the light is on, and the door opens up and there is this huge adult Halloween party. Giant! Adults are so much bigger physically than small children in the fourth or fifth grade, and who is there but Ms. Rose. She pulls us into the party and—obviously, I think she's drunk—she tells us we need to hang out a little bit, and we went downstairs, and she made us bob for apples with her friends. All of these adults saying, "Look at them, they're so cute" when these little kids walked into this adult party. I remember that event and I think: there's something in film, it's called "breaking the fourth wall." It's when the actor in the movie turns to the camera and speaks directly to the audience, interrupting the illusion. . . . I think, in a way, this event is breaking the fourth wall between childhood and adulthood, and also between school and neighborhood.

LESLIE: When I think about your question, I think about that feeling of being surveilled and how to act. People look down on you if you're younger than them, unless you have a higher status, then they'll have respect for you. It's with the assumption that the older you are the more you know and the less that you need to learn, and the younger you are the less you know and the more you need to learn. It's all based on your positioning when you're an adult and what position you hold, but that doesn't reflect how much knowledge you have.

* * *

KARISSA: Thorne (1993) says, "This is partly because information about kids and their doings seems much less consequential than information about adults, especially adults acting in a risky public arena" (18). How many students actually know the consequences that teachers face by speaking up? In my instance, whenever something went wrong, my teacher was the first person that I went to, or any adult figure, to get something resolved until I realized that it's like, "No, adults aren't the people you go to. You have to solve it on your own."

I'm not only talking about principals or teachers, I'm talking about my parents, my mom. As an immigrant, she didn't want to speak up about things that happened at school or want to take authority. Where's the agency for these children? When did you find that you have to be advocates for yourself, whether it was in elementary or middle school, when it was college, or looking back?

LESLIE: I had a similar experience with cultural barriers. My family lived in the Bronx and then we moved to where we are now. I changed school districts and that school is predominantly a white school. In order to keep up with all my siblings and live in that district and that house, my parents worked most of the time. They worked *a lot*. When I would run into issues, which I of course did, like racism between students and teachers, I had to handle it on my own, talking to teachers. I never really went to my parents with any of it because at that age I was constantly hearing about bills and money. I thought, "I shouldn't have to be thinking about bills and money at this age because it makes me so concerned for my parents." Things like that, I would never tell them about and I would always have to deal with it or handle it myself. Parent meetings: they were never involved in stuff like that. At that age, that's when I found out that I had to handle things on my own to the point that when I was in second grade, I brought a knife to school . . . You have to think about the neighborhood that I came from before I went to that school and then being in that school. I was like, "Well, if you want people to stop messing with you, you have to make a statement, obviously." What occurs to me is I was a racial and ethnic minority, and somebody could have easily understood that as me being a threat and expelled me from the school. I guess, luckily for me, that teacher did not view me as a threat because I was a really good student. I never had any discrepancies before that point so it wasn't possible I would do something like that, but knowing that where I came from . . .

KARISSA: I feel like that's for any child who is in the United States, who just have this idea about what children are. In Cape Verde, if you're five years old and your aunt gives you two dollars to go buy a cigarette, feel free to go do whatever you want with that. You can go buy that, you can buy alcohol. It's only here where we see children as innocent.

WHITNEY: Last semester when we read *Why Are All the Black Kids Sitting Together?*, Tatum (1997) gave an example of a Black boy who said when he was little, he was considered all cute but then as soon as he got a little bit older, there was the idea that people had to walk on the other side of the street as him because he was so much more threatening now that he's just a couple years older. That's what Leslie's story just made me think of.

Also, comparing my experience to Leslie's, I have never been a confrontational person. Any problems that I had, if I went to my mom, I knew it was going to get so blown out of proportion, especially because I am multiethnic—I have a white mom and a Black dad. My mom has always been very protective over any racial comments or anything. Me not wanting a lot of attention on myself, if I told my mom, I knew she was going to bring it to everyone. I was like, "I'm not going to tell her." I used to, when I was a kid, keep everything in. I just wouldn't tell people.

* * *

KARISSA: Thorne (1993) notes, "Rita's hair was quite dirty, greasy at the roots, and it smelled. There was dirt on her cheek and her hands were smudged. She wore the same clothes she had on yesterday: a too small, short blue nylon sweater with white buttons and dirt on the back, and a green cotton pant that didn't zip right" (25). I wanted to think about: When did your perspective on poverty change? Was it based on seeing your own privileges and oppressions? Are they still being developed now?

LESLIE: I feel like every day is an opportunity to learn and to grow. You have to humble yourself. Even though you think you may know what poverty looks like, poverty comes in so many different shapes, forms, and sizes. There's just certain things that we do every single day and how we navigate, and somebody else might not be able to navigate the same way. It's little things that you don't notice that you end up noticing when you have it or when you lose it. There are so many ways to be impoverished. I feel like there's a big difference. I do my best not to judge people because you never know what their upbringing was like, but then also you can't help but judge their morals, in a sense, because people judge you based on how you look, which includes your clothing and oftentimes how you smell. When I would think of poverty when I was younger, I'd think of it as more scary and inconveniencing. I mean, like an inconvenience, just something that I didn't want to necessarily relate to. Now, I look at it as a construct, a part of a construct that has been set up against people. Knowing more about sociology has really impacted my views of poverty and the things that are set into place for people to not succeed.

INGRID: To relate to teachers or other administrators at schools to children, this is something that I think a lot of them struggle with every year. You may have a student who is in the classroom and as a teacher, or some other school administrator, you know of a student who seems to check all the other boxes: be sweet, does homework, never gets in trouble. Yet, that may be the one child who doesn't shower, doesn't have any other change of clothes except for the clothes that they wear, doesn't wear socks, and wears shoes that are four sizes too big. The question is, then, what do you do in those situations? Younger teachers and younger administrators and faculty may in fact think, "I can intervene here. I can do something." As an example, one of my mom's best friends is a retired speech pathologist from school. He told a story about this exact type of kid. He said, "I decided I was going to go out. I was going to buy him a new pair of shoes. I was going to buy him two outfits. I was going to take him out to eat after class and then give him all this stuff." He said, "The next day the kid showed up, he was in the same shoes, in the same clothes." None of the stuff that he had bought this child was there. He asked the child, "What happened to it?" He said, "My parents took it and they sold it." That's something that you have to consider, which is that a struggling child also usually comes from a struggling family. In that case, poverty runs very deep in families. It's not just one member or two members, it's not just even one generation, it's multiple generations. He said that was a tough lesson for him to learn but one that he had to learn, which is that you can try to make a lot of difference but, at the same time, you have to understand that there are outside forces here besides the individual.

LESLIE: When you think of it from a community standpoint, a lot of times where somebody tries to come up in the world, especially people of color, people within that group also feel like they're abandoning their own people. Or if you come up, everybody has to come up in a lot of different groups and cultures. It's like, "You can't come up by yourself." Then thinking about the child whose parents took the clothes given to the child: *It's not yours. It's the child's.* Or getting money from grandparents or getting money from wherever you earned it as a child and your parents taking it or keeping it and feeling justified because they raised you as a parent and taking that identity away from them, and then showing how that transpires into different communities and feeling entitled to what other people have because you're within that same group and everybody raised each other.

KARISSA: It would be different if kids were asked, "What do you need? What do you and your family need?" There are things that are necessities more than just wants.

WHITNEY: My little cousin is in elementary school, and I know on Fridays and over breaks the kids come home with gift cards to grocery stores and backpacks full of perishable foods, which didn't happen when I was younger. I was just thinking about that, asking kids what they need for their families.

* * *

WHITNEY: Thorne (1993) says, "Miss Bailey didn't deliberately establish separate lines for boys and girls; she just told the students to line up. It took both attention and effort for the kids to continually create and recreate gender-separated queues" (40). How is this an example of children creating their own meanings of gender and how is it significant? In my opinion, I thought that it was them showing that they had agency and that they did recognize that there were two different gender dichotomies. I thought it was significant because a lot of the teachers, she explained, thought it was funny and didn't think of it as like, "Oh, it actually takes a lot of energy and strategy by the kids." They just downplayed it. I thought it was important that Barrie Thorne recognized how the kids were able to create their own gender meanings.

INGRID: When I was in school, it was always, "Boys on the right, girls on the left." Always, always, always. But then, our teachers were always female in grade school. We never had a male teacher. I don't even know if I had a male teacher the entire time from preschool all the way through eighth grade—I don't think so. I think the first time I ever had a male teacher was in high school. I remember that I was always being used to comfort boys, even when I was in kindergarten. There was a boy who had some behavioral issues. He was very loud, very demanding, always throwing stuff and screaming. In kindergarten, you sit at these four-to-six-person tables; at some point, my kindergarten teacher decided to put me next to this kid. My mom still remembers, she says that I came home one day and—I used my agency—I said, "Mommy, the teacher put me next to this boy." This had already been going on for a while. I was like, "I can't do anything. He keeps stealing my markers and stealing my crayons. I just want to draw. I just want to practice my letters and he keeps screaming in my ear about chocolate milk." My mom had a parent-teacher conference with the teacher, *in kindergarten*. She goes in, talks to the teacher, and the teacher says, "I put Ingrid next to him because she's the only one that when he sits next to her, he calms down a little bit." So, she *used* me for her own gain and sacrificed *my* presence in the classroom for *her* slight peace of mind, putting me next to this kid. And that wasn't the only time. In first grade, the same thing happened. In the first grade, we were out on the playground. This kid, Johnny, got hit in the mouth. Going back to what Barrie Thorne's talking about:

how kids are very physical with one another and the boys, in particular, are always pushing, and pulling, and fighting, and shoving. Somehow, he got hit in the mouth and had a bloody nose. The teacher called *me* over, of all the kids out there on the playground, over forty kids, calls me over and says, "Ingrid, go clean Johnny up." So, I had to take him into school. It was very stressful for me because at this point I'm six years old, and I was saying over and over in my head, "girls' room, boys' room," "girls' room, boys' room." Instead of me making a decision, I asked Johnny, "You want to be in the girls' room or the boys' room?" He said, "Boys' room, I guess." Then that was an added problem because I'd never *been* in a boys' room before. It gave me more stress. I had to bring him in, clean him up, and then bring him back out. This was prior to HIV and AIDS. You see how there is this gendered notion here about what it means to be a responsible girl, and how adults take advantage of that responsible girl in school even at a very young age.

BRIDGET: When I was in fourth grade the school asked me to train to become a peer mediator. I don't remember who all they asked and what the gender dynamic was, but looking back on that, I'm like, "Why did they want *me* to do this? Why was *I* responsible for mediating issues between my classmates?" It wasn't necessarily "You have to do this" but it was like a, "We want you to do this" kind of thing. Looking back on the way things were at my school, I remember there being other girls, but not other boys, involved in this.

KARISSA: I had a similar situation, but mine was my junior and senior year of high school. I actually became the only peer mentor in our school. I was responsible for dealing with other girls that were like me. I guess they'd seen my life story from freshman year. I had really bad grades, Fs and Ds, and I didn't care. Junior and senior year, when I got straight As, they were like, "Oh, this student can change or changed. So, how about we put kids that were just like her with her?" I got all these kids that literally went through similar things that I went through in life or they just didn't care about school. It was as if they were just trying to collide all these people together, combine them and be like, "Okay, you guys have all similar issues, so Karissa can help you solve all your issues." I was like, "I can't, because I have my own issues to solve."

INGRID: Did you tell anybody that?

KARISSA: No, because I felt it was a good opportunity. It's something that, clearly, I want to still do in life now. They'd seen it and were like, "Oh, well, she likes doing things like this, so we're just going to give it to her." Maybe I did have the agency but didn't use the agency to be like, "Well, I don't want to do this" or "This is too much."

WHITNEY: In fourth grade, I was also a peer mediator. It was a lot of other girls too, but also my brother was only in kindergarten and he really freaked out without my mom. Then, when we ended up being in the same school, he would not calm down. His teacher and my teacher agreed that I could stay down there for a half an hour with him. I always missed the beginning of the school day just trying to calm my brother down. I think that was similar to how Dr. Castro had to calm down another kid.

LESLIE: I tried to be a peer mediator, but they just always looked around me. I guess it was because, in a way, I never could relate to anyone—how do I say it? In my school demographic? But, any time in school if there was a new student who was African or Black or anything who had moved, I was an unofficial mediator. It was like, "Oh, Leslie, so and so is here, we want you to take her under your wing." It's like, "Okay, sure. *I guess.*" Even though I wasn't an official mediator, I was.

INGRID: Well, that's interesting. What you're saying is you were good enough for other people who had darker skin tones but not good enough for people with lighter skin tones?

LESLIE: Right. Right. Exactly. Like, I couldn't relate to the general public, but only one specific kind of person or people.

INGRID: Then did you agree every time they called on you?

LESLIE: I did, just because of the fact that it's a lonely world out here for us little Black girls. I'd take them under my wing, like, "Sure, yeah. This is this person. This is that teacher. This teacher is cool" just to be friendly, just to be friends with that person. But then, as I got older, I realized that it's not my responsibility to be the welcoming committee for every Black person that came to the school and if we naturally became friends, then we naturally became friends.

KARISSA: I see a lot of schools do that now: trying to combine all their students of color together, just so they can be like, "Well, these students of color have other students of color, so diversity isn't our problem. There has to be something else." But having two Black kids in your school doesn't make the school diverse. That's what people don't understand. It's sad.

INGRID: On the other hand, I remember I was the only girl who wasn't 100 percent white in my two grades. Each grade had two classrooms, and I was the only one. I remember at the end of third grade, a transfer student came in and she was Asian. I was so happy. She was in the other class, so I didn't really get to see her all that much, but whenever I saw her I would try and engage her. We ended up becoming best friends. She was also very, very studious, very, very responsible. We ended up being best friends for the rest of our time in that school through eighth grade. I oftentimes think, "What would have happened if she hadn't come? How would I have been different and probably a lot more lonely?"

* * *

KARISSA: Thorne (1993) says, "'The chase,' 'chasers,' 'chase-and-kiss,' 'kiss-chase,' and 'kissers-and-chasers'" (69) are just games that kids play during recess. Then she highlights, "I never saw a girl use a kiss to threaten another girl, although young girls sometimes kissed one another with affection" (71). I thought these two statements were really interesting because we constantly see kids without sexual desire. My main question is, Why do we see these kids without sexual desire? My second question: Why would it be okay for the girls to do things with affection and kiss when it wasn't okay for the boys, even starting at a really young age?

WHITNEY: We think that kids are fully innocent and pure, but in reality, they know the meanings behind things and they have more agency than we give them credit for. I think girls are always socialized and seen as more nurturing and more affectionate, where boys, they can't have that kind of affection or else they're seen as if they were gay or something like that.

LESLIE: I also feel like it's a cultural thing, depending on where you go. My dad told about when he and his cousin used to go to school together, they would hold hands walking to class. My dad is from Africa and it wasn't uncommon to see boys holding each other's hands and playing with each other. And the way that African people dance is different, and it's not unseen or unheard of to see African men dancing in what some people would classify as feminine. I think that it's cultural and it's also taught, the way that we see them and perceive them and what we expect of them.

BRIDGET: Even starting in second grade, there are very obvious signs that people have been influencing their gender presentation and how they "do gender," basically. They are already falling in line with these gender roles and how women are more nurturing and affectionate and men are supposed to be more rough and crazy.

INGRID: My best friend and I, we were in charge of bringing the mail down to the rectory because we went to Catholic school, so down to the rectory from the main building. We got out of school early, right before lunch. We always got to take this nice walk outside while everybody else was still in class. I think the boys, in particular, were really jealous of that. One day, I remember hearing one of the kids in my school up at the top floor in the boys' bathroom scream our names. We looked up, and two of them were mooning us out of the window. That was in the seventh grade, and one of them was the boy who got the bloody nose in first grade. You can see all these ways in which responsible girls ended up getting terrorized and made fun of in a sexual way for those things.

KARISSA: I thought more about my location. My boy cousins were allowed to leave the front porch, but I had to sit there and watch everyone else play. And if the girls wanted to play, they had to come onto our porch and play with our dolls and paint our nails. I always questioned, "Why do the boys get to do all of that stuff and go out?" Then I just constantly got this message, "Well, girls can get pregnant and boys can't." That was the main reason why I had to stay in, because of my parents' fear of getting pregnant and that lasted until I was eighteen or nineteen years old. That's because that's the cutoff when my mom had me, and once I hit that cutoff, that I didn't have any kids, she was like, "Okay, you passed this one regulation I had." A lot of the girls I was around had got their period already and I hadn't. My mom thought that they were fast and thought, "Well, this is what they're doing, they're probably out there already doing that and we can't get you pregnant, you guys see how hard it is and where we live and we're a lower-class working family." I grew up in the projects, teen pregnancy was all around. My mom even signed a paper saying that she didn't want them to give me condoms at school, so she knew that was our environment, that was the main thing, every single day. My mom didn't care if I wore sweatpants or if I was a tomboy or if I even liked girls, she just was like, "You don't get pregnant," that's it.

WHITNEY: When I was younger, it wasn't like my parents told me I had to do certain things or not do certain things. They encouraged me to play baseball instead of softball, but it was more like my dad was trying to control what my brother did, instead of me. I was allowed to, as Thorne calls it, "cross the boundaries," but for my brother, my dad would tell him that he couldn't play dolls with me or play dress-up. I remember one time me and my cousin dressed my brother up and we straightened his hair and put him in a dress and we even dressed the dog up and put him in a stroller and my dad was like, "No, you don't do that." It was more for my brother than me.

LESLIE: Talking about sports made me remember when I was younger and I told my dad that I wanted to do boxing and he said, "No, because that's very masculine and you're going to get hurt." I realized a lot of times fathers are worried about protecting girls' physicality and virginity and making sure they're safe. Even talking about joining the military, he encouraged my older brother to join the military and did everything so that he could join the military and be in the air force, but then when it came to me, he's like, "No, I don't want you to be in the military because there's a lot of women who are sexually abused in the military and I don't want that to happen to you." It's protectiveness over every single part of my being, in my parents' minds.

KARISSA: I actually really hated when Thorne (1993) said "wearing their breasts like badges" (72). I feel like that gave children another sexual-desired image of, "Your body shape or your boobs can get you anywhere. As long as you have a great figure, you'll make it." I thought, "I don't like this" because I was one of the kids with the boobs when they were younger. It was a bad thing. It wasn't a good thing. I used to wear big clothes or big shirts so that people didn't see them, or sports bras to push them down.

BRIDGET: I think it's also important to recognize there's this discussion of, Do boys and girls have different cultures? Do men and women? Are they inherently different? It's no, because first and foremost, men and women are not all there is. There are trans and nonbinary identities that don't fit into neat little boxes that have been created for us. Even cis men and cis women don't all fit into all these boxes. We as human beings are capable of so much, so much variation, so much difference. That can be a really beautiful thing, but we are ruining it by saying, "Yes. There are only cis men and cis women. If you feel differently then you're wrong. I don't care about your lived experience because that's not my lived experience. This is what you have to do to fit in."

* * *

INGRID: Thorne (1993) says, "In the long run, I would prefer schooling, and a society, in which gender is of minimal importance. But in the world as it exists, everyone does not start out with the same value and resources. To challenge male dominance in its overt and subtle forms, we have to change the organization and content of masculinities and femininities, recognizing their complexity and plurality, and altering forms based on opposition and domination. Paradoxically, to create an equal world, we may sometimes need to emphasize gender, for example, by promoting strategic solidarity among girls or legitimizing alternative forms of masculinity among boys" (171). My question is, Are we there yet? All of these observations remain in the late '70s and early '80s, so even your childhoods were fast-forwarded from the childhoods of these children. Have we done what Thorne was actually looking for us to do? Or, if we haven't, what could we still work on?

LESLIE: I think that we've made people more conscious of it, but there's still major pushback. In our everyday lives, I definitely see people being more conscious of it, even amongst my old-school parents. Knowing that it exists now, that there is a social construct that exists, seeing the pushback in society . . . I feel it's not implemented as much because of the fact that not everybody necessarily understands, so that means that they don't agree because most of the time when people are fighting against something, they haven't really given it a chance to understand (most of the time, not all the time). We're headed there, but I don't feel everybody understands and that's why we haven't gotten to where we need to be.

KARISSA: I feel we haven't got to where we need to be because of world ignorance, people knowing that they're doing things wrong, but yet they're like, "Whatever, it doesn't affect me. Therefore, I shouldn't care for it." Until we get out of that mindset, it's going to be like that. Also, thinking of children as they are today, and not children of the future, like, "They are the future adults." That's *not* what they are here for, let them take action because I think kids have the most agency and they are their best advocates. Therefore, we should let them live in that, and grow up with that, because there's a lot of people that are just learning to do that now.

INGRID: I think what you're alluding to is that Thorne is writing from a privileged white Westernized perspective. The concerns that Thorne has here, in terms of gender relations, are specific for, really, a population that is living amongst a developed nation that has a vast amount of resources, high levels of education, high levels of security, high levels of support. There are going to be other concerns in other places.

BRIDGET: I think that we have made some progress, but I also think that we still have a long way to go. I think there's this idea: "Oh, that's not my personal experience. I went through all of these things, and I turned out fine. I don't have to change anything about the way I raise *my* children, I can impose these really strict gender roles on my kids from an early age and they'll turn out fine too because I turned out fine." People tend to think that their personal experience negates broader societal patterns and consequences of those patterns. I think with that attitude it's going to be really, really hard to have this huge change that Thorne wants to see, and that *I* would love to see. I would love to see gender become less important than it is, but it *is* important right now.

WHITNEY: I also agree that we have made a little progress, but not a lot. After working at an after-school program for multiple years, I've seen the kids all interact in same-gender groups, they don't really drift out towards others, out of that, either. Parents think that everything should be the same way that it has been in the past; just thinking about when people get pregnant now, they still want to do gender reveals, get the pink, or the blue, they want to stick to those strict categories.

* * *

INGRID: Do you see feminism in Thorne's book, and if so, how?

LESLIE: In [the chapter] "Beyond Dualisms," I definitely feel like she's addressing the ways in which even through sociological studies, people framed girls a certain way and used certain words like "immature" (Thorne 1993:107), and how it's obviously viewed through the eyes of male scholars. When you look at how words are *framed* and how we view girls' play, it really makes a huge contribution to how we continue to see girls as "petty" and "immature." So, once we can identify how, through words, how we have ideas, and if we just simply change the words and be more objective, we can obviously have more objective studies on how children play and where their socialized actions come from.

KARISSA: In [the chapter] "Learning from Kids," she's showing it in a feminist way, in my perspective, because, for instance, kids aren't seen as going through anything, or they don't face any inconveniences, or they don't know what it means to be oppressed (that's what people believe), but they definitely do. They definitely see the difference of how they're treated from as a child to an adult. Just the fact that Thorne talks about how we should learn from children and that, at a young age, they can teach us more than we know about ourselves right now shows that feminism can start at a young age. It doesn't have to be about what we're going through or what we're facing. In general, being able to advocate for yourself and know about what's going on in society makes you feminist.

WHITNEY: I think that her attention to the separate categories of the boys and the girls in equal importance—she gave the girls just as much thought and she looked at them just as much as the boys—is feminist. Thorne talked about in previous studies sometimes they only studied the boys because they're more visible and they are easier to study. At the same time, she said, in her view, it was easier to study the boys because she was looking at them from a blind-eye view, because she didn't live those experiences. I think, for the most part, she paid just as much attention to the girls, but at the same time her acknowledging that she *did* live those experiences also helped her case.

INGRID: That's very feminist, to acknowledge your standpoint.

BRIDGET: I would say yes and no. I definitely think that the book is quite feminist for the time that it was written. But, if we're considering it from right now, the present moment, I wouldn't say it's very feminist. It does make a point to recognize that young girls are marginalized and young girls often have the worst of it. In [the chapter] "Lip Gloss and Goin' With," there's that saying that girls "got the sexiness" and that's why they always win, but Thorne (1993) made the point that, no, girls definitely don't always "win the game" (135). I appreciate that she does point out the way that girls can struggle through their childhood and into adulthood. But, I think that feminism is meant to be intersectional and in my women's studies course that I took last year, we had a lot of conversations about how you can't really end the oppression of women unless you take an intersectional approach and address that there are a lot of identities that can intersect. To write an entire book about gender at school and not really address *at all* what trans and nonbinary children go through I think misses the mark in terms of modern feminism. For that time, *totally* feminist, absolutely, but if we're looking at it from this time, not so much.

INGRID: I think one of the big points that we have to make sure we realize is that our learning and knowledge continues. This book, in and of itself, has been cited by following research almost five thousand times since it was published. It's used as a building block. So, when I get upset, when I read something and I react, "No, that's wrong!" I have to remember that, in terms of Thorne being an important change agent in sociology and in childhood studies and in feminist studies, it's the springboard from where we get to when we're here today.

Considerations

Several aspects of our roundtable on *Gender Play* merit further address. Most importantly, the conversations revealed that the sheer amount of WORK we did as girls for the institutional triangle was staggering. And that work was carework: physical work, emotional work, people work.[1] As I ruminate on the phrasing "gender arrangements" found in Thorne and Luria's (1986) article on childhood, gender, and sexuality, I realize that we, as girl children, were funneled into provisions and bargains caused by, or at least orchestrated by, parents, teachers, students, and, sometimes, ourselves. As Stacey and Thorne (1985) make clear, gender, with its social sorting, is a highly visible and highly constructed process. We were ensconced within the faulty gendered constructs that continue to govern institutions and, as children, our work within those structures obeyed and defied in (perhaps) equal measure. Here, then, we get expanded insight into borderwork: an intragenerational passing of borderwork rules—between adults with authority and girls without— dictated that we made concessions. We missed class, eschewed sex, ran errands, counseled peers, remained home, or forgot dreams. Similar to the point Nielsen (this volume) makes, there is an undeniable gendered division in work and care; but, might we also agree that girls use agency to navigate this mountainous, albeit contested, terrain?

Children's agency matters: *whether* they have it, *what* they do with it, *why* they enact it, *how* they express it. Girls' agency came up quite a bit in our talks on *Gender Play*: the students expressed views on agency that were sophisticated and highly relevant, and so I must (prefacing with a gendered apology) pat myself on the back.[2] Since my first publication (Castro 2005b) I have, with continual fascination, created alternate considerations of and new theories on children's agency, passing that knowledge on to those in the classroom. Given that Leslie, Whitney, Karissa, and Bridget had previously taken courses with me, including Sociology of Childhood, Families, Latinas in U.S. Society, and/or The Posthuman Child, I was really pleased that their expressed memories and observations integrated themes of agency in childhoods past and present. Thorne emphasized to her students that there is "a politics of time" for children (Pugh, this volume), and Gordon's (this volume) additional point that agency is intersectional brings us to an imperative nexus, the *who* and *when* of childhood agency: it is intersectional *and* intertemporal. I also must add that agency is, crucially, interspatial. Karissa's point, "Maybe I did have the agency but didn't use the agency" while at school acutely reminds us that the localized context of agency matters. *Where* children are in their lives and worlds militates decisions regarding silent/vocal or still/mobile agency: the rewards and risks affiliated with agency's potential outcomes are many.

Points made by others in this volume (and sometimes, by proxy, Barrie Thorne herself) that rule breaking can be a creative endeavor (Messner, this volume) and imagination's possibility is "seeing that there are multiple framings and ways of doing things" (Rueda, this volume) provide a good segue into the coda of this chapter. I am struck by Connell's (this volume) remark that the lyrical quality of Thorne's writing in *Gender Play* makes it read almost like a novel. Similarly, Orellana (this volume) beautifully expresses her memories of working with Thorne: taking a creative approach, even as social scientists, "Writing was an art form, as we sculpted words and ideas into shape on the page." I believe the same, and so I call on two feminist works that greatly influenced me as an undergraduate: Gloria Anzaldúa's *Borderlands/La Frontera* (1987) and Sarah Kirsch's *The Panther Woman* (1989). In *Borderlands*, Anzaldúa intersperses personal stories and historical research with poetry, calling on her "inner life of the Self" and code switching between Spanish and English to weave "a mosaic pattern" that speaks to the childhood alienation she experienced while growing up on the border of Mexico and Texas (66). *Panther* embraces an intertextual and intravocal approach to women's recorded personal accounts, lived histories, and political struggles. Kirsch does so by first presenting women's stories exactly as they were told to her during interviews; then, calling on her strengths as a poet (and perhaps shocking to those of you who do qualitative research), Kirsch excerpts phrases and sentences from those transcriptions, putting them back together to form new narratives in a sole paragraph. The book's translator explains, "These concluding distillations of each woman's words often point to *lyric*, for the descriptions and observations of the women take on a lyric quality or an aphorist weight when thus condensed and emphasized. This can be a brilliant device; it is enormously moving" (Kirsch 1989:xii).

Inspired by Anzaldúa's and Kirsch's feminist creative processes, I extract direct quotations from our focus group conversations that are (re)formed and (re)ordered into a secondary (re)imagined "Gender (re)Play"—a "story of stories" that seamlessly melds all five of our voices into the visual poem "Why She Is." I combine our words line by line or by multiplicity within line: you may recognize some phrases from our talk printed in this chapter, while many more are mined from the other eighty pages of transcription. I chose to look for phrasing that started with "it" due to "its" quality of nothing and everything, poignantly and relevantly defined as "a condition or action without reference to an agent."[3] And apparently, the online Merriam-Webster Dictionary provides a kids' definition of "it," quite apropos for our roundtable talks on *Gender Play*: "the thing, act, or matter about which these words are spoken or written." The unattributable aspects of "it" harken back to Betty Friedan's (1963) classic chapter addressing the unrecognized work of women, "The Problem That Has No Name." "It" also calls to mind Stephen King's (1986) eponymous tale of childhood's unspoken nightmares and brutal truths. While "it" is so mercurial, "it" can also be hopeful, indicating "a crucial or climactic point." For on our college's last prepandemic days of March 2020, a group of diverse women sat together finding similarity across girlhood, joining in the project of making meaning in it.

Why She Is

It does just like it is–
    it is the assumption, maybe it is that?
It is built in, but it is socialized as well;
    not knowing which one it is, I'm not sure what it is.
It's all of these things.
It's important, it's really important
                        (it's hard to deny that)
It is rare to see how hard it is.

"It's only a child!" (It's not normal. It's not normal.)
    It's much easier for you to understand.
    It's only here where we see children as innocent.
It's all based on your positioning,
    it's just a different way of thinking about it.
It's cultural and it's also taught
                       (it's really kind of the same)
It's little things you don't notice.

It's multiple generations: it's boy, girl, boy, girl.
    It's more a hidden thing–
        it's behind closed doors, or in secret.

It's not unseen or unheard, it's also in any public place.
It's like you're being shamed for it.
It's like they don't want their child

(it's okay)

It's important to recognize it's a problem.

It's not implemented, it's across the board.
It's not a problem for the guy, but
it's still a problem for the girl, no matter what.
It's the same argument of nature versus nurture and understanding
it's that they matter because we make them matter.
It's on each end of the spectrum

(it's both you, yourself)

It's at the very bottom.

It's used as a building block. It's your entryway, it's the springboard.
It's kids looking out for other kids.
It's the influence of peers:
it's not always malicious—it's just talking, it's just gossiping.
It's not mean, it's a joke. I don't know if it's a negative thing or it's a
positive thing.
It's negative?

(it's not a question)

It's not supposed to be friendships!

It's overt and subtle forms, it's also what you're saying:
it's, "What did you do to create that situation?"
It's hard.
It's really hard.
It's going to be really, really hard.
It's like we have to put up this front

(it's going to be like that)

It's a lonely world out here.

It's like, "What does this do to girls' motivations?"
It's contextual: it's a rendition, it's caricatures, it's in the music.
It's pretty easy to catch–

it's always like women are lying.
It's not that serious . . .
 It's one thing that rings strongly in my mind
 (it's this fear)
It wasn't actually what you're saying it is.

It's the parents are saying "No."
It's just one-sided a lot of times:
 it's like, "You can't come up by yourself."
It's like people will kind of look at you–
 it's like one brings them together.
It's never assumed that I'm part of my family
 (it's problematic)
It's that I was looking for attention.

It's just we tend to accept it's not really true.
 Yes.
 It's completely untrue.
It's what you're willing to teach your children,
 it's what you're allowing your children to do,
 rather than forcing your children to do
 (it's more)
It's like they'll be more likely to listen.

It's dangerous, it's exciting
 it's when people live
 it's a guilty pleasure of mine.
It's just ugly and I hate it's unladylike to swear.
It's something that, clearly, I want to still do in life now.
It's just childish! It's something you do when you're younger
 (it's insane to me)
It's not that they don't matter.

It's not so obvious.
It's much more obvious.
It's not something that it's just inherent.
It's foolish, it's different, it's weird.

It's like something that we don't really recognize until we're older:
    it's not my responsibility
                          (it's sad)
It's been discovered it's not okay anymore.

It's the work of finding one's true identity.
It's like a competition, it's a lot to do with competition, it's sink or
    swim.
It's just a matter of–
    Fighting.
    Exactly.
It's also who gets dissuaded
                        (it's harder to trust)
It's how I'm feeling.

It's a girl thing:
    it's very feminist.
It's because of that ability to have that shared emotional bond.
It's like you can break down that wall and still have a conversation.
It's important to know the context and know your audience.
It's about being comfortable with one another
                        (it's easier)
It's the same consequences but they're presented differently.

It's your job to have a certain voice, but for another person, it's not.
    It's torture.
    Yes.
It's obviously viewed through the eyes. It's very contained. It's
    definitely unique.
It's a totally different situation: it's about the figuration of the girl.
It's the other way around ↔ This is the way it's supposed to be, not
    that way!
    It's a super long story, it's all about this
                        (it's even remotely true)
It's like I can't relate.

It's like I wasn't playing my role.

NOTES

1 See also Orellana, this volume, on the importance of recognizing what children do as work, not all play.

2 See Messner, this volume, for an insider's view on how Barrie Thorne deplored such apologetic speech from female students, as I do too. Unfortunately, as a woman my recognition of the problem does not stop me from feeling a bit guilty!

3 This definition and all following come from Merriam-Webster Dictionary: https://www.merriam-webster.com. On a personal note, as an undergraduate I was taught by my favorite psychology professor, Brian Ackerman, to never start sentences with "it" outside of direct quotations or creative ventures, a rule that I pass on to my students and contributors to my volumes. If you look through my published work, I doubt you will find a sentence that starts with "It" excepting the Acknowledgements section of my books. Thus, constructing this poem was extremely cathartic.

REFERENCES

Anzaldúa, Gloria. 1987. *Borderlands/La Frontera: The New Mestiza*. San Francisco: Anne Lute Books.

Castro, Ingrid E. 2005a. "A Consequence of Inequality: Women, Race, and Friendship on College Campuses." PhD dissertation, Department of Sociology, Northeastern University, Boston, MA.

———. 2005b. "Children's Agency & Cinema's New Fairy Tale." Pp. 215–37 in *Sociological Studies of Children and Youth*, vol. 11, edited by D. A. Kinney and K. B. Rosier. New York: JAI Press/Elsevier.

———, ed. 2021. *Childhood, Agency, and Fantasy: Walking in Other Worlds*. Lanham, MD: Lexington Books.

Friedan, Betty. 1963. *The Feminine Mystique*. New York: Norton.

King, Stephen. 1986. *It*. New York: Scribner's.

Kirsch, Sarah. 1989. *The Panther Woman: Five Tales from the Cassette Recorder* (trans. M. Faber). Lincoln: University of Nebraska Press.

Rasmussen, Kim. 2004. "Places for Children—Children's Places." *Childhood* 11(2):155–73.

Stacey, Judith, and Barrie Thorne. 1985. "The Missing Feminist Revolution in Sociology." *Social Problems* 32(4):301–16.

Tatum, Beverly. 1997. *Why Are All the Black Kids Sitting Together in the Cafeteria? And Other Conversations about Race*. New York: Basic Books.

Thorne, Barrie. 1993. *Gender Play: Girls and Boys in School*. New Brunswick, NJ: Rutgers University Press.

Thorne, Barrie, and Zella Luria. 1986. "Sexuality and Gender in Children's Daily Worlds." *Social Problems* 33(3):176–90.

Zeiher, Helga. 2003. "Shaping Daily Life in Urban Environments." Pp. 66–81 in *Children in the City: Home, Neighbourhood, and Community*, edited by P. Christensen and M. O'Brien. Abingdon, UK: Routledge.

PART IV

Looking Ahead

11

Making Space

Valuation and Gender Inequality in STEM

CASSIDY PUCKETT AND BRIAN E. GRAVEL

In the basement of a diverse comprehensive high school just outside of Boston sits a three-thousand-plus-square-foot space that once housed a large woodshop. When one enters the room today, the shop still smells of dust left behind by generations of vocational students and holds what might appear to be a machine graveyard: table saws, band saws, lathes, planers, jointers, and shapers, all too heavy to move once the school decided to no longer offer woodworking courses. After classes shut down, the school debated handing the space over to the town for public works vehicle maintenance. But then the school decided to use it for something else.

A makerspace.

"Makerspaces" are creative spaces where students can design and construct objects, through activities meaningful to the learner, ranging from weaving to programming (Halverson and Sheridan 2014). In the last decade, the "Maker Movement" has gained momentum, and educators and policymakers have viewed it as an opportunity to create equity in science, technology, engineering, and mathematics (STEM) education (Halverson and Sheridan 2014; Martin 2015). As part of this movement, President Obama invited students to share their innovations at a White House Maker Faire (White House 2014). While promoters envisioned makerspaces as helping all students develop design and problem-solving skills and STEM literacies (Hatch 2013; Tucker-Raymond and Gravel 2019), many makerspaces have become white male dominated, and "making" is often represented as a technocentric, male, and American activity (Vossoughi, Hooper, and Escudé 2016).

Yet this is untrue of this particular school's makerspace and, as we show below, this surprising case reveals key undertheorized dynamics of gender inequality. In the workshop are objects old and new, combining vestiges of vocational classes together with new making activities. A "Wood Technology" sign still hangs over the door and another name—"The Workshop"—is painted in black on the back wall opposite the entrance.[1] In the center of the room is a large bookshelf piled high with woodworking supplies, digital tools, and painting paraphernalia (adding art to make it a "STEAM" space) (Peppler and Wohlwend 2018). Nearby is a bulletin board with Polaroid images from the old woodshop days. It is, by design, not clean or tidy. It is, by design, not identifiably vocational or academic. And its ambiguous status means that in the Workshop everyone is welcome.

Students in the Workshop are from a mix of racial and ethnic backgrounds—representative of the school's roughly eighteen hundred students who collectively speak fifty-two languages—and gender balanced. Around the room are several wooden worktables, where clusters of students talk, tinker, and design. One group is soldering electrical components, another is designing for 3D printing. A teacher works with a group to create an interactive art piece about Mary Shelley's *Frankenstein* (Gravel and Svihla 2021). A group of Haitian girls sit beneath a mural of the first students to inhabit and define the new makerspace. One of the girls helped paint the mural, a student we call "Roseline." Around her are eight others, including her cousins Stéphanie, Fabienne, and Marie, who immigrated to the United States after the 2010 earthquake (Horton 2012). The group came to be known as "The Ladies" by makerspace teachers and researchers, a nod to their stewardship of the space.

In the Workshop, the Ladies do as they please; the same goes for all students who enter. With Roseline's leadership, the group picked woodworking—a joyful act of rebellion for girls otherwise excluded from this activity in Haiti (Charles 1995). Why was woodworking so important? As Stéphanie, Roseline's cousin, explained, "When my dad was in Haiti, he used to build stuff . . . this, desk, cab . . . um, these [points at a cabinet] . . . I don't know most of these things, but my other brothers know these things. . . . And I watched them. But me? Nah, *I'm a girl, girls [don't] do this.*" As Stéphanie noted, women and girls in Haiti have been historically limited to the domestic domain, even as they bear the brunt of political and environmental upheaval, including the earthquake that brought them to the United States (Padgett and Warnecke 2011). But in the makerspace the Ladies can do woodworking or engage in any kind of making.

One day, three of the girls sand wooden boxes they are constructing, two work together to cut a fallen tree limb they found outside, and another girl sits exploring a Chromebook provided by the school. The girls sanding their boxes switch to woodburning, marking the wood with names, messages, and designs. These carvings/burnings are expressions of their presence and identities, reflecting their roots. In Haiti, crafting and art production are an important part of life, and played a central role in the fight for Haitian independence (Danticat 2011). The girls work diligently, laughing and chatting away in Kreyòl. Throughout the year, together with other students, they continue to visit the makerspace, marking the space and making activity as gender neutral. This contrasts with both STEM and career and technical education (CTE), where white and male students dominate, outnumbering female students in fields like manufacturing and architecture (Leu and Arbeit 2020).

Juxtaposed to the makerspace, in the same school just four floors upstairs, activities falling squarely under the STEM umbrella, like computer science (CS) classes, computer club, and robotics are dominated by more affluent white and Asian males, reflecting broader imbalances by race, class, and gender. Historical stereotypes dictate that such STEM activities are "guy things," and research shows that fewer girls participate in these educational subjects (Xie, Fang, and Shauman 2015). In college, although women outpace men in earning degrees, they are underrepresented in many STEM fields, including engineering, CS, and physical sciences (Hill, Corbett, and St. Rose 2010; National Science Foundation 2015). *So, what does the case of the Haitian girls claiming the makerspace—in the same school where white and Asian boys dominate CS—tell us about how gender inequality is constructed in STEM?*

Using findings from an interdisciplinary collaborative project between a sociologist and an education researcher,[2] in this chapter we build upon Barrie Thorne's influential *Gender Play* to argue that how activities are valued matters for gender construction and gender inequality, as well as other forms of categorical and intersectional inequalities. The value of an activity may be based on who participates, as Thorne described: girls' activities can be assumed to take less "skill" than boys' activities and therefore be understood as less valued, even when evidence shows that "girls' activities" require skill (Thorne 1993). But, educational policies and the local school context can also shape how activities are valued in unexpected ways, as in the school's makerspace, with important consequences for equity.

In terms of policy, because makerspaces have roots in both CTE and STEM, they are value ambiguous, and therefore have the potential but not guaranteed possibility of transforming engineering and technology into equitable fields—if they retain their value ambiguity in the local context. In our case study school, the Workshop upheld the makerspace's ambiguous status through the school's and makerspace designers' choices to retain the tools and materials left behind from its use as a woodshop (hand tools, small power tools, wood, varnishes, paints, sandpaper). Educators and researchers involved in its development added just a few newer technologies (soldering irons, simple robotics, circuitry kits, a 3D printer) and invited both vocational and academic teachers to the space, marking it as status ambiguous (Puckett and Gravel 2020). Finally, adults positioned students as its central meaning makers and designers of the space; the curiosities they express drive the activity and support adults provide. In contrast, CS is understood in educational policy and in the local school context as higher-status "academic" activity leading to lucrative careers. Teachers frame CS courses as elite spaces, for which students can either compete for slots or opt out of the competition altogether, contributing to inequitable participation in CS.

Overall, the case of the Workshop shows how activity valuation in local contexts shapes how gender and other categorical and intersectional inequalities operate within schools. Given these observations, we build upon Barrie Thorne's classic ideas about the social construction of *gender* to argue that the social construction of *activity* should also be a part of how we understand inequality. Analysis of the dynamic ways in which activity is valued and matched to social groups, in addition to how categories of people are constructed, can reveal how inequalities occur and, importantly, how they may be addressed. When activity is treated as contested terrain, surprising cases of more equitable technology and engineering participation, like the Ladies' participation in the Workshop, can reveal how historically inequitable dynamics can be disrupted.

Designing for Equitable STEM

Researchers have tried for decades to understand the shape and scope of gender inequities in education, to help sort out and address the problem of sex segregation in educational and occupational fields. The organization and function of space in gender construction is central to Thorne's *Gender Play*. Thorne describes how the lines between "boys' activities" and "girls' activities" are clearly delineated in physical space and serve the purpose of defining gender boundaries, with boys invading spaces and girls being thought to pollute or contaminate spaces (1993). These ideas have racialized meanings, as well. This hierarchy is made concrete in the school's CS department, located on the school's top floor: a clear white and Asian boys' domain. Along the walls outside of the CS classrooms are whiteboards covered in mathematical equations, styled to echo the elite culture of Silicon Valley, left uncleaned to broadcast a higher-status academic image for passersby to see. To similarly mirror industry, the CS department chair designed his courses using the CS curriculum of nearby universities (Northeastern and University of Massachusetts–Boston) and constructed a competitive culture.

The department chair initially required all students to receive a B or better in Algebra I to be eligible to enroll, even though he later decided this was not necessary and informally allowed some to enroll without meeting this criterion. But the policy remained in the school's "program of study" used by guidance counselors, and the chair only recruited students in higher-level mathematics classes, conveying the message that CS is a higher-value activity, with mathematics acting as gatekeeper to allow only "competitive" students. As a result, similar to Thorne's description of the boundaries delineating "boys' activities" and "girls' activities," the lack of girls' participation in computing is striking but unsurprising.

What did the CS department think about the low number of girls involved? The chair said, "Well, we have Technovation." To address the department's lack of gender diversity, the school made some efforts to recruit more girls into computing. One way it did so was through the national girls' technology program Technovation, an after-school program run by a nearby university. But teachers were not involved and it was not integral to the school's CS curriculum, and so it was largely unsuccessful in bringing girls into CS. To address the lack of gender and racial diversity in CS, the school also introduced Hour of Code, a single-day event. But, they again only invited higher-level math classes to participate, and even though they included some twenty female students of the seventy students who attended, few joined CS. In 2018–2019, no girls and very few Black and Latinx students enrolled in CS, despite the school being gender balanced and Asian, Black, Latinx, and white groups each comprising roughly a quarter of the student population.[3]

But, in the makerspace things are different. Was this an act of defiance where the Ladies walked into the makerspace and decided to swim against the current? Thorne described cases where girls participated in "boys' activity" or boys participated in "girls' activity" as children "crossing the gender divide." Thorne explained that what counted as crossing depended on how activities are gender categorized within particular contexts, such as in neighborhoods or at school, with more stringent gender boundary policing at school. Thorne said "earnest crossing" with the "intent of full participation in the activities and on the terms of groups of the other gender" could indeed challenge gender arrangements (Thorne 1993:121). But, this notion of earnest crossing does not fit the Haitian girls—even though crossing did occur at school and the girls' participation might be viewed as crossing the line delineating boys' and girls' activities. Instead, making was never gender categorized at the Workshop.

Part of the reason this was the case is the ambiguous history of makerspaces, which emerged out of long-standing historical debates about how to value human activity in general and technology and engineering specifically, mirroring debates in occupational fields (Puckett and Gravel 2020; Puckett and Rafalow 2022). Some involved in the Maker Movement hoped that with a hands-on orientation and ties to both STEM and CTE, makerspaces could be status neutral and invite equitable participation. In an effort to accomplish this goal, makerspaces are often designed to combine activities like woodworking and 3D printing (Halverson and Sheridan 2014; Martin 2015). The simultaneous categorization of makerspaces as both STEM and CTE opens up the possibility that typically marginalized students like the Haitian girls could feel a sense of belonging in the makerspace alongside boys and students from a range of racial, socioeconomic, and gender backgrounds. Instead, however, many makerspaces are distinctly STEM spaces, easily slipping into competitive male-only spaces.

But that was not true in the school's makerspace. In contrast to CS upstairs, the Workshop downstairs was designed from its inception to be a space where all types of students and teachers could explore engineering, design, expression, and creative engagements in any type of "vocational" or "academic" activity. In this way, the Workshop centered students and their own interests as the means for developing the values and commitments of the space, rather than particular technologies defining makerspace activity (Vossoughi, Hooper, and Escudé 2016). The Workshop was established in 2014 through a partnership among the school, the second author (Brian), and other collaborators at Tufts University. The makerspace team strategically placed it in the woodshop, rather than other school spaces like the library, because the physical machinery, tools, and materials left behind marked the space as faintly vocational. Then they introduced materials, activities, and people more typically connected to STEM into what was a historically vocational space to create the Workshop, making it a status-ambiguous space.

Vocational spaces can also be gender inequitable, if they are imbued with political value. Like the Ladies' experiences in Haiti, the original wood technology shop largely excluded girls. Built in the late 1970s the woodshop was maintained over time through the political will of a supportive local blue-collar community, including a twenty-year school board member who still only enters the school through the vocational program's back doors. Students could enroll in different levels of woodshop as an elective, but it was almost exclusively a space for boys and men. The long-standing teacher, Sully, was trained in vocational education to teach kids the art and skill of cabinetry production. He wore a blue denim apron over his clothing. He drank Dunkin' Donuts coffee all day long. He knew his role, his job, and how to relate to the boys who spent time in his courses.

Yet, over time, enrollments in the shop classes began to wane. The school redirected budgets toward "academic" subjects and computer labs, introducing more advanced placement courses to the school's program of study. Eventually, Sully transferred to a neighboring city's high school, where the outlook was more secure. The school hired a replacement for Sully, but he lasted fewer than two years. Finally, the shop closed and it became a dumping ground for broken furniture, old overhead projectors, and remnants of school theater productions—objects too big to destroy but too useless to keep upstairs. The woodshop sat dormant for years. Occasionally someone might use the saws still housed there for a project, like an engineering teacher or the auto shop teacher, whom the school retained to teach vocational courses valued by the broader school community (Puckett and Gravel 2020). But the lights largely remained off. That is, until the makerspace opened in 2014.

The new makerspace could have easily slipped into being understood as a distinctly STEM-focused space, like the male-oriented nostalgic images of tinkerers found in *MAKE Magazine*. An analysis of the magazine's covers from 2005 to 2013 showed that 85 percent featured men, there were no people of color, and technologies like robotics and drones were predominant rather than artistic, woodworking, or auto-mechanical activity (Buechley 2013). In contrast, some involved in the Maker Movement argued that making has long historical roots in human activity, promoting a more democratic vision of how it should be understood (Eglash 2004; Ingold 2013). Given these ongoing contestations over the value of makerspaces, how could the Workshop emerge as a distinctly equitable space?

The school's makerspace collaborators were keenly aware of this tension—between the branded, technocentric visions of making and alternate perspectives on making as shared human activity—when Brian and others worked with the school to open the Workshop in the fall of 2014. At the time, the Maker Movement's rise in popularity drove 3D printers, laser cutters, robotics, and other highly technical tools and processes into library and community makerspaces. In their proposal to the National Science Foundation to fund the effort, Brian and his team wrote, "We theorize that the emergence of the maker movement—and its public recognition as a high-status, white-collar hobby, the sort of thing that 'people who work at Google' would do—provides an unprecedented opportunity to change teachers' and students' perceptions of the capabilities of low (vocationally) tracked students and to recognize their funds of knowledge . . . as high-status" (Gravel, Shapiro, and Rogers 2014). The team carried this theory into the design and organization of the makerspace by emphasizing the blending of older craft and art traditions with newer technologies, like simple circuitry. They left the wood sitting un-touched all around the space, including in the back room, where large, ten-foot-tall racks of unfinished pine, maple, ash, and cedar were stacked. While they did install a 3D printer, it malfunctioned early in the fall and remained dormant, and students were drawn to other activities. The team called what students could do in the Workshop "engineering inquiry" in order to center designerly ways of thinking, inquiry with materials, and different computational activity (Gravel and Svihla 2021).

As a striking departure from the *MAKE Magazine* vision of making, the Workshop centered "making do," where students could use what-ever they found to engage in STEM-rich activities that interested them and kept them coming back. This broader vision of making—one an-chored in long histories of crafting, making do, and blurred disciplinary boundaries—set the foundation for different activity in the Workshop. When the team members finally recruited students to the Workshop, they explicitly spoke to students in classes designated for English lan-guage learners, "newcomer" immigrant students, students in vocational programs and art classes, and their teachers. Later that year they taught an elective course in the makerspace called "Creative Design and En-gineering." The team members asked the principal to ensure that the student composition in the elective reflected the wide diversity of the school, so no one group defined who belonged within the space.

The Ladies Make Space

In fall of 2014, the Workshop opened after school, and within two weeks, more than forty students were visiting each afternoon, many of whom were Haitian and more than half of whom identified as female. The design of the Workshop allowed students to make of it what they wanted. It was driven by interest in what might be called raw or pure inquiry—it was a space where youth could come and work on whatever they wanted, in whatever ways they wanted, as long as they did not get hurt. Provocations were laid out on tables at times: small robotics kits or a sample electric guitar made from a glass Coca-Cola bottle. But largely, students were invited to explore whatever captured their eyes.

Facilitators worked to amplify students' interests when they expressed curiosity or a desire to explore something, treating students as full-fledged cocreators of the Workshop. Some students brought in skate-boards, bicycles, or headphones needing repair. Fixing the broken wires on headphones was a meaningful introduction to soldering. The history of the woodshop reignited discussions about hand tools and woodwork-ing, which was intensely popular from the outset. The Haitian students, who came in large numbers when the Workshop opened, spent signifi-cant time making things out of wood: checkerboards, boxes, signs, and wood burnings that communicated messages to each other or evoked religious beliefs.

The Haitian girls—eventually "the Ladies"—were a noticeable and thriving presence in the space from its very beginning. They played music, made tea and pancakes on a hot plate for those who visited, and explored different forms of making. The Workshop pulsed with energy, driven largely by the Haitian students who gave it life. The Ladies visited nearly every day, starting out by exploring wood-burning projects. They learned to repurpose the soldering irons, burning patterns in pieces of wood left in the space after years of dormancy. The Workshop was a place to explore and creatively express their cultural identities while also learning something new. These activities shaped the values of the Work-shop more broadly; wood burning became a very popular activity for all students that first fall. And it was a launchpad for continued explora-tions of design, crafting, and engineering, and for building community in the makerspace.

As projects evolved, so too did the community the Ladies built; they regularly invited friends to join them in the space. Our research team noted their continued, steady participation in the space and how they claimed the makerspace and making as a part of their identity and expression of future selves. In one fieldnote from September 2015, a member of the research team wrote, "Roseline came in worried that her flower and name that she had made last year were thrown out. She found her name and heart shaped box (which was later admired by the other girls she brought down [to the Workshop]); she added hooks to her name so that it could be hung to the wall and helped her friends start designing their names for wood burning."

Characteristic of their time in the Workshop was a commitment to collective activity and collaborations, as these were ways to continue building and learning. Instead of Sully, an older white male commu-

Figure 11.1. Wood burnings, including representations of names and initials and religious symbols referring to the Bible and a love of Jesus, examples of how youth expressed their identity in woodworking. Permission of the authors.

Figure 11.2. An example of a more complex project that the Ladies collaborated on with Joe, involving glued layers of wood, cut on a band saw, to produce the heart-shaped box. Permission of the authors.

nity member named Joe, who was knowledgeable in artisan woodworking and guitar making, began mentoring youth in the space. Visiting the school one day, Joe was excited to share his love of woodworking and to nurture the girls' interests. He started coming regularly, working closely with the Ladies, helping them gain confidence with hand tools and larger power tools. Their first project was building the heart-shaped wooden box. Each afternoon, they came as a group, sometimes with additional friends in tow, asking, "Where is Joe?"

Through woodworking, the Ladies connected with each other and with others, and their interactions built the culture of the Workshop around creative explorations with technology. They also reflected on how the makerspace context was different in that it allowed their participation. In contrast to the predominantly male making activities in Haiti, the original woodshop, and CS, which the Ladies understood as not "for them," they could participate in the collaborative and communally oriented makerspace. Empowered to engage in woodworking, directed by their own curiosities and interests (including dragging a large tree limb from outside of the school into the space that they turned into bowls and coasters), the Ladies made the space their own.

They continued to participate even after school closed for the year, joining in a summer internship program at the Workshop. In that program, they chose to design and build shelving for a community group that spent time in the space. The group's name was Disability Triangle, and Roseline and Marie worked alongside two other students to design and build triangular shelves. Their motivation for the unusual shape was to make students with disabilities feel welcome at the Workshop. Marie reflected that her pastor taught her the importance of good work, and work for others. In this culminating project, their woodworking, design, and engineering skills were directed at building something that communicated a key value they had helped to construct in the Workshop: engineering inquiry was for all, and all were welcome (the Facebook page for the space is titled "Makers Welcome").

Disrupting historical patterns of gendered engagement within "making"—where forces continually reify makerspaces as competitive, technocentric, masculine enclaves (Buechley 2013)—was accomplished through deliberate and intentional practices to sustain girls' sense of "rightful presence" (Calabrese, Barton, and Tan 2019). The Ladies re-

Figure 11.3. The students building the Disability Triangle. Permission of the authors.

Figure 11.4. The completed Disability Triangle. Permission of the authors.

sisted gendered and racialized categories of engineering, woodworking, and makerspace participation in the Workshop, activities typically dominated by masculine, white, competitive, and individualistic "meritocratic" conceptualizations (Oldenziel 2001; Seron, Silbey, Cech, and Rubineau 2018). The Ladies helped define the meaning and value of makerspace activities through their persistent and rightful participation, collective activity (always collaborating on projects), and commitment to expanding participation (inviting new people to explore the space they helped build) (Costanza-Chock 2020). Small personal interactions and larger relationships to notions of home and religious identities contributed to this valuation of activity imbued in the Workshop (Massey 2005). The girls' rightful presence was sustained by the ways *they* defined practices for engaging with technology, engineering, and making, resisting gendered narratives about who can engage in these forms of learning in school, and how they do so.

Following the summer internship, Roseline reflected on what she learned in the Workshop: "I learned a lot about a lot of things. Working in a team. I wasn't very good at, but now I'm good at it. Learning a lot about how to work together, and how to share, like, ideas. And how to hear somebody else . . . basically that's what I learned." Throughout two school years as mainstays in the space, Roseline developed her interest in STEM, and explored STEM-related opportunities through a local state college's summer engineering technology bridge program. She later majored in a STEM-related program in college.

What does the contrast between CS and the makerspace tell us that is new? In *Gender Play*, Thorne argued that gender boundaries and the gendered meaning of activities is a continual, dynamic negotiation within particular spaces. For example, Thorne noted the ways different classrooms and the playground varied in the extent to which boys and girls were at odds. But, the importance of ongoing struggles over the meaning and value of activity can be lost in discussions of gender inequality. Valuation can shape participation. Cultural scholars argue that any activity—like hands-on making—is subject to ongoing valuation processes (Lamont, Beljean, and Clair 2014; Zuckerman 2012). This valuation typically involves comparison with previously valued activity, debate about how to assess value, and struggle over who is a legitimate judge of value (Bourdieu 1993; Lamont 2012). The result of this valuation process is categorizing activity into existing hierarchies and matching the activities with corresponding social groups, with important implications for inequality (Navis and Glynn 2010).

However, valuation does not simply occur out in the world somewhere, divorced from lived experience. It occurs within organizations, and in our case, within a school with a very specific history. Administrators, teachers, and students navigate uniquely local histories and politics to cocreate meaning and value around activities and who is best suited to engage in them (Coburn 2006; Datnow, Park, and Kennedy-Lewis 2012). In the school, CS was constructed as a higher-valued activity; therefore the competition was much fiercer, with gender- and race-based separation starker and inequality more difficult to address, in accordance with the findings of decades of research on CS education (Margolis et al. 2008; Vakil and Ayers 2019). But, in the makerspace, activity was status *ambiguous* because different types of teachers led activities in a space now neither vocational nor academic, involving both CTE and STEM activity. This contributed to more equitable participation.

In summary, the contrast between the makerspace and CS shows that the valuation of activities is a continual, dynamic negotiation within local organizational contexts and that this process of valuation has critical consequences for categorical inequalities in schools, including race, class, and gender. When activity is status ambiguous—as in the makerspace—there is less competition and different groups can lay claim to participation. However, when an activity is constructed as higher value, competition for participation is fierce, as it was in CS. Some students might choose to opt out altogether, rightly viewing access to these resources as likely allocated to already advantaged students and instead investing their time in places where they feel welcome.

Conclusion

In this chapter we built upon Barrie Thorne's classic ideas to argue that the social construction of *gender*—and the construction of intersectional inequality—is shaped by the social construction of *activity*. By analyzing the dynamic ways in which activity is categorized, in addition to how categories of people are constructed and activities matched to social groups, our story reveals how inequalities occur and, importantly, how they may be addressed. When activity is treated as contested terrain, surprising cases of more equitable STEM participation can reveal points of potential disruption to inequitable dynamics.

We presented the makerspace as one such surprising and relatively unique case of more equitable access to STEM educational opportunity. The categorization of technology and engineering activity in the makerspace was coconstructed by organizational actors (and students especially) within the broader, ambiguous institutional environment, where a range of interpretations of technology and engineering and how to match students to these activities is possible. This designed ambiguity, supported in the local school context through purposeful cultivation in the makerspace, allowed for the Ladies' empowered and equitable participation in the Workshop. But the opposite occurred upstairs in CS, where girls could not make the same claims to activity. Nor did they want to; girls like the Ladies explicitly said they resisted the competition laid out plainly before them by simply not participating, preferring collaborative and community-oriented work. The girls' actions and how they negotiated the makerspace provide a counterstory to the idea that STEM in general is a male-dominated space, and that engineering, innovation, and makerspaces inevitably follow these trends.

Sociological research has largely left uninterrogated how the valuation of activity shapes gender and other categorical inequalities in education, and how that shapes students' futures. While the importance of space in gender boundary making was recognized decades ago as playing a role in gender construction, the valuation of activity has largely been taken as a given. This leaves critical dynamics of inequality—and important opportunities for their disruption—largely unknown. As we showed in the contrast between the makerspace and CS, such processes can reveal ways in which inequality is maintained and how we can disrupt deeply entrenched dividing lines that shape future trajectories (Domina, Penner, and Penner 2017). Further, as demonstrated with this project, disciplinary collaborations between fields can help push research and policy forward, with the critical lens of fields like sociology informing the designed intervention approach of the learning sciences, to promote equity in STEM.

This activity-valuation framework can also be applied beyond gender inequality, to think about "activity" in deeper ways—not just what young people do but how valuation frames institutional arrangements to shape what students do now and in the future (Puckett and Gravel 2020). Indeed, by nurturing ambiguity, the makerspace was designed to be more inclusive by race and class as well, unlike CS. These same dynamics of valuation are also present in higher education and occupations. For example, universities may categorize particular fields of study as universally necessary and therefore a shared rather than scarce resource, such as a requirement that all students take English. Or universities may categorize particular fields as higher value and requiring competition for entry, with more stringent prerequisites or curriculum that demands advanced preparation for introductory courses, as has been the case in CS (Margolis and Fisher 2002). However, inequality is not inevitable. While categorizing activity as higher status can increase resource competition, the way that the ambiguous design of the Workshop allowed the Ladies to make space for themselves in STEM shows that there are clear ways to promote equity—just as Thorne argued decades ago.

NOTES

1 The names of the makerspace, students, and teachers are all pseudonyms.
2 These findings emerge from a multiyear mixed-methods interdisciplinary research project. The coauthors work in different fields that have different scholarly expectations. The first author, Cassidy, is in sociology, where many studies observe and describe phenomena, rather than intervene. In contrast, the second author, Brian, is in the learning sciences, where researchers are expected to design and study educational interventions. Therefore, project methods included qualitative observation and interviews, surveys, as well as Brian's collaboration with the school to codesign the makerspace. For more methodological details see Puckett and Gravel (2020).
3 Here we use the term "Black" to include African, Afro-Caribbean, and African American students.

REFERENCES

Bourdieu, Pierre. 1993. *The Field of Cultural Production*. New York: Columbia University Press.
Buechley, Leah. 2013. "FabLearn Keynote: A Critical Look at Making." Paper presented at the FabLearn Conference, Stanford University, Palo Alto, CA, October 28.
Calabrese Barton, Angela, and Edna Tan. 2019. "Designing for Rightful Presence in STEM: The Role of Making Present Practices." *Journal of the Learning Sciences* 28(4–5):616–58.

Charles, Carolle. 1995. "Gender and Politics in Contemporary Haiti: The Duvalierist State, Transnationalism, and the Emergence of a New Feminism (1980–1990)." *Feminist Studies* 21(1):135–64.

Coburn, Cynthia. 2006. "Framing the Problem of Reading Instruction: Using Frame Analysis to Uncover the Microprocesses of Policy Implementation." *American Educational Research Journal* 43(3):343–79.

Costanza-Chockj, Sasha. 2020. *Design Justice: Community-Led Practices to Build the Worlds We Need.* Cambridge, MA: MIT Press.

Danticat, Edwidge. 2011. *Create Dangerously: The Immigrant Artist at Work.* Princeton, NJ: Princeton University Press.

Datnow, Amanda, Vicki Park, and Briannna Kennedy-Lewis. 2012. "High School Teachers' Use of Data to Inform Instruction." *Journal of Education for Students Placed at Risk* 17(4):247–65.

Domina, Thurston, Andrew Penner, and Emily Penner. 2017. "Categorical Inequality: Schools as Sorting Machines." *Annual Review of Sociology* 43:311–30.

Eglash, Ron. 2004. "Appropriating Technology: An Introduction." Pp. vii–xxi in *Appropriating Technology: Vernacular Science and Social Power*, edited by R. Eglash, J. L. Croissant, G. Di Chiro, and R. Fouché. Minneapolis: University of Minnesota Press.

Gravel, Brian E., R. Benjamin Shapiro, and Chris Rogers. 2014. "EAGER: Engineering Inquiry for All in Nedlam's Workshop." National Science Foundation Award #1450985. Available at nsf.gov/awardsearch.

Gravel, Brian E., and Vanessa Svihla. 2021. "Fostering Heterogeneous Engineering through Whole-Class Design Work." *Journal of the Learning Sciences* 30(2):279–329.

Halverson, Erica Rosenfeld, and Kimberly Sheridan. 2014. "The Maker Movement in Education." *Harvard Educational Review* 84(4):495–504.

Hatch, Mark. 2013. *The Maker Movement Manifesto: Rules for Innovation in the New World of Crafters, Hackers, and Tinkerers.* New York: McGraw-Hill.

Hill, Catherine, Christianne Corbett, and Andresse St. Rose. 2010. "Why So Few? Women in Science, Technology, Engineering, and Mathematics." Washington, DC: American Association of University Women.

Horton, Lynn. 2012. "After the Earthquake: Gender Inequality and Transformation in Post-Disaster Haiti." *Gender & Development* 20(2):295–308.

Ingold, Tim. 2013. *Making: Anthropology, Archaeology, Art, and Architecture.* New York: Routledge.

Lamont, Michele. 2012. "Towards a Comparative Sociology of Valuation and Evaluation." *Annual Review of Sociology* 38(21):201–21.

Lamont, Michele, Stefan Beljean, and Matthew Clair. 2014. "What Is Missing? Cultural Processes and Causal Pathways to Inequality." *Socio-Economic Review* 12(3):573–608.

Leu, Katherine B., and Caren A. Arbeit. 2020. "Differences in High School CTE Coursetaking by Gender and Race/Ethnicity." *Career and Technical Education Research* 45(1):33–61.

Margolis, Jane, Rachel Estrella, Joanna Goode, Jennifer Jellison Holme, and Kimberly Nao. 2008. *Stuck in the Shallow End.* Cambridge, MA: MIT Press.

Margolis, Jane, and Allan Fisher. 2002. *Unlocking the Clubhouse: Women in Computing.* Cambridge, MA: MIT Press.

Martin, Lee. 2015. "The Promise of the Maker Movement for Education." *Journal of Pre-College Engineering Education Research* 5(1):30–39.

Massey, Doreen. 2005. *For Space.* London: Sage.

National Science Foundation. 2015. "Women, Minorities, and Persons with Disabilities in Science and Engineering: 2015. Special Report NSF 15–311." Arlington, VA: National Science Foundation.

Navis, Chad, and Mary Ann Glynn. 2010. "How New Market Categories Emerge: Temporal Dynamics of Legitimacy, Identity, and Entrepreneurship in Satellite Radio, 1990–2005." *Administrative Science Quarterly* 55:439–71.

Oldenziel, Ruth. 2001. "Man the Maker, Woman the Consumer: The Consumption Junction Revisited." Pp. 128–48 in *Feminism in Twentieth-Century Science, Technology, and Medicine*, edited by A. N. H. Creager, E. Lunbeck, and L. L. Schiebinger. Chicago: University of Chicago Press.

Padgett, Andrew, and Tonia Warnecke. 2011. "Diamonds in the Rubble: The Women of Haiti." *Journal of Economic Issues* 45(3):527–57.

Peppler, Kylie, and Karen Wohlwend. 2018. "Theorizing the Nexus of STEAM Practice." *Arts Education Policy Review* 119(2):88–99.

Puckett, Cassidy, and Brian Gravel. 2020. "Institutional Ambiguity and de Facto Tracking in STEM." *Teachers College Record* 122(11):1–38.

Puckett, Cassidy, and Matthew H. Rafalow. 2022. "From 'Impact' to 'Negotiation': Educational Technologies and Inequality." Pp. 97–113 in *The Oxford Handbook of Sociology and Digital Media*, edited by S. Sobieraj and D. A. Rohlinger. New York: Oxford University Press.

Seron, Carroll, Susan Silbey, Erin Cech, and Brian Rubineau. 2018. ""I Am Not a Feminist, but . . .": Hegemony of a Meritocratic Ideology and the Limits of Critique among Women in Engineering." *Work and Occupations* 45(2):131–67.

Thorne, Barrie. 1993. *Gender Play: Girls and Boys in School.* New Brunswick, NJ: Rutgers University Press.

Tucker-Raymond, Eli, and Brian Gravel. 2019. *STEM Literacies in Makerspaces: Implications for Learning, Teaching, and Research.* New York: Routledge.

Vakil, Sepehr, and Rick Ayers. 2019. "The Racial Politics of STEM Education in the USA: Interrogations and Explorations." *Race, Ethnicity, and Education* 22(4):449–58.

Vossoughi, Shirin, Paula K. Hooper, and Meg Escudé. 2016. "Making through the Lens of Culture and Power: Toward Transformative Visions for Educational Equity." *Harvard Educational Review* 86(2):206–32.

The White House. 2014. "Nation of Makers." Available at https://obamawhitehouse.archives.gov, accessed August 10, 2022.

Xie, Yu, Michael Fang, and Kimberlee Shauman. 2015. "STEM Education." *Annual Review of Sociology* 41:331–57.

Zuckerman, Ezra W. 2012. "Construction, Concentration, and (Dis)Continuities in Social Valuation." *Annual Review of Sociology* 38:223–45.

12

Nordic Gender Play?

Being and Doing Gender across Time and Space

HARRIET BJERRUM NIELSEN

In her book *Gender Play*, Barrie Thorne brought attention to the fluctu-
ating significance of gender boundaries in children's social interaction.
She stressed the importance of shifting the focus of gender analysis from
the individual to the group level of "collective practices through which
children and adults create and recreate gender in their daily interactions" (Thorne 1993:4). Instead of understanding gender among school
children from the perspective of girls' and boys' different behaviors or
cultures, she recommended employing the concepts of *borderwork* and
gender crossing to grasp their gender play as the ongoing shifts between
gender separation and gender integration in everyday social practices.

The concept of borderwork was inspired by the Norwegian social
anthropologist Fredrik Barth, who in a 1969 paper suggested that the
critical focus when studying ethnic groups is the "boundary that defines the group, not the cultural stuff that it encloses" (Barth 1969:15). A
boundary relies on categorical distinctions, but takes them to a meta-
phorical level that structures a sense of opposition and conflict between
groups (Barth 2000:22; Thorne 1993). Thorne's concept of borderwork
refers to the interactions undertaken to mark, activate, and emphasize
gender difference as a boundary in a given situation. Like Barth, she
promotes the idea that boundaries may be created through both contact
and avoidance. Borderwork can take many forms among children, ranging from discreet avoidance to teasing and fighting charged with feelings of thrill and excitement. Through such processes, group differences
come to be generalized and perceived as static and dualistic. As Thorne
phrased it: "the loose aggregation of 'boys and girls' in a school class
became 'the boys' and 'the girls' as separate and reified groups" (1993:65).

Gender crossing, on the other hand, is antithetical to borderwork as it describes situations where crossing the gender boundary contributes to reducing the social and symbolic significance of gender.

In this chapter, I will knit together my own research on children with Barrie Thorne's by merging a perspective of gender socialization over the life course with the perspective of borderwork. The concept of *socialization* holds a different theoretical meaning in the German sociological tradition, which is the one I will rely on here, than in the Anglo-Saxon tradition, which is the one Barrie Thorne confronted in her book and which is also the one referred to most often in this volume. Whereas the Anglo-Saxon meaning of the concept is connected mainly to Talcott Parsons and his structural functionalism, the German meaning of the concept has its roots in the Frankfurter School and refers more broadly to the often contradictory ways subjectivities come into being in a given sociohistorical context. It refers not to a top-down passive learning of social roles (sex roles, for instance) but to the historically embedded psychosocial position *from which one acts*. It highlights the sociobiographical trajectory of persons, rather than seeing social structures as something only outside a person. From this perspective, social and political change does not necessarily imply that people oppose social structures, but instead that people's subjectivities change in different historical periods due to new life conditions (Nielsen 2017).[1]

From this historical and psychosocial perspective, I will raise these questions: Are borderwork and gender crossing universal to the ways children do gender? Or could the gender order of their society affect the felt necessity to create a gender boundary? More specifically, do children living in more gender-equal societies like the Nordic countries play differently with gender? How does the time dimension of societal change interact with children's age and development? How and when do they do borderwork?

Gender Separation without Borderwork

Some of these questions emerged almost thirty years ago, when I first met Barrie. She was invited to the University of Oslo in January 1994, and at the Centre for Gender Research we took the opportunity to organize a seminar entitled "Social Construction of Gender in Children's

Worlds." *Gender Play* had recently been published, and I read it with great interest in my preparations for the seminar. The book spoke directly to me, as I was into the second year of a longitudinal study at an urban school in Oslo, predominantly serving middle-class families. I intended to follow one school class of children from first grade, in 1992, until the completion of their nine years of compulsory schooling.[2] Two-thirds of the students in the class were girls. Initially there were only two minority students (both girls, both with Arabic cultural background) in first grade, but more joined over the years, most of them children of refugees from the Balkan Wars.[3] Methodologically, I employed the same type of ethnographic fieldwork as Barrie, but over a longer time frame and with shorter periods of observation (Nielsen 2009).

Many of Barrie's vivid accounts of school life resonated strongly with me, despite the differences in time and space. However, after reading *Gender Play*, I could find little in my fieldnotes that aligned with the concepts of borderwork or gender crossing. When given a choice, the students in the class I followed did prefer to be with their own gender, but it appeared a rather peaceful separation, only occasionally stirred up by border incidents. Few episodes could qualify as intentional borderwork like teasing, competing, chasing, or invading on the basis of gender. In my talk at the seminar, I therefore suggested that we expand the concept to include the following variations of borderwork:

- *implicit borderwork*: the boundary that is created implicitly when children separate in gender groups, for instance, in the playground;
- *unintended borderwork*: when an act is interpreted by the other group as borderwork in situations where it appears unintended as such, for instance, a boy annoying randomly both boys and girls around him;
- *internal borderwork*: when a gender group strengthens its internal cohesion by focusing on gender difference, for instance, girls telling each other that they hope not to get any boys in their work group, but doing so out of earshot of the boys;
- *meta-borderwork*: when individual children challenge the idea of the salience of gender differences.

Thus, the gender separation appeared more a product of shared interests and behavioral compatibility—a pull toward one group rather than a push away from the other (Nielsen 1994). We can say that gender worked as a category, but less so as a boundary, and for this reason there was little need for explicit borderwork.

This state of affairs remained throughout the following years. During the first four years of school these girls and boys were relaxed about working together, when instructed, and otherwise kept to their own groups and mostly ignored the other gender.[4] I noticed only a few episodes of gender teasing, where some of the girls teased the boys by ascribing romantic interests to them (e.g., during a teacher-initiated play when students had to announce their choice of partner), or they teased each other about being in love with a particular boy. One girl, Astrid, appeared to take pleasure in teasing boys about all manner of things, but none necessarily about gender, and she was rarely joined by other girls. It was also Astrid who unleashed the one and only episode of gender "cooties" I saw during the whole nine-year-long project. It occurred when the boys' group was in conflict with the gym teacher, which delayed the gym activities. Astrid became fed up and yelled, "Stupid boys—boy cooties!" but nobody followed up. It is fair to say that rituals of "gender pollution" were absent in this class. The only and very few episodes I noted with strong and resentful borderwork arose from situations in which a teacher, most often a substitute teacher, divided the group by gender, and either had them compete with each other as boys versus girls or kept praising the girls in order to motivate the boys. In those situations I saw a collective rise of group identities and anger towards the other group. In addition, there was a telling episode during a lesson on gender roles, to which I will return later.

Gender Play in Fifth Grade

In fifth grade, borderwork finally emerged in my study. For some weeks during spring, the entire class, in every recess, was eagerly engaged in girls-against-boys chasing games, disguised as "Cops and Robbers." They also began to play-fight more with each other, accompanied by high laughter and excitement that could quickly morph into grievance and anger, mobilizing gender teams on each side. This increased contact across the gender boundary ran parallel to an increased fear of being seen as having romantic interests, embarrassment at being seen alone with a person of the wrong gender, and a need to express commitment to their own and aloofness to the other, just as Barrie had described in her study. In one situation where work groups were organized by a draw, resulting in a group with one girl and four boys, and another with one boy and four girls (the remaining groups turned out as single gendered), the two unfortunate students engaged in frenetic and shrewd underground negotiations to change the result, and succeeded. Often, their need to mark borders made it necessary to bend or press the teacher's gender-equality rules, as in the following episode where the class was instructed to check their homework by posing public questions to other students in the class. The student who was selected to answer first then asks the next question, and so on:

OBSERVATION (5th grade, 1996): Every second girl must ask a boy such that both boys and girls have a chance to speak (there are twice as many girls as boys present). The girls are very vigilant to the rules—not once is a boy asked too many questions, whereas it goes unnoticed if a girl is asked an extra time. Julie asks Astrid, Astrid asks Ola. Ola asks Nora, who answers and then says, "Can I ask a girl now?" [. . .] Jacob asks Tuva, Tuva asks Ida, who after her answer asks the teacher, "*Must* I ask a boy?" and then gives in and asks Halvor.

A sharper sense of opposite sides is created in fifth grade through this intensified borderwork. In the following excerpts from interviews, Ola explains to me the structure of the class as two teams, and Emily and Nora tell me what they think about having boys in their work groups:

INTERVIEW with Ola (5th grade, 1996): I think there should be one more boy in our class, and that they shouldn't . . . Not long ago they got another girl, and we did not get a boy! We were supposed to get a boy, but he didn't come. We lost a boy! They also lost a girl, but they got one back. They lost two girls, by the way.

INTERVIEW with Emily and Nora (5th grade, 1996): They don't have any sensible opinions! [laughing] When you have to cooperate, like right now in our group, Halvor, he doesn't know anything, he just sits there! And then we are expected to decide everything and that's rather boring. Girls are better in drawing and like to find out about things. Boys like to do things simple, very, very simple—they just jot down some notes and that's it. Quick and easy and they're done.

Later in the interview, Ola concedes that "I can sit next to girls, I don't care, they are human beings after all." Also, Emily and Nora's depiction of the boys' work style was more stereotypical than I had observed in practice. Here, then, we see borderwork, which is also underlined by the girls' laughter. I noted how a girl and a boy, who were friends privately, consciously ignored each other in school to prevent the boy being teased by other boys. As a girl told me in fifth grade, about the problem of mixed-gender friends, "Many people believe that you cannot be friends without being sweethearts."

The borderwork in fifth grade seems to have been triggered by a desire to lift the gender curtain of the years prior, and get in contact with each other, with hidden (or mostly hidden) sexual excitement. This new desire simultaneously created the need to mark and secure borders. In this way borderwork could be seen as the first step towards the "extreme-gender" I observed later in eighth and ninth grade, where the leading girls in the class transformed themselves into being ultra-feminine, while the leading boys strengthened their masculine position by making sexualized and often denigrating comments. At this stage there was no more need to hide a (hetero)sexual agenda; on the contrary, the aim was to position oneself as a visible and attractive heterosexual player.[5] As Frosh, Phoenix, and Pattman (2002) have also observed, this implies that gender difference often becomes eroticized and exaggerated at this age. In my class there was much talk and teasing about bodies, especially the parts of the body that signal sex. This sexualized interaction, however, did not cause the girls to give up their academic position. They kept their lead in class, but clearly struggled with the tension between being clever and ambitious girls while also wanting to be desirable in the eyes of the popular boys.

Twenty-Four Years Later: Gender Separation with
Gender Crossing

In 2016 I began a new longitudinal study at the same school in Oslo, which was still dominated by middle-class children. Here, the incidents of borderwork between first and fourth grade had decreased further compared with the earlier study, whereas gender crossing had increased.[6] This class was also middle-class dominated, but with a majority of boys and of children who had at least one parent not born in Norway.[7] Even though there was a clear gender separation in play, the significance of the gender boundary appeared to have waned even more. To sit together, to work together, to hold hands in line, or occasionally to play together were not situations that needed to be avoided or guarded against. In the four years I have now followed this class, I have noted only two episodes of a student not wanting to hold the hand of the other gender. Both cases involved the same girl, and no others seemed to have a problem with it. The same applies for the very few incidents I have seen of border alarm:

> OBSERVATION (4th grade, 2020): The task is to make posters with suggestions on how to make it easier to follow the rules of conduct of the school, for instance, that you should be quiet in the hallway or change to indoor shoes before entering the classroom in wintertime. Thomas protests to the teacher, "But it is *you* who decides the rules, not us!" Another boy follows up: "It is not our rules!" The teacher says that it is true that the rules are already given, but that they can help each other in how to follow the rules. She gives an example: buying nice pink indoor shoes. A boy frowns at the word "pink." Thomas gets annoyed with him and says in an irritated voice, "or cool black shoes then!" "Thank you, Thomas," says the teacher. Nobody else comments on the pink shoes.

Thomas, a dominant boy in class, seems to be more engaged in the power distribution between teachers and students than in gender work, which he dismisses as irrelevant. Being only one girl or boy in a work group has lost its danger; it raises no objections, and appears to be hardly noticed. The need to hide gender-mixed friendships also seems to have gone: in one case a girl and a boy appear to thrive in each other's company in class. They sit together, talking and laughing for long periods, even though the girl tends to choose girls as playmates at recess. Another girl and boy often meet outside school to play video games, and are unreserved about telling the class. The main concern here seems to be whether the two children like each other and share interests, as we saw with the video game friends, or here, where two first graders realize that they both take an interest in handball:

OBSERVATION (1st grade, 2017): The children are dressing in their outdoor clothes outside the classroom. Michael and Aisha are slow. They talk with each other about handball and tend to forget what they are supposed to do. Michael says that he is going to play on a certain field on Saturday. Aisha says she is going to be there too. Michael beams with joy towards her: "Are *you* also going there?! Then we will be the world's best childhood team ever!"

Sometimes, however, even with spontaneous sympathy for each other, there may be problems finding common ground:

OBSERVATION (1st grade, 2016): Emma and Emil sit next to each other outside the classroom, smiling at each other. Emma tries to show Emil the flowers on her indoor shoes. He looks at them, but does not find anything to say. Emma gives it another try, points at her shoes and says, "Here are my toes." But Emil still doesn't find any relevant way to respond, and the conversation fades out.

But there are also limits for gender crossing. In fourth grade, boys from the two parallel fourth-grade classes took part in a fighting game over ownership of an icy mound of snow in the schoolyard—which went on for several days. A girl from one of the classes also wanted to participate. Nobody objected, but the boys' rough treatment of her (several boys from the other class attacking her at once, giving the boys on her team a respite) showed that she was in the wrong place. Even though she fought bravely, she eventually had to quit; crying, she sought comfort among the girls. This incident aligns with what I call "internal borderwork."

The class is now in fifth grade (2020–21). Due to the pandemic, however, my observations ceased in March 2020, when they were still in fourth grade. Whether the same type of intensified gender play has emerged in fifth grade, as in the previous study, it is not possible for me to say. But my hunch is that it has. The waning significance of the gender boundary seen in increased gender crossing and decreased borderwork during the first four years of school is, however, of itself interesting. What does it mean, and why has it happened?

Doing Gender Similarly and Differently

Let us summarize what we have learned so far from comparing these studies: in Barrie Thorne's observations, as in mine, a dominant pattern of gender separation in elementary school is evident. When given a choice, girls and boys most often seek their own kind, though not to the same degree for all children. Even though gender separation may sometimes be institutionalized in schools, it is primarily a child-driven project. Gender separation is often stronger at recess than in the classroom, where teachers usually mix girls and boys in seating arrangements and work groups. This separation in the social relations and activities of girls and boys in middle childhood appears to be a relatively dispersed phenomenon. Cross-cultural research from social anthropology and psychology indicates that gender separation is the strongest and least flexible in children between the ages of five and eleven (Maccoby 1998; Whiting and Edwards 1988). There may be developmental reasons for this. Separation into same-gender groups may help children to develop and maintain collective identity, since gender is relatively simple to enact as a dichotomy and carries important cultural meaning that children try to grasp. The increase of borderwork during elementary school may be related to the growing cognitive awareness of the gaze of others in the school setting: crowded spaces with potential witnesses, as Barrie coined it. Moreover, social and emotional development increases the need for belonging to a peer group as children grow more independent from parents. As indicated by Barrie's study as well as by my 1992 study, gender separation increases until fifth grade, when it softens into an excited atmosphere of mutual approach, awareness, and physical play. This may be seen as a first step toward relations of infatuation and sexuality in youth, which is also a relatively dispersed phenomenon, although framed by different cultural codes, and not always heterosexual.

There are some differences in the social processes of gender separation between the US study and the Norwegian ones, however, and also
between the two Norwegian studies. For the first to fourth graders, the
significance of *marking* the gender boundary seems to have diminished
in the two Norwegian studies, and more so in the 2016 study than in the
1992 study. Even though gender separation persisted, and increased during these first years of school also in the Norwegian cases, the imagined
danger of being contaminated by the other gender declined, and this, especially in the 2016 study, allowed for individual children to follow their
inclinations to cross the border without being teased. It is pertinent to
ask whether this is a change in space or time—or both. Barrie Thorne's
observations in *Gender Play* concern the 1970s and 1980s, whereas the
two Norwegian studies took place in the 1990s and 2010s. There is no
doubt that studies from the Nordic countries during the 1970s and 1980s
also displayed more borderwork (Nielsen 2009). Rasmus Kleppe (2014)
noted this change among kindergarten children in a 2008 study wherein
he replicated an ethnographic study from 1967 (Berentzen 1980). He
found that both gender separation and gender boundaries in play were
far less conspicuous, when compared with the study made forty-one
years earlier. Not only was there more gender crossing in play; the children also occasionally mixed features from what is known as boys' typical rough-and-tumble play and girls' typical family play. For instance, in
one observation a group of girls and boys between four and five years of
age pretended that they were dangerous lynxes who ran around the playground to hunt prey. At night the lynxes returned to their cave, where
they were busy cooking dinner, reading bedside stories, and singing lullabies for the baby lynxes. There was no gender division of work here,
either during hunting time or during family time. All children were
thrilled by all parts of the play.

Studies of Nordic school children indicate that the behavioral rep-
ertoire of both girls and boys has broadened during the last decades,
and support the idea that space—as well as time—may play a role in
this change. I saw this already in the 1992 study: girls who combined
their traditional relational orientation and interest with ambition and
an active and self-assured manner in class, and boys who combined
their traditional focus on competition and status with more relational
competence and softer values. This was also present in Kleppe's (2014)

kindergarten study wherein boys, compared with the study from 1967, had become more aware of younger children's needs and could engage in taking care of them, and where girls in princess outfits could take pleasure in playing Superman. In my two studies, the boys were not afraid of showing feelings and vulnerability, or giving their mom or dad a hug if they suddenly appeared in the classroom with a forgotten lunchbox. Boys could also comfort and praise each other. Within a context of girls and boys becoming more alike in their behavior, *the boundary itself* is not perceived to be so significant, leading to a decline in explicit borderwork and an increase in gender crossing. However, if the gender boundary is less marked among younger children in the Norwegian context, then the intensified and sexualized gender focus that still appears from fifth grade onwards may represent a different transition than would be the case were a stronger awareness of the gender boundary already present. One might say that in the Norwegian case, it is sexuality that promotes gender boundaries, and not gender boundaries that produce heterosexual games. Further, one might speculate whether the gender identities from childhood and the experiences of heterosexual gender may be more split in the Norwegian case. They do not grow "naturally" out of each other, but represent a disruption in the gender-separated, but also rather gender-equal, world of childhood. But why is this the case? To understand this, we should leave the classroom and take a look at the wider social structures that have framed the experiences of Nordic children.

Changing Nordic Childhoods

Whereas reporting on new "active" girls from the 1980s onwards is not specific to the Nordic countries, reporting on the new "relational" boys seems to be. To my knowledge, it is only in Nordic classroom studies from the last decades that this new pattern of young masculinity emerges, a pattern that might well be related to class and ethnicity, but that needs to be further investigated (see, for instance, Eriksen and Lyng 2017; Godø 2014; Nielsen 2009; Overå 2014; Öhrn and Holm 2014). Compared, for instance, with a study by Frosh and colleagues (2002) of boys from the United Kingdom in the same period, concluding that there is "something missing emotionally in the lives of boys" (259), and in light of the impoverished emotional contact with their fathers that these boys often reported, the Nordic studies of boys gives a quite different impression.

This makes sense in relation to the gender-equality policies of the Nordic region, where fathers have become much more present in early childcare, and the absolute majority of mothers work outside the family. During the 1980s women's economic possibilities were supported by the implementation of gender quotas and other antidiscrimination legislation with regard to education and work, and the expansion of parental leave and public day care for families. From the 1990s onward, the political model of the universal breadwinner was extended to the idea of the universal carer (Fraser 1997). Men's rights as fathers received increasing attention, and a special and mandatory father's quota for parental leave was introduced in 1993. Today more than 70 percent of Norwegian fathers take this leave of now fifteen weeks (on the condition that the mother returns to paid work), and it is very likely that this early bonding between father and child benefits their future relationship. These policies have changed Norwegian family life in profound ways and, thus, also the lives of children. Being exposed to less gender division in work and care in their families may have reduced the prominence of the gender boundary in their life experiences, and men's presence in the care of babies and toddlers may have had an impact, particularly on boys' identity development. Intimacy, feelings, and care will no longer be so clearly connected to women and the symbolic feminine, but will also become a part of what it means to be a man. Similarly, ambitiousness and competitive behavior have become part of what it means to be a woman. Thus, care and work have moved in the direction of social and symbolic degendering. Despite there remaining clear differences in the average behavior patterns of women and men, or girls and boys, the gendered worlds are becoming less distinctively different. Gender as a boundary, but not necessarily as a category, may therefore be waning.

But what of the return of pronounced gendered meanings in fifth grade, accompanied by burgeoning love and sexuality? These developments may, in fact, also mirror Nordic gender policies targeting the areas of politics, education, work and care, sexual violence, and sexual rights (Nielsen and Rudberg 2007; Oinas 2001; Skilbrei 2020; Widerberg 1995). Meanwhile, love, desire, gendered imaginaries, and consumption have been elephants in the enlightened Nordic room. More could be done to encourage conversations on these topics. In the same period when men's and women's lives have become more equal in areas of work and care, we have also seen an increasing sexualization of the public sphere, and a market-driven exaggeration of gender difference related to appearances, consumption, and lifestyles. The same children who engage in more and more gender crossing are also exposed to an increasingly stereotyped market of the "pink or blue" in clothing and toys. Global social media, often imported from the United States or China, and with a very different take on gender difference, lands out of context among the little Nordic lynxes. Thus, one might say that Nordic children are brought up on the belief that gender is not important, but with little awareness of how gendered expectations and gender imaginaries permeate their own consumption—and, later on, of what gender equality could mean in relation to bodies, appearances, love, and sex. The greater gender polarization in eighth and ninth grade, and the increasing stress reported by women striving to be successful young professionals while feeling obliged to perfect a feminine and sexy appearance, may be some of the outcomes (Eriksen, Sletten, Bakken, and von Soest 2017; McRobbie 2009; Nielsen 2020).

Nordic Gender Play

The Norwegian case suggests that age-related borderwork and gender play may exist in tension with experiences of gender equality as practice and norm. According to Barth (1969), a boundary, depending on its social and psychological function, may persist despite the groups on either side becoming more alike. However, the mismatch between the boundary and the experiences may also trigger reflections on gender stereotypes. In the following three examples we see how age-related gender play, under given circumstances, can move towards gender reflection.

The first is taken from Rasmus Kleppe's kindergarten study (2014), in which girls and boys played lynxes singing lullabies for their babies at night. The children are playing "Raise-your-hand," a game that the teachers (both in the 2008 study and the 1967 study!) tend to dislike for the unruly excitement it provokes. While seated at the lunch table, for instance, one child starts asking the other children questions in the format "Everyone who likes [whatever], raise your hand!" The game is

often used for the purposes of borderwork, and in the 1967 study it provoked not only laughter but also an angry and competitive atmosphere
between girls and boys. In 2008 the same game did not become aggressive, and could even be used to poke fun at stereotypical borderwork. In
one such episode, a four-year-old girl first alternates between presenting typical boys' things and typical girls' things—like pink, blue, Spiderman, dresses—and the other children raise their hands accordingly.
Some girls also raise their hand to some of the "boy things," whereas the
boys moan when "girl things" are mentioned. But the lead girl has a trick
up her sleeve: "Everyone who likes *Spiderman dress*, raise your hand!"
obviously thrilled by the confusion it creates among the boys. Kleppe
concludes that the relaxed relation to the gender boundary among
these children also makes it possible to test out the border in playful,
transgressive, and humorous ways, something that may contribute to
increased awareness of gender stereotypes. We recognize here the emotional excitement of relating to the boundary that Barrie described so
aptly, but here the outcome differs.

The same mixture of fun and reflexivity is seen in the next example,
taken from the 1992 study in Norway. Here, again, the gender separation of childhood has to be negotiated with the children's actual experiences of gender. This became quite clear one day in third grade when the
teacher taught a lesson on gender roles. She first encouraged the pupils
to write down individually how they would describe girls and boys, and
then tell the class:

OBSERVATION (3rd grade, 1994): Nora speaks first: "Boys are violent,
crazy, afraid of showing anything." Emily protests: "My little brother is
not like that!" Nora modifies: "Well, it might not apply to everyone." The
teacher writes Nora's suggestions on the blackboard. Astrid trumps this
remark, saying, "Boys are stupid, goofy, weird, nutty and silly." Halvor
and Alek look a bit perplexed. Halvor adds, with a little smile on his face,
"Boys are cool, nice, and kind." "Some boys or all boys?" some of the girls
ask. "All boys," he says, still smiling. "Do you agree?" the teacher asks.
"NO!" the girls yell. Kaja does NOT think that all boys are cool, nice, and
kind! Nora: "Only the little ones." Lisa: "Girls are nice, but some girls are
stupid." Emily: "Right, many girls are stupid!" Alek thinks boys are tough,
cool, and nice.

The task given by the teacher elicits stereotypes that ignite the otherwise sporadic borderwork among the children. However, this gender play of childhood is not well attuned to their experience of gender. The children are split between the fun of borderwork and their actual knowledge of gender, and this split seems to lead to reflections on the variation in gendered behavior.

The last example details the tension that arises in the "extreme-gender" period, characterized by traditional secondary school tropes: the boys' sexual gaze towards girls' bodies, and the girls' contradictory demands of the boys. However, these traditional gender games still have to be negotiated in relation to the girls' academic lead, their higher degree of feminist awareness, and the boys' own inclination towards egalitarian ideals. Astrid belongs to the girls in class who play on the seductive "babe look." She often takes pleasure in the hetero games and is also good at fighting. She is among the best students in class, and displays feminist attitudes both in class and in this interview in eighth grade:

> INTERVIEW (8th grade, 1998): I know I have also talked a lot of bullshit, but you just get it back twice as hard. So then it becomes a bit hopeless. I don't always feel that I can be me, and say exactly what I want, because I'm afraid that they will throw in a cheeky comment, but . . . most of the boys in our class have not yet really understood what discrimination of women is all about. They don't care.

Based on my observations of Astrid's classroom behavior, she appears here to exaggerate the extent of her victimization. However, her words expose the tension she feels between the exaggerated, sexualized, and sometimes exciting gender play of adolescence, and her ideals of gender equality. One might also say that the argument of "understanding discrimination of women" takes the borderwork to a meta-level. According to my observations and not least in the interviews, the boys also voiced their support for gender equality. For instance, when imagining their future lives as adults, and also when they took it as a matter of fact that the girls often performed better than they in school.

In all three examples, we may see how variation in space and time results in specific culturally and historically conditioned tensions in relation to the gender play and borderwork of specific ages. Such tensions may be difficult and confusing to live with, especially in adolescence. However, they may also represent a push towards change.

Situating Gender Separation and Borderwork in Time and Space

What I have tried to demonstrate so far through the Norwegian studies is that changing family patterns lead to changing childhoods, and thereby changing gender identities, gendered subjectivities, and gender cultures, in new generations of children.[8] These connections between social structures and gender identities/subjectivities and cultures are what the concept of *gender socialization* means to convey: children also *become* gendered during the process of growing up, and this in turn affects how they do, and create, gender with their peers. The relation between "being" and "doing" gender has been a recurrent theme for Barrie and me in our long academic and personal friendship. I agreed that children's group practices are a necessary, albeit insufficient, way to understand how they do gender, and Barrie accepted the perspective of identity formation as relevant, but also found that, as a sociologist, she could not focus mainly on this. In our coauthored article from 2014 we knitted these perspectives together:

> The gendered identities and behaviors that girls and boys bring with them into new settings will have an impact on how they participate in these situations. But their contributions will also be met and evaluated, implicitly or explicitly, by others, and thus never left unchanged. Studies of "being" gendered and "doing" gender could thus be seen as functionally related, revealing different aspects of social processes involved in constructing gendered identity. Studies of individuals cannot give any full account of the collective process of doing gender since something new is accomplished/created in this process. But the reverse is also true: the analysis of collective praxis does not tell us anything about the different motives of the individuals who engage in processes of meaning making, what positions they choose or get pushed into assuming, and what consequences this has for their sense of self over time. (Nielsen and Thorne 2014:111)

The comparison of how school children "do gender" over time and space may add, to the above, that gender cultures, gender identities, and gendered subjectivities are not static; they are, in fact, important vehicles of variation and social change. Furthermore, they are to be understood not only as accidental individual traits but also as social patterns of subjectivity, identity, and practice that shift with passing generations (Nielsen 2017). These patterns tell us something about the historical and subjective position from which the children engage in the typical gender play of their age. Where the concepts of gender play and borderwork give us access to situational processes and how they change with age, the perspective of gender socialization focuses on longer processes of transformation that exceed this immediate context. What we have here are two different aspects of temporality and change, and instead of choosing between them, we should ask how they interact. In Barth's later writing we find a similar point: "We need to distinguish between the cognitive premises that construct the boundary . . . and the sociology of people living and acting around that boundary and thereby shaping an outcome. Those contingencies produce the effects from which people in turn reconceptualize boundaries . . . that derive from what actually happens along that particular boundary as a result of the connections that people spin by their actions and by the consequences of those actions" (Barth 2000:30–31).

What Barth says here, as I read it, is that the "cultural stuff" on either side of the boundary can change, and this may sometimes affect how the boundaries are constructed and acted upon. When children's experience with gender in their society changes, the need for borderwork, or the danger of gender crossing, may also change. And when a gender boundary is waning, this may further encourage gender identities and gender cultures to loosen. If this relation to historical structures and subjectivities is separated out from the analysis, the concepts of borderwork and gender play risk becoming static themselves, reducing the growing child to the image of a universal negotiating agent (Halldén 2007). Children *do* interpret and construct, and they do negotiate and act; but where did they come from, and where do they go? How do their historically and biographically shaped motivations interfere with the ways they take part in social construction processes with their peers, and what consequences do such constructions have for their further development?

An intriguing aspect of Barrie's concepts of gender play and borderwork is that she does not only see them as cognitive processes of boundary maintenance. She also sees how they are "marked by conflict, intense emotions, and the expression of forbidden desires" (1993:85). Whereas feelings of excitement probably are universal, that which are experienced *as* conflicts, intense emotions, or forbidden desires are not only age related but historical. Some aspects of the borderwork, and some dimensions of the gender identities and the persistence of gender as a categorical distinction, appear to be less open for change, however. There seems to be a developmental drive towards gender separation and gender play in children at certain ages, but the way these are acted out depends on the social and psychological meaning of gender at a given time and in a given space. Thus, gender play appears to be related in complex ways to different motivational formations, which gradually emerge and change historically; to different rates of maturity; and to the always ongoing constructions of meaning in the peer group.

NOTES

1 See also, in this volume, Smette and Eriksen's chapter and the concluding sections of Best's and Connell's respective chapters, which in different ways invite a more historically embedded analysis of the relationship between agency and structure.

2 The children attended a public school. In 1992, 98.2 percent of seven- to fifteen-year-old children attended the public school system (Statistics of Norway, https:/www.ssb.no). The social profiles of public schools differ according to their locations. The particular school in my study had a majority of urban, middle-class students.

3 The history of immigration in Norway is very different from that of the United States. As late as 1970, only 1.5 percent of the population consisted of immigrants and their children, most of them from other European countries. The figure had risen to around 4 percent when this class started school. This specific demographic history explains why there were few immigrants or nonwhite students in Norwegian schools when I started my longitudinal study. Furthermore, the immigrant students were not equally dispersed in different school areas, and my school was located in a district with relatively few. However, from the early 1990s, there was a marked increase in immigration (mainly refugees from war zones or people reuniting with their families), and in 2016 the number of immigrants and their children had risen to 16.3 percent, half of them from other European countries (Statistics of Norway, https:/www.ssb.no).

4 I am focusing on separation and borderwork in relation to gender in this chapter and will not consider the intersection with ethnicity. Generally, minority and majority students related in the same way to gender separation and borderwork; however, among the girls there was also a discreet, but notable, exclusion of the

two minority girls all the way through school. This was the case neither among the boys nor among the girls when it came to minority girls who joined the class later. The inclusion of these new minority girls may have had to do with their middle-class background and that they were permitted by their parents to dress and behave like the Norwegian children and take part in extracurricular activities, unlike the other two girls. Other Nordic studies from this period have also found similarity to be more important for girls' friendships than for boys', but it varies what dimension of similarity that is decisive (see, for instance, Gordon, Holland, and Lahelma 2000; Rysst 2008).

5 This does, of course, not imply that all the students identified as heterosexual. However, other sexualities were not made visible in class; thus to be heterosexual was an unquestioned norm. I do not have information about the sexual orientation of the students, neither at this point in time nor later. (I was in contact with them the last time when they were twenty-three years old, in 2008.).

6 In the following I will refer to the first longitudinal study as the 1992 study and the second as the 2016 study, after the year the students started in first grade.

7 This ethnic and racial mix, in combination with the fact that most of the students spoke Norwegian fluently, had attended Norwegian kindergarten, and more or less wore the same style of children's clothes and accessories, meant that ethnic and racial borders had less significance than in the 1992 study and rarely were made objects of comment or behavioral boundary marking. However, I did observe that some of the minority girls—even when coming from very different cultures—tended to seek each other's company during the recesses. For the boys, ethnic and racial belonging or race did not seem to play any role in their interaction, often organized around football.

8 "Gendered subjectivities" refers here to the ways a person's general motivational structure is influenced by gendered experiences, whereas "gender identities" refers to the more conscious identification with specific gender norms and gender cultures (see Nielsen [1996, 2017] for a more thorough discussion of this distinction).

REFERENCES

Barth, Fredrik. 1969. "Introduction." Pp. 9–38 in *Ethnic Groups and Boundaries. The Social Organization of Difference*, edited by F. Barth. Oslo: Universitetsforlaget.

———. 2000. "Boundaries and Connections." Pp. 17–33 in *Signifying Identities: Anthropological Perspectives on Boundaries and Contested Values*, edited by A. P. Cohen. London: Routledge.

Berentzen, Sigurd. 1980. *Kjønnskontrasten i barns lek* [The Gender Contrast in Children's Play]. Skriftserie nr. 3, Sosialantropologisk Institut, Universitetet i Bergen.

Eriksen, Ingunn Marie, and Selma Therese Lyng. 2017. "Relational Aggression among Boys: Blind Spots and Hidden Traumas." *Gender and Education* 30(3):396–409.

Eriksen, Ingunn M., Mira A. Sletten, Anders Bakken, and Tilmann von Soest. 2017. *Stress og press blant unge* [Stress and Pressure among Young People]. Oslo: NOVA.

Fraser, Nancy. 1997. *Justice Interruptus: Critical Reflections on the "Postsocialist" Condition*. New York: Routledge.

Frosh, Stephen, Ann Phoenix, and Rob Pattman. 2002. *Young Masculinities: Understanding Boys in Contemporary Society*. Basingstoke: Palgrave.

Godø, Helene T. 2014. "Skolemotstand: Betydninger av kjønn og relasjoner på ungdomstrinnet" [Resistance in School: The Meaning of Gender and Relations in Lower Secondary School]. Pp. 118–35 in *Forskjeller i klassen*, edited by H. B. Nielsen. Oslo: Universitetsforlaget.

Gordon, Tuula, Jane Holland, and Elena Lahelma. 2000. *Making Spaces: Citizenship and Difference in Schools*. London: Macmillan.

Halldén, Gunilla, ed. 2007. *Den moderna barndommen* [The Modern Childhood]. Stockholm: Carlssons.

Kleppe, Rasmus. 2014. "'Spidermankjole!': Fra kjønnskontrast i barns lek til kjønnskontrast i barns klær" ["Spiderman Dress!": From Gender Contrast in Children's Play to Gender Contrast in Children's Clothes]. Pp. 54–75 in *Forskjeller i klassen*, edited by H. B. Nielsen. Oslo: Universitetsforlaget.

Maccoby, Eleanor E. 1998. *The Two Sexes: Growing Up Apart, Coming Together*. Cambridge, MA: Harvard University Press.

McRobbie, Angela. 2009. *The Aftermath of Feminism: Gender, Culture, and Social Change*. London: Sage.

Nielsen, Harriet Bjerrum. 1994. "Boys and Girls from Grade One to Grade Nine." Pp. 29–41 in *Social Construction of Gender in Children's Worlds*. Arbeidsnotat 3. Oslo: Senter for Kvinneforskning.

———. 1996. "The Magic Writing-Pad: On Gender and Identity Work." *Young: Nordic Journal of Youth Research* 4(3):2–18.

———. 2009. *Skoletid. Jenter og gutter fra 1. til 10. klasse* [School Time: Girls and Boys from 1st to 10th grade]. Oslo: Universitetsforlaget.

———. 2017. *Feeling Gender. A Generational and Psychosocial Approach*. London: Palgrave Macmillan.

———. 2020. "Bodies and Boundaries in Three Generations." Pp. 53–77 in *Aging: The Body and the Gender Regime*, edited by S. Pickard and J. Robinson. London: Routledge.

Nielsen, Harriet Bjerrum, and Monica Rudberg. 2007. "Fun in Gender: Youth and Sexuality, Class, and Generation." *NORA: Nordic Journal of Women's Studies* 15(2–3):100–113.

Nielsen, Harriet Bjerrum, and Barrie Thorne. 2014. "Children, Gender, and Issues of Well-Being." Pp. 105–30 in *Handbook of Child Wellbeing*, edited by A. Ben-Arieh, C. Ferran, I. Frønes, and J. I. Korbin. Heidelberg, Germany: Springer.

Öhrn, Elisabet, and Ann-Sofie Holm, eds. 2014. *Att lyckas i skolan. Om skolprestationer och kön i olika undervisningspraktiker* [Succeeding in School: School Achievement and Gender in Different Teaching Practices]. Göteborg: Göteborgs universitet.

Oinas, Elina. 2001. *Making Sense of the Teenage Body*. PhD thesis. Åbo: Åbo Akademi University Press.

Overå, Stian. 2014. "Nye gutter? Maskulinitet og sosial klasse på barnetrinnet" [New Boys? Masculinity and Social Class in Elementary School]. Pp. 94–117 in *Forskjeller i klassen*, edited by H. B. Nielsen. Oslo: Universitetsforlaget.

Rysst, Mari. 2008. "'I Want to Be Me. I Want to Be Cool': An Anthropological Study of Norwegian Preteen Girls in the Light of a Presumed 'Disappearance' of Childhood." PhD thesis. Department of Social Anthropology, University of Oslo.

Skilbrei, May-Len. 2020. "Criminological Lessons on/from Sexual Violence." Pp. 357–71 in *The Emerald Handbook of Feminism, Criminology, and Social Change*, edited by S. Walklate, K. Fitz-Gibbon, J. Maher, and J. McCulloch. Bingley, UK: Emerald.

Thorne, Barrie. 1993. *Gender Play: Girls and Boys in School*. Buckingham, UK: Open University Press.

Whiting, Beatrice B., and Carolyn P. Edwards. 1988. *Children of Different Worlds: The Formation of Social Behavior*. Cambridge, MA: Harvard University Press.

Widerberg, Karin. 1995. *Kunnskapens kjønn: minner, refleksjoner, teori* [The Gender of Knowledge: Memories, Reflections, Theory]. Oslo: Pax.

13

Changing Youth Worlds

On Prom, Cars, and Other Things

AMY L. BEST

Barrie Thorne's imprint on youth scholarship is indelible. Her attention to children's group life and the lattice of social relations that construct children's social world pressed for a fundamental reconceptualization of socialization as the prevailing explanatory framework for thinking about children's relation to society and its utility for the discipline. *Gender Play* highlighted peer socialization as gender socialization and in doing so disrupted the notion that adults are children's only teachers. Thorne exposed the adult bias pervading academic work, and made a convincing case that this bias left us with little understanding of how youth actively shape their own worlds and, by extension, ours. Most attention to children narrowly conceived of them in terms of their "adult futures" and eventual adult status. Thorne offered a cautionary note about what came to be called an "adult ideological standpoint," calling upon sociologists and other youth and childhood studies scholars to critically reflect on the limits of their own adult logics and the singular focus on children as learners. Her work helped to capture and amplify the agentic dimensions of youth worlds and offered reasoned challenge to developmental approaches that had defined the experience of childhood through a prism of biological determinism that pervaded much of the literature on youth and childhoods at the time of the publication of *Gender Play*. "Children's interactions are not preparation for life; they are life itself," Thorne declared in the opening pages to *Gender Play* (1993:3). For a graduate student like me, this declaration was revelatory.

This attention to children outside a framework of socialization provided a loose outline for conceptualizing the worlds from which particular actions spring by excavating the social relations that organize young people's everyday world as they move in and around it. Operating outside an interpretive schema that narrowly defined children as "adults in the making" who are "acted upon more than acting," Thorne pushed for consideration of the entanglement of age and gender and rendered visible the complex array of gender doings in children's world. She did so without reproducing "the big man bias" in gender research that took gender conformity expressed by those residing at the center as a reflection of the whole.

In centering children's group life and its symbolic constructions, and by bringing "children from margin to center" (1993:4), *Gender Play* opened up inquiry to consider formerly excluded topics, once cast as too trifling and decidedly unserious to warrant scholarly consideration. And in this way, Thorne helped to pave a new path for young researchers. I was a relatively new graduate student the first time I read Barrie Thorne's *Gender Play*. Inspired by the groundwork laid by Thorne, my own work has sought to detail the constraining effect of an adult ideological standpoint, deconstruct and denaturalize categories of adolescence and childhood, counter the implicit bias of biological determinism as a dominant explanatory framework for understanding youth behavior, and identify the sociohistorical processes by which age categories are inhabited. In the three ethnographic monographs I have published in the twenty-plus years since I was a graduate student, I have sought to push against naturalized and totalizing frameworks of "the adolescent" by centering youth themselves and the tangled worlds they construct, taking the very things of relevance in their lives, even if unimportant in adult worlds, as my starting point. In what follows, I detail Thorne's influence in these ethnographic projects. To many youth scholars, Thorne's ethnographic and interpretive sensibilities offered new possibilities for seeing and sorting children's actions and interactions. The second half of this chapter considers the enduring value of the conceptual tools Thorne's *Gender Play* gave us, as it attends to a transforming context where children and youths' worlds-making happens. I argue that the conceptual tools Thorne's *Gender Play* imparted remain as critical and relevant as ever, but the warrant for them has changed. This is the case because the landscape where children and youth organize themselves has also changed.

The Collective Life of Youth

The notion that youth actively construct social worlds led me to the high school prom for my dissertation, a topic that by the mid-1990s had curiously received only passing mention by youth, educational, and gender scholars. The project began, but only after some wrangling to persuade my dissertation advisor that (1) the high school prom did merit scholarly attention; (2) its omission from the scholarly record had been a disservice to our understanding of youths' engagement in school and American cultural life, as well as our analysis of gender and the role of schools in reproducing gender identities and gender inequalities; and (3) a dissertation focused on the prom would not foreclose a tenure-track job. To her credit, my advisor threw her full support behind a dissertation focused on the prom, and the dissertation ultimately became a book, *Prom Night: Youth, Schools, and Popular Culture*, published in 2000. In it, I investigated how the high school prom, an event paradoxically cast as both trivial and lasting, operates as a site where youth negotiate the process of schooling, solidify their social identities, and struggle against the structural limits that bear down on them, which included, in my view, prevailing and parochial ideas about the adolescent. Channeling Thorne, in the book's introduction, I wrote, "The rendering of youth perched at the threshold of adulthood (favored not only in popular thought but in scholarly literature) provides limited understanding for how kids experience school life today. Not only does this rhetoric of becoming have little relevance to how kids define the experience of being young, it deflects by glossing over the contested and contradictory practices through which life inside and outside school is made meaningful" (2000:2).

Prom Night was concerned with the self-organization of youth in and around school and was guided by four core concerns: (1) What do proms tell us about school today? (2) How do proms relate to youth cultures and identities? (3) How have consumer markets and culture elevated the prom as an event? (4) Why are proms so steeped in gender and heteronormative rituals and what are the consequences for youths' feminine and masculine identity projects? For a long time, proms have been an important focal point for high school students. I was interested to understand why the prom had come to assume such cultural significance, specifying historical periods and social and institutional structures but centering young people, and like Thorne, as they existed in collective life.

Then and now, I conceived of schools as spaces of contention, organized around contradictory cultural pulls that reproduce elements of social power, and at the same time inspire challenge to that very order. This is well in line with Pierre Bourdieu's formulation of fields. The prom, itself a field of struggle, exists at the nexus of two fields where power and its counter are deeply entangled: school and consumer markets. I sought to map how schools maintain forms of social domination by gaining students' willingness to "play by the rules" yet also inspire students' challenge. Proms provide a perfect occasion to examine these tensions. Proms are steeped in heteronormative romantic convention. Cast as belonging to the domain of girls, the prom compels a sort of deep investment in all things feminine, including dress, make-up, hair. Work on the body for the prom is part of the prom's appeal, and self-transformation is its promise. "The prom is your night to shine," as the saying goes. Most of the girls I hung around embraced this fully and for varied, and often unexpected, reasons. On prom night, a girl can dress in a revealing outfit and escape being labeled a "slut" because the sexual norms that rein girls in in school are temporarily suspended at the prom. This possibility of gender identity play explains the event's continued popularity and appeal for girls. Of course, this pulls them into the consumer market fold and sometimes forces them to navigate the tricky waters of sexuality.

Yet, just as kids are engulfed by imperatives to consume a litany of prom essentials, they also transform these essentials (tuxedos, limos, dresses, music, and corsages) into something else. Kids work hard to locate the prom outside an adult-controlled lexicon of school and middle-class adult culture, and instead to position it as an event squarely lodged in a youth world. Some kids playfully mock the idea of the prom as a "sophisticated" occasion for pre-adulting. The clever assemblages of clothes and objects were resources kids seized to express their individuality in a scene that is seen as annoyingly mainstream. These kids went to the prom, but did not get swept up in its trappings, enabling them to navigate the prom's bizarre place as both celebrated and totally dumb. This tension narrows teen's range of choices: to embrace this highly normative adolescent rite, reject it outright, or disrupt the way culture defines adolescence as inferior.

Lots of kids played with these conflicting definitions of being an adult and not being an adult, of the prom as important but stupid, by importing objects that contradicted the faux sophistication adults layered on the prom. Students used irony and creative play to cast the prom as a youth event, responding to the oppressive weight of "youth playing at adults," an adult view of the prom that is hard to shake. One girl at one prom gave her date a boutonniere made of two bright red radishes, instead of the expected carnation or rose. At another prom, a teenage boy wearing a tuxedo blew large bubbles while chewing his bubble gum as he checked into the prom. At one school whose proms I observed, kids in the beginning of the evening carried around backpacks over both shoulders, over tuxes and bedazzled dresses. At yet another prom, I spotted four girls who wore brightly colored athletic socks beneath their dresses. Youth use these strategies of dress because few other resources are available to them to disrupt the idea that youth are image conscious and insecure about how they are perceived by their peers. These often creative, sometimes funny, small actions that I came to see as fragments of play shifted social meanings around, which loosened adults' hold on things. In attending proms and interviewing high school students about proms, I came to see in these moments of play the grip of social constraints give way to small ruptures of possibility.

The tools Thorne offered to think through the shifting ground where social meanings take hold have provided useful direction to think more fully about the constellation of actions that create the life of groups. For Thorne, the focus on actions and play helped shift adult attention from "unfolding of individuals" to "group life" and "social relations" (1993:4). In this formulation, individual actions are anchored in a set of social relations that carry collective consequence. An important feature of group life that Thorne provided a vivid sketch of in *Gender Play* was the underground economy of food and objects. Understanding these as "materials for an oppositional underlife" often found in "total institutions" and building upon Goffman's recognition that an underlife is part of every institution and not adjacent to it, Thorne offered insight into how children actively reconstruct gender worlds through play. For Thorne, underground objects revealed the lattice of group life. Artifacts smuggled from home and stowed away in desks, or a piece of gum furtively passed between two slightly soiled little hands on the blacktop during a heated game of four-square, expressed patterns of social engagement. Thorne captured the significance of material objects and their symbolic weight for decoding a whole complex of social relations by which young people include and exclude others, sort each other through gender's lens, and reinscribe gender hierarchies.

Thorne's work also hints at the ways kids craft an oppositional register of meaning that eludes adults, talks back to adult authority, and establishes an alternate system of cultural authority. Many youth researchers have seized on this point. dana boyd's (2014) notion of "hiding in plain sight" captures how youth engage in meaning making that evades adult understanding in the highly public online worlds of Facebook, a space that had once been a relatively autonomous youth space. "Hiding in plain sight" speaks to the fact that a dynamic world of meaning can unfold, and can be the basis of group belonging, and can also remain entirely unintelligible to adults. This idea also animated my interests in all three ethnographic projects I have undertaken as a sociologist. My most recent book, *Fast-Food Kids: French Fries, Lunch Lines, and Social Ties* (2017), examines youth's engagement with fast food in school and the commercial realm. Like Thorne, I treated food consumption and food sharing as small actions that are part of the scaffold of group life shared among youth and animated through play. Thorne's attention to play as "little oases of imagination in dryly routinized scenes" provided a lens through which to see "growing up as a process of reining in bodily and imaginative possibilities" (1993:15–16). Thorne offers a framework of play, what it is and what it does, to think with.

In *Fast-Food Kids*, I detail the varied ways youth used play to craft cultural scenes bearing a distinctly youth imprint and, in doing so, transformed *fast food* in commercial settings like McDonald's into *slow food*. Engagement with fast-food settings served to collectively anchor youth identity and solidify social boundaries. French fries and Big Macs emerged as objects of exchange, often bearing distinct gender traces. Commercial foods like McDonald's fries, which are easily shared and also easily pilfered, become in these contexts social resources for "borderwork," a term Thorne developed to capture the elaborate and loaded interactions through which gender boundaries are built, traversed, broken down, and rebuilt.

Just as food is seized for different youth-cultural ends in fast-food settings, that can also be observed with school food. Food play, what I mostly regarded as food antics in the school cafeteria, was seized to pass the time and provide comment on school itself, especially its most routine features. From observations in the school cafeteria and interviews with kids about school food, I learned that food play is also a means to express ambivalence toward *public* school. The objects seized for food play and food antics were almost always school-based food, only rarely lunch brought from home, and never food imported from commercial outposts like Panera, McDonald's, or Chipotle. I came to understand that this is the case because school food, unlike coveted commercial foods, holds little, if any, sacred value—and certainly not in the way homemade food eaten with family does. School food is institutional, is mass produced for public consumption, holds no status-conferring power, and is stripped of its emotional value for the students who consume it. Little care is afforded to school food. It is tossed around, thrown in the trash, eaten without comment, which helps to explain why school food can become an object of play, which was especially common for youth at the public high school in the upper-middle-class community I studied and much less common at the high school where 60 percent of the students were free and reduced lunch eligible.

In the more privileged school, I watched as boys stacked empty milk containers and attempted to build models from contorted plastic forks. I watched kids mix foods together: pretzels and apple sauce, for instance. Kids playfully pretend to shove food into each other's mouths and pretend to throw small milk cartons, apples, and other food items at each other. The antics were minor affairs, small pranks. I came to see this type of food play as a limited liability action for these youth. They can express indifference to school lunch without running the risk of any real trouble that might undermine their future mobility, and at the same time render visible the boredom that characterizes much of school.[1] Yet, in the school where 60 percent of the kids were free and reduced lunch eligible, school food almost never transformed into play and was rarely discarded, even when other forms of play did emerge. For these kids, school food was an object to be eaten, not batted around. In this sense, school food and its meaning materialize in the context of inequities that exist beyond the cafeteria doors.

Understanding kids' relationship to food in school also means understanding their relationship to school. In contrast to school food, commercial food is prized and usually seized as an object for sharing and gifting, much like the small objects in Thorne's underground economy. Commercial foods were not gifted to just anyone. They were shared with close friends and usually status equals. Girls were usually the ones to offer the gift of food. I watched girls bring cupcakes, bags of candy, popcorn, and chips, all brought with the intent to be shared. At one lunch, I observed a table of girls host a mini–birthday party, replete with a giant Mrs. Fields chocolate chip cookie trimmed with red icing. Plenty of research has demonstrated how deeply invested girls are in relationships and the sense of self they derive from the bonds of friendships formed through the sharing of food, clothes, and make-up. That I saw these everyday actions as a type of play can be traced to Thorne's *Gender Play*. For Thorne, play is "grounded in possibility."

In her attention to various and open-ended features of group life that materialize in play, Thorne was able to detail social meaning communicated in social action, and document the role of social action in reproducing enduring social arrangements, in particular gender as a social structure. This is an important point since sociologists have often thought that social arrangements derive from broader social structures. The tools of interpretive sociologists like Thorne help identify patterned arrangements, bound by social logics, constructed by symbolic exchanges and small behaviors that comprise the up-close scenes of everyday life from which social life is built. In the case of Thorne's playground, gendered logics prevailed, organizing and structuring how boys and girls inhabited space. Thorne's notion of borderwork drew our attention to the unequal arrangements in the division of space: boys claimed the large, expansive field spaces that represented the largest parcel of playground real estate. Girls fashioned themselves along the perimeter, close to school, the seat of institutional power and hemmed in by it.

Children participate in their own socialization, Thorne reminds us. This most basic observation opened the door to consider how youth and children create worlds through what Erving Goffman famously called "small behaviors" that solidify specific social realities. Thorne detailed how power shows up in small group exchanges and is reinscribed in and through small acts. *Structure passes through them but is also built by them*. For Thorne, these small behaviors were windows through which to explore broader patterns of group encounters as they organize and are organized by institutional context. In a 2009 piece, some years after *Gender Play* was first published, Thorne wrote, "Childhood is constituted as both a set of institutional arrangements and a powerful and emotionally charged set of ideas" (2009:20), suggesting a push and pull of constraint in historical terms, with impact on the collective life of young people. For Thorne, childhoods were lived in school, family, and neighborhood. Thorne's work amplified the important role of context in shaping meaning: "An emphasis on social context shifts analysis from fixing abstract and binary differences to examining the social relations in which multiple differences are constructed and given meanings," she wrote (1993:109). In this formulation, "ultimate outcomes are uncertain and often amazingly various. Children, like adults, live in present, concretely historical and open-ended time" (1993:3). This set of insights probes us to see children as acting upon history and being shaped by it.

Eroding Autonomy and Changing Youth Worlds

Much has changed in the structure of youth and children's group life in the twenty-five-plus years since *Gender Play* first appeared in print. In what remains of this chapter, I sketch some of the new coordinates shaping youth worlds and the social organization of children's lives that have generated an emerging tension between this notion of youth as "acting" and "being acted upon" referenced at the chapter's beginning. In a global context of growing anxiety about the precarity of an unknown future, one could argue that elements of children's relative autonomy that *Gender Play* captured so effectively have eroded. Childhood has been recast.

It has long been true that children of the upper-middle class remain the set point against which childhood is more generally framed. Today, these children spend a greater portion of day-to-day life in adult worlds and adult-organized settings engaged in the work of "becoming." The relative autonomy of childhood for these children, outside the world of new media, has shrunk, and the pressure to align children's activity with adult futures has grown. This has also left behind a large swath of children whose autonomy is instead limited by the heavy structures of race and class sorting systems that result in vastly unequal childhoods. These changes raise questions about how we study youth worlds as historically bounded entities and suggest that traces of earlier frameworks that focus on children's adult futures may have utility for understanding contemporary children's lives, not in ahistorical terms, as had once been the case, but in historically bracketed terms.

Given a changing set of experiences of "being" and "becoming," I want to sit with the notion of "adult futures" here, a concept Thorne sought to shelve in an effort to amplify and understand the agentic and collective dimensions of childhood. Arguably in this historical moment, a preoccupation with "adult futures" has come to play an *outsized role* in children's lives, narrowing the spaces across which they once traversed, and reining them in physically, socially, and even mentally. An idle child without purpose or direction is seen today as headed for trouble, hence the impulse to overschedule children's waking hours among upper-income parents especially, given their resources. Worry among adults about children's untended time and an endless focus on cultivating the child has meant an increase of parental and institutional mechanisms tracking children's time use (see Lareau 2003; Calarco 2018), their engagements with places and spaces and interactions. It has also meant that activities are narrowly evaluated in terms of their return on learning and educational utility. This is deeply patterned by class resources and reproduces stark class inequalities.

Two broad trends, well documented by youth scholars, have profoundly eroded children's autonomy: intensive parenting and increases in surveillance across various settings occupied by youth, as Dinsmore and Pugh (2021) persuasively suggest in their recent article. This means that the worlds kids collectively construct, that Thorne so carefully detailed, has grown smaller, more fragmented and fleeting. Dinsmore and Pugh identify contradictory aspects of what they term "cultivated" and "criminalized" childhoods and their differential consequences for children's autonomy and mental health, as well as possible adult outcomes. They advance the argument that young people have become increasingly and "intensely surveilled over the last 30 years" as a result of "the intensification of parenting, the rise of scrutiny in schools, the spread of surveillance technology, the restrictions upon children's use of public space, the privatization of risk, and the rise of fears about safety—trends

[that] have converged to limit children's autonomy and participation in public life" (2021:1).

This, they argue, produces what they term the "constrained well-being paradox." The question of whether the kids are alright has been batted around for some time among youth scholars, but only recently, with the uptick in youth suicide and the more significant reported increases in anxiety and depression among youth, has the question gained the urgency it has. On several measures of well-being, kids are better off than they were thirty years ago. Public health data have consistently shown that youth are less likely to smoke, drink, or do drugs and are more likely to have completed school, Dinsmore and Pugh report. But with the pretty dramatic increase in reported anxiety and depression, the rise of school refusal suggests that kids' emotional and mental health is suffering. Certainly, college counseling centers, often overwhelmed, can testify to this.[2] For Dinsmore and Pugh, this is the paradox of well-being. Some of this appears to have direct links to the question of youth autonomy and the pace at which kids move through childhood, with consequences for how we study the scaffold of youth worlds.

Dinsmore and Pugh make the point that declines in autonomy and increases in surveillance, mostly relating to criminalization and student discipline, are largely responses to framings of modern childhood, which presume need for greater protections from the menace of the modern world. Changes in how schools operate, from lock-down drills to locked doors, contribute to a growing unease and anxiety for children in going to school, a place where they spend most of their day. Peer worlds increasingly function either online or in adult-organized settings.

What is the consequence for children's collectively experienced autonomy, by which I mean the extent to which children are able to construct what Gary Alan Fine termed in his 1987 ethnography of boys' Little League baseball "idioculture"? Idioculture delineates the linguistic and social coordinates of children's worlds through which autonomy is collectively created and shared, or what youth (as opposed to childhood) scholars once called "youth subculture." Arguably, today there is a more seamless transfer between adult culture and youth culture, suggesting a usurpation of *collective* autonomy of youth culture, especially given the sizable role commercial media (largely crafted by adults) play in shaping the perimeters and production of youth culture. Given this, I do wonder if the relatively autonomous youth culture(s) of yesterday, even for mainstream kids, was a release valve for youth for decades, against adult pressures to conform. Categorically, it is more difficult to find distinct and autonomous youth cultures whose very existence is in opposition to adults. Consider this in conjunction with the fact that research on family life has increasingly found that the storm and stress that defined the teen/parent couplet for the greater part of a century has given way to cooperation and collaboration (see Kurz 2002), another possible indication of eroding autonomy for youth and childhood. The dark and stormy conflicts between adult and child were certainly manifested by the relatively separate and semi-autonomous worlds the two once occupied. All this points to the shrinking autonomy of children and youth.

I attempted to grapple with some of these transformational developments in youth worlds in *Fast Cars, Cool Rides* (2006). In it, I explored how kids engage with an American car culture, creating meaning through and about cars, and examined what these meanings might reveal about the physical and symbolic boundaries organizing youths' social worlds. Cars are a ubiquitous feature of modern life, upon which we endlessly depend. Without them, we are often quite literally stuck in place. Cars also carry tremendous identity value, expressing who we are and who we aspire to be. I wanted to understand the place of cars as youth solidify their sense of self, participate in consumer culture, and pursue the elusive American dream. Through cars, young people lay claim to public space, struggle against structural limits, and attempt to resolve the dilemmas of a rapidly changing world where the once reliable constants of a stable life are increasingly uncertain. In *Fast Cars, Cool Rides* I argued,

> Today's youth live in a world "of changing relationships between public and private, between local and global, between structure and movement, between bodily experience and subjectivity, between self and other."[3] They live in a world organized by what sociologist Anthony Giddens has called a "post-traditional order" where time and space are radically altered and abstract systems increasingly mediate local life, transforming our most enduring relationship: the relationship of the self to society. . . . "The self is seen as a reflexive project for which the individual is responsible," argues Anthony Giddens.[4] "Identity moves from a 'given' into a

'task' . . . such that needing to *become* what one *is* is a feature of modern living," explains Zygmunt Bauman (Best 2006, 161–63).[5]

In this context youth are called upon to fashion their own identities—an imperative that intensifies their existential angst. Crafting a self is increasingly elaborate work as young adults are drawn into the folds of a culture of consumption. Yet, the sense of endless possibility to construct and reconstruct identity through things like cars also engenders a field of play. Like Thorne's school playground, where play prevails, the public streets where car cruising is concentrated become settings within which to try out and try on different identities. Young women test out different ways of being girls, rowdy and loud, hanging out of their cars. Young women who cruise relish the chance to try on different ways of doing gender, of performing different sexual selves, as they transgress the moral boundaries that exist elsewhere. Yet, young women must carefully manage these presentations of self. This hinges upon their ability to invert and invoke the cultural codes that define femininity and female sexuality. This is the case because the streets, just like playgrounds and proms, are gendered spaces, and are made meaningful through the interactions within them.

At the same time, kids' engagement with cars demonstrates some of the perils of venturing into public spaces. In a context of elevated panic over risk exposure, as youth move beyond the private space of home, they encounter repeated attempts to curtail and limit their movement and mobility in and between public spaces. This is especially pronounced for youth of color. Policies such as curfews, and other sorted surveillance strategies that restrict youths' engagement in public life and criminalize youth for engaging in commonplace activities adult engage in freely, also undermine children's relative autonomy, but with very different consequences for student of color than for white students. Students of color come up against tight controls in school, and punitive policing as they walk to school, or even play in parks, with consequences for the worlds they actively work to construct (Gonzalez 2016; Jones 2010; Ray 2018; Rios 2004). These racial patterns of autonomy are certainly not new. But as the field of autonomous action tightens for children overall, we must also contend with how racial inequities continue to be relevant, show up in unexpected ways, and differentially impact worlds-making by youth.

All of this suggests a rethinking of autonomy as a historically bounded reality and recognition of the shrinking space where youth exercise autonomy. At the same time, the tools Thorne offered played a critical role in building an analytical framework for children's actions to be understood in terms other than their relevance for who they would become. Those tools were central to delineating the new childhood studies and set in motion an entire rethinking of childhood as a social experience and a social construct, giving rise to countless ethnographic inquiries that enabled us to see and know children and youth in their full humanity, with greater complexity and sensitivity, as thinking and acting, little-worlds creating—even in the context of constraint—with empathetic understanding, and outside the categories that hem them in. In a context of increasing surveillance, these ways of seeing and knowing remain ever important, providing counter to the limiting worldview about youth and youth worlds that is so readily available and so widely circulated.

In this chapter, I have sought to trace the reach of Thorne's *Gender Play* across ethnographic cases, considering the utility of the conceptual tools she developed to document the small behaviors and interpret the social meanings out of which young people's collective life is forged and specific gender realities materialize. I have argued that *Gender Play* helps us to understand how social structure works through the social worlds young people create. Thorne made the point that youth carve out autonomous spaces in the face of constant encroachment. And as young people's autonomous worlds narrow, I want to suggest that the distinctly empathetic understanding that emerges from complex and up-close renderings of children and youth's world-making, wherein their humanity is on full display, takes on new importance. The conceptual tools Thorne's *Gender Play* offers, then, remain indispensable, not simply despite youth's shrinking autonomy but because of it.

NOTES

1 Amy Wilkins's (2008) excellent analysis of the Goth scene also identifies the theme of limited liability for upper-middle-class kids, who can broker in a type of marginalized cool without forfeiting later mobility that other forms of youth rebellion threaten.

2 Much has been written in recent years about the social organization of youth, with attention to the new realities they confront and the meaningful economic and

social changes responsible for these new realities. Mari Sanchez, Michèle Lamont, and Shira Zilberstein's (2022) recent inquiry provides further support of a changed landscape. They suggest that children born in the late 1990s and after, a generational group sometimes called Gen Z, confront compounded challenges in coming of age. Sanchez, Lamont, and Zilberstein point to destabilizing generational and period effects for Gen Z as they are forced to contend with an unprecedented period of crisis and uncertainty, punctuated by an imploding mental health crisis, eroding pathways for mobility, and declining fabric of social and institutional trust.

3 McDonald 1999:11.

4 Giddens 1991:75.

5 Bauman 2000:31.

REFERENCES

Bauman, Zygmunt. 2000. *Liquid Modernity*. Cambridge, UK: Polity Press.

Best, Amy. 2000. *Prom Night: Youth, Schools, and Popular Culture*. New York: Routledge.

———. 2006. *Fast Cars, Cool Rides: The Accelerating World of Youth and Their Cars*. New York: NYU Press.

———. 2017. *Fast-Food Kids: French Fries, Lunch Lines, and Social Ties*. New York: NYU Press.

boyd, danah. 2014. *It's Complicated: The Social Life of Networked Teens*. New Haven, CT: Yale University Press.

Calarco, Jessica. 2018. *Negotiating Opportunities: How the Middle Class Secures Advantages in School*. Oxford: Oxford University Press.

Dinsmore, Brooke, and Allison Pugh. 2021. "The Paradox of Constrained Well-Being: Childhood Autonomy, Surveillance, and Inequality." *Sociological Forum* 36(2):448–70.

Fine, Gary A. 1987. *With the Boys: Little League Baseball and Preadolescent Culture*. Chicago: University of Chicago Press.

Giddens, Anthony. 1991. *Modernity and Self Identity: Self and Society in the Late Modern Age*. Stanford, CA: Stanford University Press.

Gonzales, Roberto. 2016. *Lives in Limbo: Undocumented and Coming of Age in America*. Oakland: University of California Press.

Jones, Nikki. 2010. *Between Good and Ghetto: African American Girls and Inner-City Violence*. New Brunswick, NJ: Rutgers University Press.

Kurz, Demie. 2002. "Caring for Teenage Children." *Journal of Family Issues* 23(6):748–67.

Lareau, Annette. 2003. *Unequal Childhoods: Class, Race, and Family Life*. Berkeley: University of California Press.

McDonald, Kevin. 1999. *Struggle for Subjectivity: Identity, Action, and Youth Experience*. Cambridge: Cambridge University Press.

Ray, Ranita. 2018. *The Making of a Teenage Service Class: Poverty and Mobility in an American City*. Oakland: University of California Press.

Rios, Victor. 2004. *Punished: Policing the Lives of Black and Latino Boys*. New York: NYU Press.

Sanchez, Mari, Michèle Lamont, and Shira Zilberstein. 2022. "How American College Students Understand Social Resilience and Navigate towards the Future during COVID and the Movement for Racial Justice." *Social Science & Medicine* 301:114890.

Thorne, Barrie. 1993. *Gender Play: Girls and Boys in School*. New Brunswick, NJ: Rutgers University Press.

———. 2009. "Childhood: Changing and Dissonant Meanings." *International Journal of Learning and Media* 1(1):19–27.

Wilkins, Amy C. 2008. *Wannabes, Goths, and Christians: The Boundaries of Sex, Style, and Status*. Chicago: University of Chicago Press.

14

When Kids "Play" Politics

Gender Play *and Young People's Activism*

HAVA RACHEL GORDON

When Barrie Thorne documented the gendered rituals of children's play in the schoolyard, her groundbreaking study underscored two monumental insights: the first is that children's play is sociologically important and worthy of scholarly analysis, and the second is that feminist scholars in particular should take children's play seriously. Up until that point in sociology more broadly and feminist theorizing more specifically, children's socialization was considered important only insofar as this socialization gave rise to adult behavior, or as a process of gendered adult becoming. In short, the conventional wisdom was that children are socialized by adults in order to reproduce a broader social order, or to perpetuate a set of gendered behaviors that are rooted in childhood and reinforced in adulthood. With her ethnography of children's gender play, Thorne upended these assumptions of children's passivity replete throughout previous sociological and feminist theorizing, and brought to life children's rich worlds of play, which alternately create, reinforce, and resist gender boundaries. Children have agency: they are active agents and creators of their worlds. Her work deftly picked apart children's play to reveal profound social processes, some of which provide insight for considering youth activism. In this chapter, I will outline the ways in which Thorne's dissection of children's "play" can serve as a road map for understanding what youth activism is, how we should explore it, and what it can accomplish. We can use her illuminating work to rethink young people's activism as another variety of play: one that exhibits youth agency, is structured by rituals and institutional constraints, and is consequential for young people's lives and the larger world they inhabit. I will also outline how we can use her insights as a springboard to continue the important work she began. We can take her theorizing even further as we evaluate the meaning and impact of young people's activism.

Children's Play as Serious Stuff
Conceptualizing Young Activists' Agency

I do not know if Thorne ever imagined that the children she studied (or their peers) might one day grow into teens and young adults who would launch anti-apartheid, anti-sweatshop, and ethnic-studies campaigns in the 1990s (e.g., Rhoads 1998) or would join youth advocating for LGBTQ+ liberation and gay-straight alliances in their schools, or would march in antiwar protests in the early part of the millennium. I do not know if Thorne imagined that *their* children, or their children's contemporaries, would become the vanguard of internet activism and gun-control, immigrant-rights, or Black Lives Matter movements. And why would she? Her resistance to analyzing children only in terms of their futurity was one of the remarkable signatures of Thorne's work: she refused to analyze children's worlds as a means to an adult end. In Thorne's worldview, children are important and remarkable in their own right. This fundamental refusal to see children as adults-in-the-making has paved the way for scholars to study the origins, conditions, and impact of young people's activism as both distinct from and implicated in the activist life worlds of adults. Thorne insisted that children's worlds of play are far from inconsequential, mundane, or passively innocent. Play is not simply the background chatter to the formal institution of schooling. Rather, children's play represents the situated interplay of agency, resistance, social change, and social reproduction. Play is consequential not just for the children themselves but also for the adult world they navigate. It is consequential for the ways in which gender categories become ossified or resisted in everyday life. In this same sense, we can draw on these insights to understand young people's activism as serious play. It is not just passive socialization, nor is it training for the ultimate moment when a young person becomes a fully evolved adult political subject (Lesko 2001; Gordon 2010). Thorne insisted that children's play is "serious" not for what it signifies about an eventual finished adult subject but for what it reveals about the boundaries of large-scale social inequalities and how these are negotiated, reified, and contested through ritual and interaction.

Thorne's playground children did grow up. It is worth it, just for a moment, to think about how these agentic children not only navigate gender boundaries but also contend with and wield political power. They are active social agents not only on the playground but also in neighborhoods terrorized by police violence and within families navigating draconian immigration laws. They are active agents in school shooter drills; some of them even live through actual gun violence. They stand at the interface of nature and society, and survive wildfires, hurricanes, displacement, and other markers of climate change. Their lives too are profoundly shaped by these political crises. Just the fact that they are children and teens does not mean they bear these political impacts passively, nor do they observe them—as uninformed and unfinished beings—from a distance.

Children's Activism as Horizontal Socialization

The insight that children are not passively socialized by adults into gender categories—but that they also socialize each other—is a profound lesson Thorne offers for understanding how children's play can translate into young people's political power. Thorne prods us to stop assuming that adults are the only competent actors who do all the socializing, and the kids (presumably incompetent by comparison) are the passive recipients of this socializing. Instead, her ethnographic work implores us to pay attention to the actual mechanics of children's interaction as it unfolds on the ground. Despite the hand wringing about young people's waning interest in civic participation and electoral politics at the beginning of the millennium (Delli Carpini 2000) and the renewed calls for more robust civic-education programs and top-down political socialization, children often face backlash from powerful adults when they insist on using their political voices before they reach the "appropriate" age. The vicious adult backlash against the Parkland gun-control teen activists (Olmstead 2018) and against the environmental activist Greta Thunberg (Di Placido 2020)—especially from powerful politicians—symbolizes the extent to which precocious-youth political mobilization confronts and offends adult expectations for children's political passivity

(Gordon and Taft 2011; Gordon 2010; Taft 2019). This happens in big ways that splash across news media, as in the case of the adult backlash against Parkland activists X (born Emma) González (Bent 2020) and David Hogg, or in the publicized vitriol against Greta Thunberg. But adult opposition to youth activism happens in small, everyday ways as youth dare to interject their voices into "adult politics," as in my study of how confrontational youth antiwar activism in Portland triggered the withdrawal of parent and teacher support (Gordon 2010) or in Jessica Taft's study of how teen girls in particular experienced belittling adult patronizing that denied their agency (2011). Adults may express dismay with young people's waning belief in civic participation, but teenagers' actual struggles to confront politicians or otherwise transform systems of injustice tell another story. Adults are critical role models and teachers, and are vital to young people's developing political consciousness (Ginwright 2010; Ginwright, Noguera, and Cammarota 2006; Gordon 2010; Kirshner 2007, 2015), but in other capacities adults also stand in the way of youth political development. After all, we live in a society in which young people are not seen as fully finished human beings (Lesko 2001), and formal political participation is popularly imagined as the right to vote at eighteen years of age. Too often everything else is considered to be mere practice for the "real thing."

This means that young people find ways to cultivate their political consciousness horizontally, through politicized peer networks, and develop innovative strategies to exercise political authority. As Jessica Taft and I have outlined elsewhere (Gordon and Taft 2011), youth politically socialize each other; the socialization process is not unidirectional from adults to youth. They do this by identifying and confronting adultist rhetorics, by rejecting adult-constructed models of "appropriate" civic-participation training in favor of more confrontational politics, by redefining and reconfiguring emotions and gendered stereotypes in order to cultivate their political voice (Taft 2011), and even by resisting criminalizing schooling practices that deny children of color the freedom to play (Ferguson 2000). In her chapter on how youth activists of color use various forms of play to politicize and resist criminalization in school, Jessica S. Cobb writes, "If curtailing play is an enactment of power in service of white supremacy, engagement in play by children and youth of color can also serve as a form of resistance to racist oppression." Thorne's ethnographic approach captured the richness of children's horizontal interactions, and the importance Thorne gave these in her work has provided a basis for understanding how children become political beings in a profoundly adultist society (Checkoway 1996), one that insists on imaging them as cute policy sprouts and prepolitical at best (Gordon and Taft 2011), or entitled, naïve, spoiled, criminal, or downright dangerous at worst.

Getting around Adults

Because it can be an uphill struggle to develop political consciousness, voice, and power as a young person given the adultist ideals of political civic personhood in the United States and elsewhere, young people often need to "get around" adult authority in order to leverage political power. Thorne's ethnographic research captured children's agency as working within, under, and around adult authority, revealing that children's agency is shaped, but not wholly determined, by adult-imposed boundaries. In line with feminist standpoint theory, children have a unique vantage point on power relations, and are often able to see things that fall outside of adults' awareness. Thorne's deeper insight—that children's agency in constructing gendered boundaries contains a subversive element—is vital to understanding how young people navigate not just gender but also a deeply age-stratified society. Thorne's work instructs youth researchers to look beyond young people's complicity in gender socialization; we must also look for their subversiveness. Shifting our focus to young people's strategies to "get around" adult power does not mean we view them through a simplistic lens of delinquency or deviance. Rather, we look at subversive behavior to better understand the roadblocks to political power in our society, and how the forces of age stratification bear responsibility for some of these roadblocks. As with all good ethnographic work, we examine children's worlds using Thorne's guiding principle of "respectful discovery" (Rueda, this volume) to activate the sociological imagination (Mills 1959) so we can find the contours of the social structures, historical processes, and reigning cultural ideologies that we cannot see but that nevertheless form the boundaries around what are often mistakenly viewed as our own (or in this case, children's) private and personal struggles. In this sense, we can study young activists' subversive struggles to claim political power as instances of how they wrestle with the forces of age inequality. As Thorne noted throughout her work, these forces are not static; rather, they are historically specific. For example, Amy L. Best's chapter in this volume highlights the rise of intensive parenting and increasing surveillance that has eroded children's autonomy since Thorne wrote *Gender Play*. Young people's struggles to engage politics reflect back to us the contours of age inequality as it unfolds in real time.

Children as Impactful Agents

Thorne's *Gender Play* opened up a powerful vantage point on the complicated and sometimes contradictory dimensions of youth agency. Even children's agency alternately subverts adult authority, reproduces inequality, and then works to resist this same inequality under different conditions. In taking children's gender play seriously, Thorne implored social researchers to take youth agency seriously, and to view kids as competent social actors rather than inert objects waiting to be socialized. For scholars and youth advocates wanting to understand the genesis, mechanics, and impacts of youth activism, the ability to see youth as competent social actors is foundational. In the age of #MeToo, Black Lives Matter, gun-control activism, DREAMer activism, and international Fridays For Future climate school strikes (just to name a few), we have good reason to see youth as competent social actors. Youth activists have leveraged their status as survivors of gun violence to challenge the powerful US gun-rights movement. Undocumented youth have challenged lawmakers to legislate immigrant rights for adults and youth alike, and have centered intersectional identities in these very same movements for inclusion, justice, and social visibility (Terriquez 2015a). Their globally coordinated school strikes have leveraged their positions as students in schools in order to gain control over the institutions that depend on them (Piven and Cloward 1979) in the name of global climate justice. Indeed, as digital natives they are on the cutting edge of activism through social media. Movement scholar Jennifer Earl writes, "Youth are as close to crystal balls as we are going to get at glimpsing into protest's future. . . . They are going to continue to remake new models of activism" (Earl 2013). It is becoming clear that youth accelerate cultural and even political change in ways that outpace some of the more traditional mobilizing strategies used by adult activists. Thorne reminds us that these accomplishments by youth help to weave the social and political fabric we all share.

Ageism and Gender Inequality

Finally, Thorne's emphasis on the ways in which gender and age coconstitute each other is also essential for mapping the complicated worlds of youth activism. Thorne argued that a deeper study of gender politics in children's worlds must be accompanied by a larger critique of adultism in child research. This was a challenge to feminist theorizing as well. In order to study how children engage in reproducing and resisting gender systems, we need to first interrogate adultist rhetorics that have long dominated scholarly work on both gender *and* children. We can see this through the dominance of the developmental model in studies of youth, for example (Lesko 2001). As Thorne richly demonstrated through her fieldwork, children structure gender within the inescapable context of age segregation and age inequality. By spotlighting the critical nexus of age and gender, Thorne established the necessity of adopting an intersectional lens to understand children's gendered worlds. As we study youth activism, this critical insight reminds us that we cannot entirely view young people's politics as a more generalized microcosm for understanding adult mobilization politics. Because youth develop political consciousness, shape mobilization strategies, and wield political power in the belly of a deeply adultist society, their political tools must inevitably contend with ageism. This layer of age segregation and stratification fundamentally shapes youth activism in a unique way that is distinct from adult politics. The study of young people's politics can illuminate parallel machinations found in adult political organizing, but these studies cannot collapse these segregated and unequal worlds together into a more generalized theory of social movements, just as her study of children and gender cannot entirely explain gender politics among adults. Indeed, ageism shapes the political tools, mobilization strategies, and outcomes of youth organizing in ways that are connected to but distinct from those in adults' political worlds. And of course, gender and age inequality conspire to create both the possibilities for and the constraints on girls' political agency in ways that are distinct from the political lives of boys (Gordon 2008; Taft 2011). With this insight, Thorne's *Gender Play* reminds us that "children" or "youth" cannot be conceptualized as an undifferentiated category within sociological study. Even as mainstream media coverage of gun-control, immigration, or climate-change activists spotlights the salience of age status in their coverage of what is often perceived as young people's "exceptional" activism (Gordon and Taft 2011), Thorne's foundational study reminds us to consider youth as a variegated category, one in which gender is still a driving force that shapes the strategies and successes of youth activist movements.

Future Directions in Youth Activist Research: Where We Go from Here

Youth Activists Also Socialize "Up"

Feminist studies of youth activism can expand on Thorne's insights into the possibilities for social change, which is where her classic book ends. Youth not only socialize each other and circumvent adult power: their agency can potentially impact adult publics, politics, and approaches to social problems. While Thorne implores us to consider how children construct gendered worlds horizontally through their active agency instead of simply through their passive receipt of adult socialization, we might also consider taking this insight one step further: socialization—especially *political* socialization in the case of youth activism—may not only germinate in horizontal youth networks; it could also operate vertically from the bottom up to impact adults. This is to say that young people's mobilization strategies and their political impact on the world can "socialize" adult activists and reshape adult politics. Kennedy (2018), for example, documents the impact that youth participatory action research (YPAR) has on adults. Schwiertz (2016) argues that the undocumented DREAMer movement counters the dominant discourses that criminalize undocumented people more broadly. Negrón-Gonzales (2015) notes that the DREAMer coming-out story, the *testimonio*, is a powerful form of "counter-spectacle" that challenges the broader trope of undocumented migrant illegality. In this sense, undocumented youth have reconfigured the wider immigrant-rights movement, incorporating coming-out stories, new forms of civil disobedience, and other youth-centered innovations that have served as new tools in the immigrant-rights movement's toolkit. Surely this kind of vertical impact accounts for some of the most virulent backlash against young activists. The backlash marks youth activism not only as "deviant" but also as *threatening*. The ability of these activists to capture global media attention threatens to upend what are usually assumed to be the adult provinces of gun rights, citizenship rights, or global corporate-led resource extraction. With their activism, teens threaten global power relations, become central nodes of broader movements, and even force countermovements to change their tactics and develop new ones; adults even mobilize to thwart youth activism. Youth climate-justice, gun-control, and immigrant-rights activism all stand as powerful reminders that youth who are not of voting age can still change adults' political conversations and policymaking. Thorne's emerging ideas on social change in her influential book's conclusion can serve as a springboard from which to think through how gender and age intersections also shape adults' political strategies.

Taking Youth Activism Seriously: Developing a Critical Analysis

If we are to consider kids as active political agents and competent social actors, we must take their movements seriously. If children are competent actors, then their worlds and their movements deserve critical analysis. This seriousness is at the very heart of *Gender Play*. Thorne insists that children's play is not simply irrelevant, light, and inconsequential. Rather, children's play is *serious* work. It is the very essence of how children reproduce, resist, and navigate some of the most salient social divisions in our society. Critically analyzing young people's political activism—including analyzing why and under what conditions young people's activism falters—is a tough enterprise for youth scholars and adult allies who want to use our scholarship, policy, and practice to interrupt adultism and further empower youth. Many of us want to counter the hegemonic discourses that dominate young people's lives. But this critical analysis is precisely the spirit of Thorne's ethnographic research on children. A critical analysis of the various dimensions of children's gendered worlds reveals more than just their strategic agency. As competent and complicated social actors, they are neither one-dimensional heroic resisters, nor are they inert and passive social objects. Their agency reflects the broader institutional and cultural bases for dynamic webs of social power and inequality. By understanding these, we understand how inequality is in some instances reproduced, and in others, disrupted. We use this multifaceted analysis to map what could be possible routes to social change.

Adult reactions to youth activists are often polarized: either youth are lambasted and chided by powerful adults, or their efforts are championed by more sympathetic adults. But adult allies need to go beyond simply applauding youth for their efforts. As Taft and I have argued elsewhere (Gordon and Taft 2011), this uncritical praise in itself reflects an ageist bent: we applaud kids for caring because we assume they won't. We praise kids for fighting for change because we assume they are lazy, uneducated, and uninformed. We view their efforts as admirable and even precocious because we assume their activism is practice for the "real thing," a longer evolution of political subjectivity that will eventually become more serious and more *legitimate* when they become an eventual adult political subject, the "real thing." As youth scholar and historian Nancy Lesko (2001) has argued, age stratification rests on an assumption of human evolution that will always view the child or teen as inferior because they are "unfinished" while the adult stands as superior because they are presumably fully evolved. This is compounded by gender: as Bent (2020) argues, media coverage of activist girls often perpetuates the idea of "girl power" as "exceptional" girlhood. But scholars and adult allies need to move beyond this polarizing reaction, and should take young people's organizing as seriously as they would take adults' activism. Scholars should begin to ask not only what youth accomplish with their organizing but also why youth activists sometimes fall short of producing social change. What are the invisible institutional or cultural constraints on their agency? What are the barriers to their activism? What do these barriers reveal about the possibilities for a fully realized youth political subjectivity, and about age inequality more generally? This does not mean criticizing youth activists themselves for their better or worse strategic choices, or labeling them as better or worse activists. Rather, it means viewing their successes and failures as equally consequential for understanding their role in shaping the present and future of our politics.

There are concrete questions we can ask that lead to such a comprehensive critical analysis: What happens to young people's backstage political conversations as their activism shifts towards the front stage? Nina Eliasoph's ethnography *Avoiding Politics* (1998), for example, charted the disappearance of political conversations in front-stage settings. Does this same political erasure happen to young people's political conversations? Are the mechanisms for this political silencing the same for youth as they are for the adults featured in Eliasoph's work? Or are there more specific mechanisms—related to age inequality—that are responsible for filtering out some elements of youth political dissent as it drifts into public debate?

What about the institutional bases for youth political activism? Thorne inspires this question with her insight that gender polarization or integration is contextually based and even institutionally and organizationally specific. Some institutional arrangements can structure interactions that polarize gender, and others can encourage the emergence of gender-integrating rituals. In this same way, institutional contexts like schools inspire forms of youth activism that differ from those cultivated in other institutional contexts, like community-based nonprofit organizations. Some political- and civic-organization scholars emphasize that civics education is key to cultivating young people's lifelong civic and political engagement (Youniss et al. 2002), and therefore schools and carefully constructed curricula hold the potential to cultivate youth political consciousness and action. In my own ethnographic research, however, I found that schools as institutions also contain specific mechanisms that inhibit more radical forms of youth voice and dissent: youth clubs often require adult sponsors, school spaces for young activists to organize might be few and far between, and student organizers are under the watchful eyes of teachers, principals, and, in some schools, even police. The curricular turn towards high-stakes testing has narrowed the curriculum in many schools, especially those serving low-income BIPOC communities. This curricular narrowing has also eliminated opportunities to explore critical thinking, sociopolitical development, and civic-participation skills in schools.

Similarly, a host of scholars have written about community-based organizations as critical spaces for youth political education and activism. Others and myself have documented the ways in which community organizations provide youth of color with critical social-movement educations that contrast sharply with traditional school curricula. Even though these settings are not schools per se, they are potent sites for impactful and activating educations (Ginwright 2010; Ginwright, Noguera, and Cammarota 2006; Kirshner 2007, 2015). Veronica Terriquez also lauds these organizations for seeding lifelong commitments to activism (2015b). On the other hand, Soo Ah Kwon's study of youth organizing in the Bay Area (2013) highlights the neoliberal context of so many youth community-based organizations. Structured through foundation grants, the demand for deliverables, and professionalized staff, these organizations, she argues, end up channeling youth away from more confrontational forms of dissent and instead foster an "affirmative governmentality": a kind of self-containment and management of supposed youth criminality that masquerades as youth empowerment. In this way, these organizations and their funders deflect attention away from the role that state divestment has played in curtailing young people's lives, which further weakens young people's ability to challenge state oppression. Youth workers in these organizations struggle to negotiate and subvert the broader deficit narratives that ultimately control youth of color—especially Black youth—even while purporting to support them (Baldridge 2019).

In this sense, institutional contexts can be contradictory: schools can provide political education but can also blunt youth organizing. As Amy L. Best points out in her chapter in this volume, schools are spaces of contention, "organized around contradictory cultural pulls that reproduce elements of social power, and at the same time inspire challenge to that very order." Similarly, community-based nonprofits can facilitate youth activism but can also channel youth activism away from critiques of the state. Youth scholars and allies should be attuned to these institutional differences, and to the forms of youth activism that arise from these. This helps us to better pinpoint what youth can win with their organizing, and under what conditions they win. This also helps us to make sense of how these institutions can be reimagined or reformed in order to better enable young people to realize their political power.

Expanding Intersectionality in Imagining Youth Resistance

As Thorne admits in the conclusion to her book, she did not theorize race and class in her gender and age analysis of children's play as thoroughly as she would have liked. To be sure, she established the groundwork for an intersectional examination of children's agency in *Gender Play*, and she attended to broader intersections more fully in her later feminist work. Similarly, future scholarship on youth activism can and should consider how more complicated intersections of race, class, gender, and sexuality shape youth as competent social and political actors. Given that adultist presumptions of children's innocence, deviance, or criminality operate along racial, class, and sexual lines (Ferguson 2000; Fields 2008; Lewis 2003), we can apply these feminist insights to key questions in the study of young people's activism. For example, how does racism structure young activists' relationship with different media (newspapers v. different types of social media)? In my own research, white, middle-class radical youth in Portland played on images of young people's innocence in order to advance their educational-justice aims, while working-class and poor Latinx and Black youth in Oakland—already hypervisible in dominant media images of criminality and deviance—did not strategize to harness mainstream media attention as a social movement resource in these same ways. BIPOC youth in Oakland politicized academic achievement as resistance against school push-out and the school-to-prison pipeline, and school achievement buffered adults' attempts to delegitimize their political claims. Meanwhile, white, middle-class youth in Portland perceived academic failure as a personal, more private struggle between parents and themselves, but not as a struggle implicated in broader social and political legitimacy. Adult allies in Oakland played a key role in mitigating sexism in youth activist movements, which was especially helpful for BIPOC girl activists. The presence of adult allies prevented girls from exiting the movement entirely, as many white, middle-class girls did in Portland without adult allies to perform these critical feminist interventions.

Intersecting disadvantages are not the only animating nexus that shape youth activist movements, however. Intersecting identities also give rise to new strategies and tactics within movements in ways that facilitate social-movement spillover and even knit together broader movements, such as LGBTQ+ and immigrant-rights movements (Terriquez

2015a). Taft (2019) demonstrates how child workers in Peru politicize their own identities as children as they organize labor movements. Through their organizing, they highlight the perils and hidden exploitation embedded in notions of childhood innocence that in the end fail to recognize children as *workers*, and thus strip them of labor protections. Young water protectors fuse Indigenous histories, their own futures, and the future of the planet in their fight for native sovereignty and their intersectional challenge to the ongoing project of settler colonialism (Elbien 2017). Parkland organizers, such as Emma Gonzalez, enact public feminism by linking gun-control activism to gender and racial justice, as well as LGBTQ+ rights (Bent 2020). Young activists leverage their intersecting identities to redefine labor movements, climate justice, and immigration justice on a global scale.

Youth Politics and the Possibilities for Age-Diverse Coalitions

We can also investigate youth organizing as it interfaces with adult organizing. Youth use their agency to socialize each other and even to influence adults, but they also use this to *coalesce* with broader social-change efforts. Youth activist scholars can explore the instances in which youth successfully cultivate coalitions with adult activists, and where they fall short. Are these coalitions explained by the confluence of certain movements? Are there points of interest convergence between activist kids and adults that better predict age-diverse coalitions? Are there key social issues in which young people hold a certain legitimacy or centrality that adults do not? If so, what are these and why might they help to contextualize the formation of age-diverse coalitions? Finally, how strong are these coalitions, given the prevalence of adultism in our society? How does adultism play a role in movement demobilization, and what might be models for counteracting adultist methods of organizing or ageist behavior within movements so that age-diverse coalitions can survive? Taft's (2019) work on intergenerational relationships in the fight for working children is one example of this fascinating and important strand of research on generational alliances within movements.

In line with Thorne's analysis, these questions lead us beyond understanding youth as a distinct group. We can examine youth activists' struggles in order to illuminate some of the same historical, organizational, and relational dimensions of social power that structure adult worlds, too. Ultimately, youth-activist energy, innovation, and vision in social movements that span generations, issues, and identities hold the power to radically change politics as we know it. Thorne's analysis of children's play as agentic and consequential has laid the groundwork for understanding youth activism as more than just a process of political becoming. Youth activism is the "serious" play—the play that creatively and courageously engages possibility—that we must take seriously as a legitimate and transformative force in our politics.

REFERENCES

Baldridge, Bianca. 2019. *Reclaiming Community: Race and the Uncertain Future of Youth Work*. Stanford, CA: Stanford University Press.

Bent, Emily. 2020. "This Is Not Another Girl-Power Story: Reading Emma González as a Public Feminist Intellectual." *Signs: Journal of Women in Culture & Society* 45(4):795–816.

Checkoway, Barry. 1996. "Adults as Allies." Detroit, MI: WK Kellogg Foundation.

Delli Carpini, Michael. 2000. "Gen.com: Youth, Civic Engagement, and the New Information Environment." *Political Communication* 17(4):341–49.

Di Placido, Dani. 2020. "Angry Reactions to Greta Thunberg's Activism Speak Volumes." *Forbes*, January 7.

Earl, Jennifer. 2013. "Not Your Father's Social Movement Studies." *Mobilizing Ideas*, March 11.

Elbien, Saul. 2017. "The Youth Group That Launched a Movement at Standing Rock." *New York Times*, January 31.

Eliasoph, Nina. 1998. *Avoiding Politics: How Americans Produce Apathy in Everyday Life*. Cambridge: Cambridge University Press.

Ferguson, Ann Arnett. 2000. *Bad Boys: Public Schools in the Making of Black Masculinity*. Ann Arbor: University of Michigan Press.

Fields, Jessica. 2008. *Risky Lessons: Sex Education and Social Inequality*. New Brunswick, NJ: Rutgers University Press.

Ginwright, Shawn. 2010. *Black Youth Rising: Activism and Radical Healing in Urban America*. New York: Teachers College Press.

Ginwright, Shawn, Pedro Noguera, and Julio Cammarota, eds. 2006. *Beyond Resistance! Youth Activism and Community Change*. New York: Routledge.

Gordon, Hava Rachel. 2008. "Gendered Paths to Teenage Political Participation: Parental Power, Civic Mobility, and Youth Activism." *Gender & Society* 22:31–55.

———. 2010. *We Fight to Win: Inequality and the Politics of Youth Activism*. New Brunswick, NJ: Rutgers University Press.

Gordon, Hava Rachel, and Jessica Taft. 2011. "Rethinking Youth Political Socialization: Teenage Activists Talk Back." *Youth & Society* 43(4):1499–1527.

Henn, Matt, Mark Weinstein, and Dominic Wring. 2002. "A Generation Apart? Youth and Political Participation in Britain." *British Journal of Politics and International Relations* 4:167–92.

Kennedy, Heather. 2018. "How Adults Change from Facilitating Youth Participatory Action Research: Process and Outcomes." *Children and Youth Services Review* 94:298–305.

Kirshner, Ben. 2007. "Introduction: Youth Activism as a Context for Learning and Development." *American Behavioral Scientist* 51(3):367–79.

———. 2015. *Youth Activism in an Era of Education Inequality.* New York: NYU Press.

Kwon, Soo Ah. 2013. *Uncivil Youth: Race, Activism, and Affirmative Governmentality.* Durham, NC: Duke University Press.

Lesko, Nancy. 2001. *Act Your Age! A Cultural Construction of Adolescence.* New York: RoutledgeFalmer.

Lewis, Amanda. 2003. *Race in the School Yard: Negotiating the Color Line in Classrooms and Communities.* New Brunswick, NJ: Rutgers University Press.

Mills, C. Wright. 1959. *The Sociological Imagination.* New York: Oxford University Press.

Negrón-Gonzales, Genevieve. 2015. "Undocumented Youth Activism as Counter-Spectacle. Civil Disobedience and Testimonio in the Battle around Immigration Reform." *Aztlan: A Journal of Chicano Studies* 40(1):87–112.

Olmstead, Molly. 2018. "The Public Attacks on the Parkland Teens Are Getting Nastier." *Slate,* March 29.

Piven, Frances Fox, and Richard A. Cloward. 1979. *Poor People's Movements: Why They Succeed, How They Fail.* New York: Vintage.

Rhoads, Robert A. 1998. *Freedom's Web: Student Activism in an Age of Cultural Diversity.* Baltimore, MD: Johns Hopkins University Press.

Schwiertz, Helge. 2016. "Transformations of the Undocumented Youth Movement and Radical Egalitarian Citizenship." *Citizenship Studies* 20(5):610–28.

Taft, Jessica K. 2011. *Rebel Girls: Youth Activism and Social Change across the Americas.* New York: NYU Press.

———. 2019. *The Kids Are in Charge: Activism and Power in Peru's Movement of Working Children.* New York: NYU Press.

Terriquez, Veronica. 2015a. "Intersectional Mobilization, Social Movement Spillover, and Queer Youth Leadership in the Immigrant Rights Movement." *Social Problems* 62(3):343–62.

———. 2015b. "Training Young Activists: Grassroots Organizing and Youths' Civic and Political Trajectories." *Sociological Perspectives* 58(2):223–42.

Youniss, James, Susan Bales, Marcelo Diversi, Verona Christmas-Best, Milbrey McLaughlin, and Rainer K. Silbereisen. 2002. "Youth Civic Engagement in the Twenty-first Century." *Journal of Research on Adolescence* 12(1):121–48.

ACKNOWLEDGMENTS

We thank all the contributors for sharing their expertise and stories, and for helping build our feminist community during what has been an extraordinarily challenging time for many people. From Berkeley, Abby Thorne-Lyman gave generously of her time and helped us stay in touch with Barrie. We are grateful for the helpful suggestions we received from our anonymous reviewers. The NYU Press team has been a delight to work with. We are honored that our volume could join such esteemed titles in the Critical Perspectives on Youth Series, and are grateful for the support of series editors Amy L. Best, Lorena Garcia, and Jessica K. Taft. We thank Sonia Tsuruoka and Yasemin Torfilli for their assistance in helping prepare the volume for production, Emily Wright for her exquisite copyediting skills, and Alexia Traganas for shepherding the book through the production process. Our editor, Ilene Kalish, shared our enthusiasm for the book and its vision. We are deeply grateful for Ilene's support. And our families provided love, support, and laughter as we worked to complete the volume.

This book entered production ten years after Barrie's retirement in 2012, when we first tossed around the idea for what would become *Gender Replay*. As we were putting finishing touches on the book, we finally had an opportunity to meet with Barrie to talk to her about it. That meeting was shortly before her eightieth birthday. Barrie was pleased and honored. That brought us immense joy. Barrie's scholarship, teaching, and mentoring were the inspiration for our volume and so *Gender Replay* is our gift to her. And if you have been inspired by Barrie's writings, then we hope you also find some inspiration in *Gender Replay*.

ABOUT THE CONTRIBUTORS

KARISSA M. BARBOSA graduated from Massachusetts College of Liberal Arts with a major in Sociology and three minors in Anthropology, Social Work, and Women, Gender, and Sexuality Studies.

AMY L. BEST is Professor of Sociology and Chair in the Department of Sociology and Anthropology at George Mason University. She is the author of *Prom Night: Youth, Schools, and Popular Culture*, which was selected for the 2002 American Educational Studies Association Critics' Choice Award; *Fast Cars, Cool Rides: The Accelerating World of Youth and Their Cars*; and *Fast-Food Kids: French Fries, Lunch Lines, and Social Ties*, all ethnographic tales about youth, social inequalities, and culture. She is the editor of *Representing Youth: Methodological Issues in Critical Youth Studies* and is coeditor of the NYU Press book series Critical Perspectives on Youth with Lorena Garcia and Jessica K. Taft.

BRIDGET M. BROYLES graduated from Massachusetts College of Liberal Arts with a major in Sociology and three minors in Anthropology, Social Work, and Women, Gender, and Sexuality Studies.

INGRID E. CASTRO is Professor of Sociology at Massachusetts College of Liberal Arts and was the 2022–2023 Chair of the Children and Youth Section for the American Sociological Association. She is the editor of *Childhood, Agency, and Fantasy: Walking in Other Worlds* and coeditor of *Researching Children and Youth: Methodological Issues, Strategies, and Innovations*; *Representing Agency in Popular Culture: Children and Youth on Page, Screen, and in Between*; and *Child and Youth Agency in Science Fiction: Travel, Technology, Time*.

JESSICA S. COBB is Policy Manager for the Education Civil Rights Alliance, convened by the National Center for Youth Law. She holds a

PhD in Sociology from the University of California—Berkeley and a JD from UCLA School of Law. Her work has appeared in *Sociology of Education*, *Social Science Quarterly*, and *City and Community*.

RAEWYN CONNELL is Professor Emerita at the University of Sydney, and Life Member of the National Tertiary Education Union. She is the author of *Gender and Power: Society, the Person, and Sexual Politics*; *Masculinities*; *The Men and the Boys*; and *Southern Theory: Social Science and the Global Dynamics of Knowledge*. Her recent books include *The Good University: What Universities Actually Do and Why It's Time for Radical Change* and *Gender: In World Perspective* (currently in its fourth edition).

WHITNEY EASTLAND graduated from Massachusetts College of Liberal Arts with a major in Sociology and two minors in Criminal Justice and Child and Family Studies.

INGUNN MARIE ERIKSEN is Research Professor at Norwegian Social Research (NOVA) at Oslo Metropolitan University. Eriksen has worked on a number of studies that involve youth culture, peer relations, and identities. She has written extensively on school environment, bullying, and student well-being in school, with particular attention given to the meaning of gender, ethnicity, and social class.

HAVA RACHEL GORDON is Professor of Sociology at the University of Denver. She is the author of *We Fight to Win: Inequality and the Politics of Youth Activism* and *This Is Our School! Race and Community Resistance to School Reform*.

BRIAN E. GRAVEL is Assistant Professor of Education and Director of Elementary STEM Education at Tufts University. He is the coauthor of *STEM Literacies in Makerspaces: Implications for Learning, Teaching, and Research* and coeditor of *"Show Me What You Know": Exploring Student Representations across STEM Disciplines*. His research has been funded by the National Science Foundation, the LEGO Foundation, and the Spencer Foundation, and has appeared in the *Journal of the Learn-*

ing Sciences, the *Journal of Science Education and Technology,* and the *Journal of Pre-College Engineering Education Research.*

MARGARET A. HAGERMAN is Associate Professor of Sociology at Mississippi State University. She is the author of *White Kids: Growing Up with Privilege in a Racially Divided America,* which won the 2019 William J. Goode Book Award and was Finalist for the 2019 C. Wright Mills Award, given by the Society for the Study of Social Problems. Her work has been featured by a range of mainstream media outlets, including *PBS Newshour, Good Morning America,* the *New York Times,* the *Atlantic,* the *Guardian, Time, Good Housekeeping, Libération,* and the *Los Angeles Times.*

AMANDA E. LEWIS is Director of the Institute for Research on Race and Public Policy and College of Liberal Arts & Sciences Distinguished Professor of Black Studies and Sociology at the University of Illinois at Chicago. She is the author of *Race in the Schoolyard: Negotiating the Color Line in Classrooms and Communities* and coauthor of *Despite the Best Intentions: Why Racial Inequality Persists in Good Schools* and *Challenging Racism in Higher Education: Promoting Justice.*

MICHAEL A. MESSNER is Professor of Sociology and Gender Studies at the University of Southern California. He is the author and editor of nineteen books, most recently *Unconventional Combat: Intersectional Action in the Veterans' Peace Movement.* His honors include the Pursuit of Justice Award from the California Women's Law Center; the Feminist Mentoring Award from the Sociologists for Women in Society; and the Jessie Bernard Award, presented by the American Sociological Association in recognition of contributions to the understanding of women's lives.

HARRIET BJERRUM NIELSEN is Professor Emerita at the Centre for Gender Research at the University of Oslo. She was the Director of the Centre from 1993 to 2009. She has written extensively on children, youth, and gender in perspectives of social, developmental, and generational change. Her latest book is *Feeling Gender: A Generational and Psychosocial Approach.*

MARJORIE ELAINE FAULSTICH ORELLANA is Professor of Urban Schooling, Associate Director of the International Program on Migration, and Codirector of Faculty for the Teacher Education Program at UCLA. She is the author of *Translating Childhoods: Immigrant Youth, Language, and Culture*; *Immigrant Children in Transcultural Spaces: Language, Learning, and Love*; *Language and Cultural Practices in Communities and Schools: Bridging Learning for Students from Non-Dominant Groups*; and *Mindful Ethnography: Mind, Heart, and Activity for Transformative Social Research*.

CASSIDY PUCKETT is Assistant Professor of Sociology at Emory University. She is the author of *Redefining Geek: Bias and the Five Hidden Habits of Tech-Savvy Teens*. Her work has appeared in sociological and interdisciplinary journals, including *Harvard Educational Review, Qualitative Sociology, Social Science Computer Review*, and *Social Science & Medicine*. Her research has been funded by the National Science Foundation, the American Council of Learned Societies, the Mellon Foundation, and the US Department of Education.

ALLISON J. PUGH is Professor of Sociology and Chair of the Department of Women, Gender, and Sexuality at the University of Virginia. She is the author of *The Tumbleweed Society: Working and Caring in an Age of Insecurity* and *Longing and Belonging: Parents, Children, and Consumer Culture*, which won the 2010 William J. Goode award and the 2010 Distinguished Contribution award from the ASA section on Children and Youth. She is also the editor of *Beyond the Cubicle: Job Insecurity, Intimacy, and the Flexible Self*.

ERÉNDIRA RUEDA is Associate Professor of Sociology and Director of the Latin American and Latinx Studies multidisciplinary program at Vassar College. Her work has appeared in *Children and Society* and the *Journal of Latinos and Education*, and in the edited volumes *Why Kids Love (and Hate) School: Reflections on Difference* and *The Education of the Hispanic Population*. She was Barrie Thorne's research assistant, student, and advisee in the sociology doctoral program at the University of California Berkeley from 1999 to 2008.

CHRISTO SIMS is Associate Professor of Communication and affiliate faculty in Science Studies, Ethnic Studies, and the Design Lab at the University of California–San Diego. He is also the founding member of the Studio for Ethnographic Design at UC–SD and the University of California Collaboratory for Ethnographic Design. His first book, *Disruptive Fixation: School Reform and the Pitfalls of Techno-Idealism*, won the Best Book Award from the Communication, Information Technologies, and Media Sociology Section of the American Sociological Association.

INGRID SMETTE is Researcher at Norwegian Social Research (NOVA) at Oslo Metropolitan University and is currently a postdoctoral fellow at the University of Oslo. Her work has appeared in the *Journal of Youth Research* and she has coedited a special issue on cross-cultural perspectives on parenting and class in the *British Journal of Sociology of Education*.

LESLIE TAYI graduated from Massachusetts College of Liberal Arts with a double major in Psychology and Sociology and two minors in Women, Gender, and Sexuality Studies and Child and Family Studies.

The editors, Freeden Blume Oeur (*left*) and C. J. Pascoe (*right)*, with Barrie Thorne (*center*) at Barrie's retirement party in Berkeley, California, April 2012.

ABOUT THE EDITORS

Freeden Blume Oeur is Associate Professor of Sociology and Education at Tufts University. He served as lead editor of the present volume and is the author of the award-winning book *Black Boys Apart: Racial Uplift and Respectability in All-Male Public Schools* and (with Edward W. Morris) coeditor of *Unmasking Masculinities: Men and Society*. Freeden is a feminist researcher of children, masculinity, and African American politics and intellectual history.

C. J. Pascoe is Associate Professor of Sociology at the University of Oregon. Her work focuses on young people, inequality, and education. CJ is the author of *Nice Is Not Enough: Inequality and the Limits of Kindness at American High* and the award-winning book *Dude, You're a Fag: Masculinity and Sexuality in High School*, and (with Tristan Bridges) coeditor of *Exploring Masculinities: Identity, Inequality, Continuity, and Change*.

INDEX

academia: barriers to family life for faculty in, 126–127, 140–142; experiential learning and, 52–55; immigrant achievement and, 102–106; mentoring in, 130–132, 150–151; minority student achievement and, 53–54; as play, 46; race, gender, and class hierarchies in, 143–144; Thorne's care work in, 149–150

Ackerman, Brian, 182n3

ACLU of Southern California, 74–75, 81

activity and activism: of children, 38–39, 90–94, 242–245, 247–248; critical analysis of youth activism, 250–253; group interactions in, 230–234; horizontal socialization and, 244–246; race and class issues and, 254–255; socializing up of youth activists, 249–250; Thorne's evaluation of, 187–188, 213–215, 242–245; valuation-activity framework and, 200–202; youth politics and age-diverse coalitions, 255–256. *See also* agency: ambiguity in STEM and CTE programs

adult futures, erosion of child agency in relation to, 235–239

adult ideological viewpoint, 36; childhood studies and, 16, 226–227

adultism and adult authority: backlash against children's activism, 244–246, 250; children's agency and, 60–64, 66nn8–9, 93–94, 246–247, 254–255; children's research and role of, 248–249; reactions to youth activism and, 251–253

affirmative governmentality, in youth, fostering of, 253

affordances of boundaries, 100

African Americans. *See* Black Americans

age divisions and hierarchies: Thorne's work with, 48, 213–215; youth politics and age-diverse coalitions, 255–256

ageism, gender inequality and, 248–249

agency: ambiguity in STEM and CTE programs and, 188–193; backlash against children's agency, 244–246; of children, 38–39, 121–123, 176–181, 242–245, 247–248; gender in school life and, 32–34; knowledge construction and, 85; of minority students, 54–55; race and class issues and, 254–255

Ahmed, Sarah, 151

Althusser, Louis, 34

American Sociological Association, 140, 155

anger, feminist scholarship on, 123–125

anthropology, gender and, 7, 21n8

antiracist activism, play and, 78–80

Anzaldúa, Gloria, 177

autonomy, erosion for children of, 234–239

Avoiding Politics (Eliasoph), 252–253

Bachmann, Laurence, 119, vii

Bad Boys: Public Schools in the Making of Black Masculinity (Ferguson), 72

Barbosa, Karissa M., 155–181

Barrie. *See* Thorne, Barrie

Barth, Fredrik, 3, 20n3, 97, 99, 112, 205, 217, 221–222